Dear Dinah

TIME FOR A HOUSEHOLD PARTNERSHIP

Jeannie Seeley-Smith

Authors of Unity Publishing
New York, NY

Dear Dinah: Time for a Household Partnership
© 2003 by Jeannie Seeley-Smith

All rights reserved. No part of this book may be reproduced in any form whatsoever without permission in writing from the publisher, except by a reviewer, who may quote brief passages in critical articles or reviews.

Authors of Unity Publishing
575 Madison Avenue
10th Floor
New York, NY 10022
www.authorsofunity.com

Author photo by Joel Larson
Book design by Sara Patton
Back cover copy by Susan Kendrick Writing
Printed in the United States

ISBN 0-9725250-2-5
LCCN 2003100024

Contents

Prologue: Who is Dinah? ix
Introduction: A Subtle Awakening 1

Chapter 1
The Thanksgiving Day Caper 12
    When Mere Words Don't Work 12
    A Common Complaint 14
    Righting a Wrong 15
    The Search Continues 19
    I Won't Give Up . . . I Won't Give Up 20
    Eureka! 21
    The Thanksgiving Day Caper 21
    Dear Abby . . . Do You Have a Solution? 23
    Hmm . . . Perhaps the Problem Is Not the Men, After All 26

Chapter 2
Our Lost Dreams 28
    When We Wish upon a Star 28
    Validation 29
    Life Is Like a Baseball Game 30
    Excuse Me—Is It My Turn to Play Yet? 31
    What about My Dreams? 32
    I Guess That's Just the Way It Is 32
    So—What Is a Partnership? 33

Chapter 3
The Woman's Household Personality 35
    Who Am I in My Home? 35
    Your Household Personality Questionnaire 37
    How to Determine Your Household Personality 44

Chapter 4
It's No Wonder I Do What I Do 47
    The Rebel, the HoneyBee, the Sojourner, the Stargazer,
        or the Tigress? 47
    The Rebel 47
    The HoneyBee 51
    The Sojourner 54
    The Stargazer 58
    The Tigress 62

Chapter 5
I'm Running As Fast As I Can 66
    The Thou Shalts 66
    Who Has It Worse? 68
    On Your Mark, Get Set, Go! 69
    Thou Shalt Run ... Always 70
    A Running Partner 71
    What's in It for Him? 71

Chapter 6
The Man's Household Personality 73
    Who Am I in My Home? 73
    Your Household Personality Questionnaire 74
    How to Determine Your Household Personality 82

Chapter 7
One Man's "Castle" is Another's
"Home on the Range" 85
    The Emperor, the Philosopher, the Hunter, the Dapper,
        and the Partner 85
    The Emperor 85
    The Philosopher 90
    The Hunter 95
    The Dapper 100
    The Partner 104
    A Question for the Woman: On a Scale of 1 to 10,
        How Does My Mate Rate As a Partner? 108

Chapter 8
Two Become One — But Which One? 110
Are you Assertive, Even-tempered, or Passive? 110
The Assertive Female with the Assertive Male 111
The Good News and the Bad News 113
What to Do Differently? 114
A Letter from Dinah to the Emperor and Hunter 114

Chapter 9
It's Not Always What It Seems 116
The Assertive Female with the Even-tempered
    and/orPassive Male 116
The Good News and the Bad News 118
What to Do Differently? 120
A Letter from Dinah to the Philosopher
    (the Passive) 121
A Letter from Dinah to the Dapper
    (the Even-tempered) 122

Chapter 10
Don't Fence Me In 124
The Even-tempered Female with the Assertive Male 124
The Good News and the Bad News 126
What to Do Differently? 127

Chapter 11
Why Mess Up A Good Thing? At Least For Him 128
The Passive Female with the Assertive Male 128
The Good News and the Bad News 130
What to Do Differently? 132
One More Letter from Dinah to the Assertive Males 134

Chapter 12
If It's Not Broken, Why Mess with It? 136
The Even-tempered Female with the Passive Male
    and/or Even-tempered Male 136
What to Do Differently ... Or Should They? 138

Chapter 13
No Waves, No Storms **140**

   The Passive Female with the Even-tempered
      and/or Passive Male 140
   So What's the Beef? 141
   What to Do Differently? 143
   As You Can See, Intimacy Involves a Lot of "We" 144
   Parent/Child versus Adult/Adult Relationship 145
   Let's Both Be Grown-ups 146
   Insanity Is Doing the Same Thing Over and Over Again
      but Expecting a Different Result 147

Chapter 14
Blessed Be the Beliefs That Blind Us **148**

   Kindred 148
   Watch Their Feet 150
   What's Wrong with This Picture? 150
   Different Job Descriptions 152
   The Risk of Change 153
   I Told You So! 154
   Changing a Sacred Belief 155

Chapter 15
Your Beliefs and Actions Inventory **158**

   First Things First 158
   Beliefs and Actions Inventory 159
   Your Belief Type 173
   Your Action Type 176
   Your Range of Conflict (Personal and Couple's) 178
   Congratulations! 183

Chapter 16
Let's Dance to the Light of the Moon **184**

   The Calm after the Storm 184
   Carpe Diem 185

It's Time to Tango 185
Step Two: A Shared Action 186
Head to Heart 187
"You Count, But I Count, Too" Behavior 188
It's Not As Easy As It Seems 189

Chapter 17
Let's Make a Deal! 191

The Art of Negotiation 191
Viewing the Win-Lose Style through a Matrix 191
The Win-Lose Negotiator 193
The Win-Win Negotiator 195
Returning to the Matrix 196
Let's Meet Halfway—"The Compromise" 197

Chapter 18
The Time Has Come 199

It's Either Time to Dance or to Sit This One Out 199
Wannabee, but Not Gonnabee 200
Gonnabee Someday, Come Hell or High Water 201

Chapter 19
The Household Partnership 202

Signing the Code of Ethics 202
A Time of Celebration 203
Negotiation of Labor 203
The Happy Face Game 203
Signing the Household Partnership Contract 204

Chapter 20
The Thanksgiving Day Revelation 205

A Year Later 205
The Turkey Dance 207
Sometimes We Come Full Circle 209

Chapter 21
The Stages of Household Partnership 210
    Life Can Be Like a Game of Hopscotch 210
    The Stages of the Household Partnership 210
    Stage One: The New Toy 211
    Stage Two: Buyer's Remorse 212
    Questionnaire to Determine Your Category 213
    Interpreting Your Quiz Results 214
    Moving into Stage Three 222
    Stage Three: The Point of No Return 222

Chapter 22
The Harvest is Here 225
    Stage Four: Deeper Trust 225
    Stage Five: Partnership 227
    Like A Garden, It Will Always Need Work 227

Epilogue 229
    Ten Years Later 229

Appendix A   Code of Ethics 232
Appendix B   The Happy Face Game 233
Appendix C   The Household Partnership Contract 246

PROLOGUE

Who is Dinah?

Let me tell you about Dinah. You'll meet her later in the book, and you'll discover that she has a lot to say about household personalities and relationships. As you get to know her you'll learn that she doesn't dwell much on issues. She's more of a problem-solver than a problem-dweller, and her specialty is what she likes to call "win-win" solutions. It is only fitting, then, for her to make her debut in the how-to chapters of the book.

I first met Dinah while struggling through some of the household issues addressed early on in the book. As I worked on the manuscript, I came to know her better and better. She began to influence the way I looked at things even before I knew her name. Some of her thoughts, I now recognize, begin to appear as early as the end of Chapter 1. By the time I finished Chapter 2, Dinah and I were actually collaborating with each other. In fact, she often knew what I would say before I said it myself. She then took a larger role and began to ghostwrite the rest of book for me. By the end of Chapter 8, she stepped out of the closet and wrote under her own name. I give her full credit for the remaining chapters of the book. I hope you like Dinah. I do. She cares, she makes sense, and she's fair.

A little more than ten years ago, I began to feel something wasn't quite right in my life. At first, this feeling took an amorphous form, like some uneasy stirring from within. Gradually, it came into full focus, and began batting around the room like a frisky puppy. I worked full-time outside my home but—the puppy yapped—and the realization came that I was totally responsible for everything that took place within my home. Why? That's no great mystery. I was responsible because I'm a woman and, as we all know, social expectations of women had been carved in granite and stuck in the back room of a Moose lodge somewhere for the last thousand years. And they include no provisions about women working full-time outside the home.

Such injustice! In the early chapters you will find me kicking and screaming about it. I embark upon on a mission, and that is to take a sledgehammer to those chiseled-in-granite expectations, and the Moose lodge along with it. Gradually, however, I began to hear another voice—Dinah's voice—more reasoned and compassionate than my own shrill battle cry. It came not as an epiphany, but more like a gradual awakening. Eventually, she helped me realize that the world is not populated totally by downtrodden women and denigrating men. Contrary to my initial convictions, no sinister plot is afoot; no conspiracy brews. No brotherhood of perpetrators is victimizing womankind. Dinah made me realize that all of us, male and female alike, are just trying to carry on the best we know how as we all adjust to this socio-cultural environment of dual-income households.

But, even though good intentions abound, we're still lost in a fog. With all the hoopla about balancing our lives, about taking care of ourselves first so we can take care of others, we still have not come up with Plan A, let alone Plan B. We remain as bewildered as our sociologists seem to be as we try to figure out how to run our households when no one's at home.

Who, for example, takes care of the kids? Who irons shirts, mends socks, shops for groceries, mows the lawn? What about the bills, the bank deposits, the reconciliation of the checkbook? Who prepares the spread for entertaining the Burtons on Saturday? Who takes care of Grandma? What about the school clothes, the weddings, the birthday gifts? And who, for God's sake, will plant the tulips? Call the plumber? And don't forget about Johnny's tutoring, or that discussion with his daycare provider, or the babysitter for Friday night. Who fed the dog this morning? Who will take him to the vet this afternoon, or talk to the neighbor about her four-year-old who throws stones at Fido? Who is going to have time for the children, their friends, our friends, our community ... now that all of us are working full-time jobs?

We plan, but the stress keeps building. We hate the conflict; we find ourselves spending an awful lot of time arguing about who does what and when. Nothing, of course, erodes our intimacy as quickly as unresolved issues and brewing resentments. But, nevertheless, we soldier on with both hanging around our necks.

You men. You're tired of feeling unappreciated. Nothing you do or say is good enough. Her complaining drives you crazy. Sometimes you don't want to come home. You women. You're tired of feeling unappreciated. Nothing you do or say is good enough. His uncaring attitude drives you up the wall. Sometimes you don't want to come home.

Dinah came into this book just in time for me. She began to make her presence known in the midst of my most stressful years: full-time job, teenagers, husband's job demands, community responsibilities, aging parents. I yelled at the monitor in front of me as I was typing the first chapter of this book, "Forget why! Tell me how!" That's when Dinah appeared. She told me how. She introduced me to a new life — one called "household partnership." My husband, Gary, and I developed and implemented it, and so can you, once you discover your own household personalities.

Dinah, as you may have surmised by now, is me. Or, at least my alter ego. My awakening. I appropriated her name from the song, "Someone's in the Kitchen with Dinah," because yesterday no one was, and today someone is.

If you struggle with an unfair division of household labor, if you want to work with your partner in *true* partnership, if you want to create harmony and intimacy in your relationship, this book is for you. However, it comes with a caveat. After reading this book, you never again will think of your household in the same way. That's true if you only skim the pages.

If you take a larger step, and actually do *all* the exercises—learn about your household personalities, take the Belief and Action Inventory, play the Happy Face Game—and, through it all, keep *communicating* with each other, an exciting, life-changing household partnership will develop, a relationship of harmony and intimacy, beautiful to behold, joyful to live.

Dinah

Dedicated to

*My husband Gary, the true Partner,
for your inspiration and example.*

*My children David and Kristina,
for the immense joy and sunshine you bring to my life.*

*My son-in-law and daughter in-law Bill and Molly,
for adding such enrichment and happiness to our family.*

*and
In loving memory of Jo.*

INTRODUCTION

A Subtle Awakening

Once Upon a Time

I was born on a cold, blustery March morning in 1946. It was the first year of the "baby boomers." I arrived a full seven minutes before Kathryn, my "younger" sister. My brothers, Gary and Allen, were already tottering around at the time. Our mother, who by now was exhausted, seemed nevertheless thrilled. Amazingly, six weeks after our birth she had the energy to write her beloved Aunt Evelina the following letter:

Dear Aunt Evelina,

Thank you for your gifts. It seems as tho' the four-leaf clovers you attached to the children's bonds have brought us all very good luck. Ever since the twins were born, Durward and I have been awfully happy. We have bought a neat five-room house on an acre of land on the Clinton River. Nice landscaped lawn, fruit trees, garden spot, swimming hole in the river — everything we'd dreamed of — $6,500 with $2,700 down. The house is well-built — nice bathroom, good furnace, and foundations laid for two extra rooms. Now with a home of our own, we really do have "everything." We feel we have a perfect little family now.

Your loving niece,
Elizabeth

Yes, I guess from all accounts, we looked pretty good. In truth, our family read like a fairy tale:

INTRODUCTION

> *Once upon a time there was one happy Dad, one peaceful Mom, two darling playful boys, and two absolutely adorable baby girls. The perfect six of them lived in a cozy, modest cottage, surrounded with apple trees, alongside the Clinton River, in the small perfect Midwest town of Utica, Michigan. And they lived happily ever after.*

Or so I thought.

I especially remember those barefoot summer days.

"There he is," I noted, squinting up into the sky. "There's Sol."

When Sol rose over the back woods in the early mornings, he'd find Kathy and me sitting on the hill by the river, eating our morning cereal while patiently waiting for him. When he arrived, we knew it wouldn't be long before his "good morning" rays spilled into the Clinton. We glanced at each other in anxious anticipation as we watched Sol rise inch by inch. We knew what was coming. By midday, Sol's rays would warm Coward's Hole, our secret swimming hole.

Lying back into the tall grass, I visualized my hands slipping off the old, worn rope that hung from the fat maple branch above. My fall would drop me fifteen feet into Coward's Hole below. Twelve feet deep into the Clinton, eyes wide open and gulping for air, I was secure, knowing that the faithful rays of Sol would guide me up and out. He definitely was a true and devoted friend—and, like all good friends, worth waiting for.

However, after the heat of the day, we hid from him. It was all very clandestine. And poor Sol never knew whether to search for us in our tree house (Angel Hall), our teepee (Firelight), or our underground fort (Forbidden Grave). Usually long after the evening supper, old worn-out Sol would find us across the road, hiding and giggling in the farmer's wheat field, better known to us as the Land of Swish. Angry that we had dodged him for so long, he retaliated by lighting the Land of Swish on fire, or so we liked to say. Actually, the farmer's field was where Sol slept. To this day, forty years later, I still have sweet far-away memories of our old friend Sol and the

Land of Swish whenever I see an evening sunset "go out in a blaze of glory." But back then, Sol retiring for the night did not mean *our* play was over.

The moon (Mr. Wink) was also our friend. Playing scary night tag, hide and seek, and smoking stalks of dried weeds were all part of the day. Later in bed, after evening prayers with our mom, the night-light (a jar of freshly caught fireflies) kept us company.

Ah, indeed. Life was good. In fact, it was more than good. It was perfect.

Loss . . .

The one thing that we can absolutely be sure of is that life changes. Sadly, my family found out about this truth earlier instead of later. On a warm September Friday afternoon in 1955, our perfect life tragically came to an abrupt halt. Quite unexpectedly, my mother died. She was only forty-one years and ten months of age. My brothers were thirteen and eleven; Kathy and I were nine.

Our deep sense of loss was felt everywhere and in everything. Nothing was the same. All the good times had drastically changed or were completely gone. Even Sol could not light the morning or make us smile in the same way he had so many times before. And as far as Mr. Wink, for years afterward I dreaded even his shadow, much less his appearance. He no longer accompanied moonbeams, sweet dreams, or innocence. Now he ushered in long, lonely, and empty nights. I'm afraid there are no other words to describe this "happening" except to say that it was a knife to the heart that left us all bleeding and scared. As you might suspect, my life and my family's were altered from then on out.

Ten weeks after my mother's death, my father wrote the following words to Aunt Evelina:

> *We bought a big evergreen blanket with a big red ribbon wrapped around it, and other red boughs running through it for our darling's grave for Christmas. We miss her so much.*

My father went on to write:

> *I just received the autopsy report. It says she died on September 5 from carcinoma of the pancreas, which metastasized to the lungs. The doctor said he did not understand how she kept going for so long and not tell anyone, because she was very sick for a long time. I am so happy she and the twins made the trip to Louisiana to see you in August. It seems she could not leave this world without saying goodbye to you, and showing off her girls.*
>
> *I've got to see that the children get to bed now.*
>
> *With love,*
Durward

As I look back, Dad (left alone at forty-three with four young children and a house to care for), like us kids, found it easier to live in denial. None of us wanted to let her go.

For months, her robe lay draped over the hook in the bathroom. The sewing basket sat on her nightstand. Her sheet music lay gathering dust on top of the piano. In her closet, her clothes waited faithfully on their hangers. It was there, in my mother's closet, that I sought comfort.

When no one was around, I would sneak into the closet and quietly shut the door. Then, after finding her favorite housedress, I would wrap it around me. Sometimes I'd stand for an hour draped in the soft cloth. I had discovered that by taking in deep breaths, I could capture lingering fragrances that took me to her. It helped fill the hole in my stomach—at least for those moments.

One day, "well-meaning" family members arrived to help Dad "move on." My heart ached as they gently folded and packed her clothes—including *my* comfort dress—in brown cardboard boxes. Words that could have explained my wants stuck in my throat. Fearing I would be deemed foolish if they discovered my secret shroud, I remained silent as her clothes left the house. The days in my grieving closet were over. Life "moved on."

An Observation

When Mom was alive, Dad was this "happy-go-lucky" sort of guy whom you could always hear whistling in the distance, especially while he gardened—his (and our) favorite pastime. Early in the spring, Kathy and I would trail behind him while he moved deliberately along, dropping seeds in the garden furrows near the banks of the Clinton. As I think back, I'm sure we had more fun helping him outdoors, planting the garden and whistling, than we did doing housework with Mom on the inside. Watering and fertilizing the tomatoes, feeding the cackling chickens, and playing catch with my brothers were far more to our liking than helping Mom do dishes or hang the wash. Everyone referred to us as tomboys. We smiled and took it as a compliment.

Typical of the '50s, men's and women's household roles had deep roots that grew undisturbed. Men worked outside, women worked inside. It was simpler back then. Everyone knew what was expected of them ... and, it appeared, everyone liked it that way. And even if they didn't, no one knew how, or wanted to go through the hassle, to change it. My home was no exception, except my mom was a kindergarten teacher and consequently struggled with the same issues of balancing home and work that working moms do today.

Just Like a Daisy

It was sad to watch, but after Mom was gone, Dad quit whistling and worked long hours trying to make up for the loss of her teaching salary. As far as the upkeep of the house ... well, it was left solely in the hands of us kids. I'm not sure if it was from watching the TV show *Father Knows Best* or just from repeating what Mom had been doing, but early on I was aware that housework was "the girls' job"—and, to our brothers' good fortune, there were two girls left in the household.

I never questioned this role. It never occurred to me to ask why women (or, in our case, two little girls) were better suited for cleaning, making beds, and ironing clothes than men or boys were. As I look back, female socialization had already flowered in my

INTRODUCTION

young mind. My new role felt natural to me, and I settled in with no questions asked.

Mary, Mary Quite Contrary

I equate this comfort to that of a garden. All gardens begin with seeds. Even if you plant three-foot-high tomato plants, those plants began as seeds at some point. Now, we can all agree that it's not unreasonable for a gardener to have some expectations concerning seeds. For example, if a gardener plants daisy seeds, he or she expects to see daisies a few weeks later.

Let's consider the mindless daisy seed. From its perspective, there's no questioning, no contemplation, and no forethought. It is expected to grow and blossom as specified on its envelope. It's as simple as that. I don't think that's too much to ask—of a daisy seed—but what about a person's gender?

It almost seems like genders come in "envelopes," like seeds. Obviously, my envelope read "girl." And, just like different types of flower seeds, girls and boys come with different expectations of them, too.

Have you ever noticed how uncomplicated life can be when everyone does exactly what is expected of them? Without too much thinking, that is. It's always that asking "why?" stuff that separates us from those mindless seeds and gets us into deep trouble. Yes, once we start pondering, we can mess up a plan that's flowing along pretty darn well. But you see, in our case, the flowing along pretty darn well applied more to my brothers than it did to Kathy and me.

It became noticeable once we entered high school, especially on weekends. My brothers darted out in the morning and darted back in the evening. In between morning and evening, the housework got done. That's what Kathy and I were for. Not a bad plan, at least for Gary and Allen.

To be fair, my brothers deserve credit. At first they attempted to share in the cooking. Gary, the oldest, had this passion for cooking wild game. He loved hunting rabbit in the backwoods, or trapping "whatever" along the Clinton. I think it was a Daniel Boone thing.

He liked to pretend we wouldn't eat unless he provided the food. But it all came to an end on the day of the possum.

The Day of the Possum

Gary beamed with pride as he carried his "kill" into the dining room. His gait was that of a proud warrior delivering the head of the enemy on a platter to his king. But there was no hero's welcome. The three of us met him with stony silence while he placed the dish of cooked "something" down in the middle of the table. As he pulled out his chair, we could feel his eyes searching our faces for the signs of the praise that he was so sure would be forthcoming. A minute passed. Finally, with just the slightest hint of impatience, Gary broke the silence. "Well ... what do you think of it?"

"That depends ... what in God's name is it?" Allen asked in sarcastic horror. (At age twelve, Allen had already developed a certain attitude. Food was more than a necessity. Even then, he desired a presentation. For instance, he put out china and candles for hot dogs.)

"Why, it's dinner," I said, quickly jumping in to protect Gary's feelings. "This is not something he just cooked, Allen. He hunted it, prepared it, and now it's ... it's our dinner." I smiled proudly at my oldest brother, reassuring him that at least one of us was aware of his efforts. "It is dinner ... right, Gary?"

"Yeah, it's dinner." Gary said, clearly annoyed. He looked at his younger brother. "What the heck do you think it is?"

"Dinner?!?!" Allen sneered. "You've got to be kidding! It looks like something you dug up from the back dump. I'm praying right now it's at least dead!"

"Knock it off, Allen!" Kathy snapped. "You're not funny. You don't have to eat it."

"Yeah," hissed Gary, angrily. "Don't do me any darn favors! Don't eat it, you stupid crybaby!!"

Sometimes this was all it took. "Stupid crybaby" were fighting words. In the past, they had taken this opportunity to leap at each other's throats, throwing wild punches and yanking each other's hair.

Not willing to sit on the sidelines and watch, Kathy and I usually joined in. We'd jump around hysterically, screaming at the top of our lungs for them to stop. Since Gary was bigger and stronger, we usually directed our outrage at him. "Let go of his neck! You ugly, rotten bully, leave him alone!" It was not a pretty picture.

But this day, Allen's mind overruled his emotions. He calmly said, "Oh, don't worry, Gary, I don't think there needs to be any concern about me eating this ... this ... thing."

"Oh, Allen," I pleaded. "Couldn't you just try some?"

"Yeah, try it. What's the big deal anyway? What are you ... a chicken baby?" Kathy asked as she bravely reached with her fork to stab a piece from the platter.

Except for Allen's snickering, a full forty-five seconds of silence passed as Kathy slowly pushed the "kill" around her plate. It was a grand effort, but try as she did, she couldn't actually put the "thing" on her fork and bring it to her mouth.

The three of us started to giggle. The charade was rapidly dissolving. Gary grabbed the plate from the middle of the table. As he circled his arm around his kill to protect it from further insult, Allen, Kathy, and I exploded into laughter.

It was laughter at its most gut-wrenching level — laughter 'til the tears rolled, laughter so hard and for so long that we all fell to the floor helplessly, holding our sides and kicking our feet to relieve our aching stomachs. I can't remember how long we laughed that day. I only know it lasted long after Gary yanked the platter from the table and retreated to the backyard. Avoidance humor works, and we became experts at it. To this day, it's still one of my family's favorite coping mechanisms.

From that time on, the writing was on the wall. Besides the housecleaning and laundry, Kathy and I took over cooking the majority of dinners. Not that our burned potatoes were going to taste any better than the "thing," but somehow they evoked less ridicule.

A Sense of Fair Play

As time passed, Kathy and I became fully entrenched in the belief that it was our job to take care of the house. As I've said, it just seemed natural that girls did housework and boys hunted and fished.

No doubt, my family needing me satisfied some deep desire. It also built my self-esteem. Today, however, we are better informed. We now know that this deep feeling of satisfaction that comes from being "needed" all too often becomes troublesome for women. The mental health community has educated us that this "need to be needed" can easily keep women stuck doing much more than their fair share.

Fortunately, over the last decades, because of necessity, awareness, or a little bit of both, men are becoming more and more comfortable with their feminine side ... the side that allows them to also be "needed" in the same nurturing manner that women are. There is a new generation, a new consciousness, but it must be embraced by both men and women to truly survive. If we don't all work together to capture this opportune time of redefining our gender roles and new relationships to one another, we could easily slip back to the old lifestyles of the past, which kept us working apart instead of together. The other reason we don't want to slip back is that now that women are also in the work force the old roles, simply, are no longer fair.

Twins are great examples of how fairness can play out in relationships. Certain thoughts that are formulated get mirrored back and reinforced on a daily basis. Soon these thoughts become beliefs. One of Kathy's and my early beliefs was the concept of fairness. At some point it became very obvious that my wants and needs were every bit as important as hers were, and hers were every bit as important as mine. In other words, if she "counted" so did I. This worked particularly well with housework. I came to expect that if I needed help doing a chore, Kathy would pitch in. If she needed help, I pitched in. Soon it was not only a habit but also a way of life. Therefore, the seed of sharing housework and fair play was planted in my brain at a very early age, but for some unknown reason, after adolescence, it never flourished.

INTRODUCTION

Later in Life

It was only years later, after I was well into my second marriage, that I began to experience the feeling that something was missing. There was this sense that even with a husband and my two kids, when it came to the housework, I was on my own.

I, of course, given my childhood, felt an expectation. There was a voice that kept telling me that taking care of the home was *my* job. I should enjoy cooking a whole dinner by myself, doing all the laundry and ironing, entertaining, and organizing all the holiday preparations ... alone. My family believed I would enjoy this role because I would just naturally adore being needed and having such a deep sense of purpose. And even though this was partially true, I sensed it wasn't fair. But once again, our society's expectations of gender roles determined my fate.

The ability to adapt can be women's strength. It's also their weakness. If you are one of those "lucky" women who are gifted with this ability, you will find yourself adapting most of the time. In addition, if you are a working woman with a family at home, chances are that there are certain expectations that your family has of you, and you have "adapted" so as not to disappoint them. This great ability you have to adapt has now been translated into the great myth that you need to "do it all."

My enlightenment was a slow process. Awareness eventually came when my twin-based belief concerning a sense of "fair play" awoke and Dinah, my alter ego, was born. Along with this awakening came the realization, to both my spouse and I, that partnership is the key to a contented, well-run, loving household. A household partnership is a relationship that embraces what is fair and just; it's created between a male and female by ignoring the strict rules that have in the past defined the household gender roles.

So, you ask, "How do we get there?" No worry. Dinah will lead you there.

Just Because He Thinks You're a Daisy

Early one summer morning, a gardener went down to the valley to see how his garden was growing. As he walked through his rows, he felt quite pleased that his efforts had produced such abundance. One could see him smile as he occasionally bent down to pull a weed, pick off a slug, or test the ground for moisture. Yes, all and all, he was quite satisfied that everything was growing as expected.

Suddenly, in the far corner, growing next to the corn, he noted something quite extraordinary. Where he had planted daisies, out had popped an entire row of sunflowers. "How could that be?" he asked aloud. "I planted daisy seeds. My expectation is daisies—not sunflowers!"

The following chapters are written for all you sunflowers.

CHAPTER 1

The Thanksgiving Day Caper

> *As so often happens in marriage, roles that had begun almost playfully, to give line and shape to our lives, had hardened like suits of armor and taken us prisoner.*
>
> – Molly Haskell, *Love and Other Infectious Diseases* (1990)

When Mere Words Don't Work

So much has changed since then. Yet, it only seems like yesterday when I was sitting in a restaurant complaining about my inability to balance my life.

It was the lunch hour, now over ten years ago. We were sitting by the large glass windows at Palomino's, an upscale "yuppie" restaurant in downtown Minneapolis. The dining room was filled with its usual active, noisy lunch crowd. Across from me sat a young, attractive woman, the CEO of a successful Twin Cities marketing firm. While large round snowflakes filled the air and drifted down onto Hennepin Avenue three floors below, Jan and I talked about our hectic lives of trying to balance home and work. We both agreed that the upcoming holidays felt like added weight on the scales. We dreaded them.

"I have love/hate feelings for this time of year," I moaned. "I feel pulled in ten directions. I'm consumed with the upcoming shopping, cleaning, entertaining, decorating ... if only I could get Gary more involved. It just seems that he doesn't care as much as I do."

"Boy, do I have a story for you!" Jan interrupted, twirling her fork through a mound of linguini.

"Oh, really?" I replied. Smiling while tearing a generous piece from a halved baguette, I looked up and said, "I am all ears."

"Complaining doesn't work. You have to have a revolution," declared Jan with a glitter in her eyes.

"We used to have a problem with dirty dishes," she began. "I hated seeing them piled up in the sink. But do you think Dave ever noticed? Heck no. If I didn't wash them, they would have sat there for days. When I complained, he always had the same comeback. 'Hey, they don't bother *me.* Leave them there!'" Jan paused to capture more strands of linguini before continuing. "Let me tell you— I was growing pretty weary of his reasoning, which said if something didn't bother him, it didn't need to get done."

"I know," I nodded, "it's frustrating." As I glanced around trying to spot the dessert tray, I asked nonchalantly, "Were you able to resolve it?"

"As a matter of fact, we did," she said. "But it took a drastic measure. What do you think I did?"

"You gave up, stopped complaining, and did the dishes," I responded. I hesitated a bit, then added in my most sympathetic tone, "It happens all the time. Women just give in." I turned around and motioned for the waiter to bring coffee. I won the battle with the dessert tray and reluctantly decided to forego the raspberry tart. As I turned back to Jan, I asked with a confident grin, "So, am I right?"

Jan leaned toward me and chuckled. There was a long pause. "You could not be more wrong," she said, smiling. Her eyes danced in anticipation, as if they held some great secret.

"Really?" I asked. Now I was intrigued.

"You see, Dave has an office at home—which, by the way, he keeps immaculate. So, one day I packed up all the dirty dishes, carried them into his office and dumped them on his desk." Jan picked up her goblet of sparkling water to announce a toast. With a gleam in her eye, she proclaimed, "Here's to creativity."

I raised my glass to salute such determination. "What was his reaction?" I asked eagerly.

"He was shocked." She giggled. Then, shrugging her shoulders to show her feigned nonchalance, she said, "But my comment to him was, 'Hey, leave them—they don't bother me—*there!*'"

I chuckled, visualizing Dave's look when he found the pile of dishes on his desk. "Certainly an interesting strategy," I observed, "but did it work?"

"Well, it brought the issue to a head. It certainly got his attention. And guess what? I'm not the only one doing dishes anymore," she said triumphantly.

A Common Complaint

As I said, a lot has changed over the last several years. But that day I remember driving back to my office feeling a certain satisfaction over Jan's technique in bringing the issue to a head. Although I knew that as much as I was impressed with Jan's guerrilla tactics, "win-lose" methods don't always produce positive results. In some households, those "come on, don't mess with me" tactics only make matters worse. In my situation, I could picture Gary thinking "Whoopee, we have a game going . . . time to play." I visualized him gleefully tossing the dirty dishes back on the desk of *my* home office, piling them on my side of the bed, or stacking them in the trunk of my car. Full-fledged win-lose would break out, with our personal areas becoming the battlefields. I had visions of dirty dishes in his bookshelves and in my lingerie drawer. It would get ugly.

But back then (and in many homes still), the dilemma of how working women would get help with their households was an ongoing, irritating, festering problem. Even though working women all reacted and responded differently, many felt the same frustration.

I was then, and still am today, the president of a Minneapolis nonprofit called Perspectives, Inc. Our mission is to improve the quality of life for at-risk and homeless families and children. Our major program is to provide supportive housing to women who are both homeless and recovering substance abusers. Because of my work, I had been introduced to all kinds of economic lifestyles. These lifestyles include very wealthy women, middle-class women, poor women, very poor women, and those who fall in between. But even though all these women's lives differ considerably, I had noted that they all had a great deal in common when it came to trying to balance home and work. The frustrations were abundant and they crossed all economic and cultural lines.

Righting a Wrong

Now back to that auspicious day. As I drove into my office's parking lot, I thought back to a recent newspaper article I had read which cited the statistic that 90 percent of married women consider taking care of the family to be their job. The report stated, "Even the women who claimed to earn half or more of the household income generally carry the lion's share of the load at home."

I sat in my car thinking of the upcoming weeks and the dreaded holidays. I did not feel ready to do what would be expected of me. Anxiety mounted as I thought of the countless tasks that lay ahead. It did not help that I was also feeling pressure at work. The agency still had 25 percent of the budget to identify and I needed to find additional funding sources. As I stepped out of my car, I slammed the door. Frustration was building. "There must be an answer to this inner feeling that I must be responsible for it all. But what is it?"

My frustration escalating, I looked for someone to take it out on. So naturally I went into my office, shut the door, and called my husband Gary. "Listen, honey," I began, "I've been thinking. With the holidays coming up and all, and with all the demands at work, I'm feeling stressed. I can't do it all. I need you to be more involved." (I smile as I write this. Since that time, I've learned so many better ways to gain support than creating confrontations... and you will as well.)

There was a pause at the other end of the line. I could hear him clicking away on the keys of his computer. I waited. When he spoke, it was in a matter-of-fact tone. "Sure, sweetheart, what do you need? Just tell me what you want me to do. I'll be glad to help you out.

CHAPTER 1

But bear in mind, it's you who always has to have everything so perfect. You bring a lot of this stress on yourself."

"Well, that's sort of the problem." I took a deep breath. I did not want to minimize his offer to help, but I was also feeling blamed for needing it. "Now that's part of my point. It seems whenever I do ask you to help, it is my problem for needing it—that somehow I have created this mess. The other problem is why is this viewed as *helping* me? Let's rephrase it. Let's say I'm helping you out."

"Good point," I thought to myself. Jan would be proud.

"Huh?" Gary was confused.

I plunged in, hoping to drive my point home. "Well, you see, I feel there is this expectation that the house, family, and holidays are my responsibility. Even though you help, I feel like it's up to me to orchestrate it. I don't know how this has evolved, but apparently you view even changing a bed as helping me out with *my* job. Since when did it become *my* job? I have a job—one that takes up at least 50 hours a week." My voice was starting to rise. "Why is the house not considered both of our jobs? Don't you see? I feel like I'm the conductor. It seems like it is always my job to keep everyone on the same page!"

There was another pause. "Okay, sweetheart, I hear you. Uh-huh ... hmmm ... You having a bad day at the office?"

Immediately I took the stance that he didn't get it. Obviously he was still confused. "We'll talk later," I sighed.

"No problem, sweetheart. Now do me a favor. I know it's hard with that job of yours, but I wish you would let go of that stress. I get worried about you when you get like this, so try to relax, okay?

"Uh-huh," I responded. I had no time to get into it.

"So—what's for dinner?" Gary said cheerfully.

I pointed my index finger to my head and pulled the trigger. "Bye, dear."

That evening, on the way home, I stopped at a bookstore. I told myself there had to be a self-help book that would address the issues of working women, a "how-to" book that would advise me on how I could stop this crazy cycle of believing everything within the house was my responsibility. Considering how many homes have dual incomes, I reasoned that there had to be some expert who had come up with a solution for creating a home where a woman does not feel totally responsible for "doing it all."

A half-hour later, I had walked up and down over twenty aisles of Barnes & Noble. I had browsed through the business section, the women's section, the family section, and the self-help and psychology sections. My frustration built. I could not find what I was looking for. There were numerous books on improving a couple's communication, sex life, parenting, and financial status, but none specifically addressed women getting help with housework. I couldn't figure it out. In a nation in which 75 percent of all households are dual-income, I must be missing it.

I decided to ask the clerk, a middle-aged woman with salt-and-pepper curly hair and large brown eyes. "Where's the book that tells a woman how to get help with her home, kids, and the holiday shopping?"

She furrowed her brows, "Well, dear ... I'm not sure. But what an interesting notion!"

"Maybe the experts are stumped," I responded, somewhat discouraged. "Maybe no one has found the answer. I'll keep looking."

I went back to the self-help shelves. I found books on how to become a better wife, lover, mother, employee, housecleaner, cook, organizer, and gardener. I also found books that promised to improve my coping mechanisms while I implemented the "becoming better" ideas. I was frustrated. I didn't want to learn "how to" do things better. And I didn't want to learn new coping mechanisms. I wanted to learn how to *stop* "doing it all." I went back to the clerk.

"Perhaps it's a plot designed to keep the status quo in check. Has it ever occurred to you that maybe all these professionals are in on it?" I raised my eyebrows quizzically as I gestured back toward the self-help aisles.

"In on what?" she inquired, with a puzzled look.

"In on making sure that nothing changes, even though *everything* has changed. Half the women I know are in the work force. They

CHAPTER 1

aren't at home, taking care of everyone. We resigned but no one knows it. Don't they get it? Our homes have changed. It's not 'leave it to Beave' anymore. We need a new plan ... Plan B!"

The clerk tilted her head and stared at me. Finally she observed, "You sound like you've had a bad day."

I forced a smile, sighed, and walked away before she, too, asked me what I was going to make for dinner. I continued my hunt, going back and forth through the aisles. In the end, I became convinced a conspiracy was brewing.

"I know what these experts are doing," I said as I saw the clerk straightening a group of books. "They know women are suckers for 'making it better.' They know that no matter how well we're running our lives, we can improve on them. So, knowing how predictable we all are, they write how-to-do-it-better books. Nothing here is about changing what *is*. It is all about maintaining and coping with the status quo."

The clerk smiled pathetically and nodded. As she walked by, she patted my shoulder and said, "Sounds like you could use some help at home, dear."

"No one gets it," I thought. "I don't want help. I want what's fair. Why don't *I* help *Gary* out? Why is it *he* helps *me*?" I continued looking. Finally, refusing to go home empty-handed, I bought a book on couples' communication.

Later that evening, while lying in bed, I read, "Perhaps you should share your feelings with your mate. Tell him calmly why you need his help. Maybe, if he hears your statement more as a need instead of a complaint, he'll respond." I thought it made sense. Besides, I was beginning to feel desperate. I was ready to try anything.

The next night after dinner, feeling encouraged by my reading, I made a fire in the fireplace. The book had instructed me to set the mood. I wasn't going to mess this up. I would follow the instructions to the letter. Speak *rationally*, wrote the author, and use "I" statements with non-defensive, non-arousing tones. The author was very convincing. I was becoming persuaded that how I asked for something could make the difference. I envisioned Gary having a conversion experience. The book said to visualize or "give life" to

THE THANKSGIVING DAY CAPER

what you wanted, so I went on to imagine Gary confessing all his past sins of omission. I felt a sense of peace come over me as I pictured him rushing into the kitchen to clean the oven. I couldn't wait to try it.

It was about 9 P.M. Gary and I were all "snuggy" on the couch in front of a fire with a hot cup of tea. I felt confident. He seemed relaxed and ready to listen. I began with the "*I*" statements.

"Honey, *I* feel tired. *I* feel exhausted. *I* feel overwhelmed. *I* don't like the feeling that *I* have so much of the responsibility with the house. *I* am feeling very frustrated. *I* don't understand how this all got set up. *I* am confused. Did *I* happen to sign something when we were married that *I* have forgotten about?" The monologue ended with, "*I* just don't know how *I* am going to be able to keep doing it all."

I have to give the book credit. It worked. Gary was not the least bit defensive. He listened well. He patted me on the hand, sighed at the appropriate times, and nodded his head occasionally, indicating to me that he understood the whole time that I was "*I-ing.*" But even better, the next day he came home with a delightful surprise. He had reserved two nights at a lovely lakeside bed-and-breakfast inn for the weekend. It was a wonderful two days! I became convinced those experts were really onto something. I had overreacted; there was no plot afoot after all.

But when we got home on Sunday evening, I stayed up till midnight cleaning, unpacking, and washing clothes. Something wasn't quite right. Maybe I had missed it. As I climbed into bed exhausted, I picked up the communication book from my nightstand. I decided I needed to go back and reread the chapter about speaking in the "I's." But I never found a section where it said, "If a man is not made to feel defensive, he will do the laundry and the grocery shopping." I began to panic; I realized I had not changed anything. The holidays were coming in six weeks. I still had no answer.

The Search Continues...

Each evening that week, I returned to the bookstore. (I had tapped out my book allowance and was now financing the project with the

CHAPTER 1

grocery budget.) The smiling, brown-eyed clerk had definitely joined my mission and we were now on a first-name basis. "Alice, what did you find for me today?" I would ask anxiously. I was never disappointed. Every time I arrived, she had a new book to offer. In spite of my skepticism, I was learning. I found out about men and how they are cave dwellers and how women like company. I learned that women are more sensitive, desire intimacy, and need to talk. (Apparently men like to figure it out all by themselves.) I learned men don't like to be blamed, criticized, or corrected. They want to be treated like they are all grown-up. Yet, I learned that men can act like little boys, and love to collect and play with toys. It was confusing.

But something was working. I found that Gary and I were not arguing about the household as much. We seemed to be talking more and experiencing greater intimacy. I thought it was great. But after a couple of weeks, I began to realize it was very tedious to always be thinking about saying the "right" thing and acting the "right" way. I noticed something else. I still felt I was doing it all.

I Won't Give Up ... I Won't Give Up

I plodded on, still believing that an answer would come. In the meantime, I kept practicing a few newfound discoveries that guaranteed a new promised land. Even though there was no breakthrough, I would not give up. I remained confident that the *real* answer was right around the corner.

But time was slipping by. It was only a couple of days before Thanksgiving when I walked back into the bookstore. Alice appeared particularly excited to see me. "I have found you a great book! You've got to try it. I'm sure we are now onto something."

But that evening after reading it, I concluded that it was really a perplexing book. It was all about how *not* to blame. But I wanted to blame! At that time in my life I felt it was the only way to change things. I read statements in this captivating book that claimed, "If this sounds as though I am blaming you, I am sorry. It is definitely not your fault." According to the author, that phrase "it's not your fault" is all the man needs to hear. I was starting to feel irked. "How is anything going to get better," I asked myself, "unless he understands how wrong he is?"

Eureka!

And then it happened. I realized what I had just asked. There was a flash from above; I knew "the answer" was not going to be found in a book.

I started to think that changing my communication style changed nothing. Learning new coping mechanisms also had little effect, except for the fact that I now had more resentment than I had previously had. Yes, I was now convinced that the answer was really within me. If I truly wanted to change my life from "doing it all" to developing some sort of equity, fairness, and a partnership, I needed to change my thinking.

"Maybe there really doesn't need to be blame, after all." I said. "Everyone knows that blame only drives the problem deeper into the consciousness of the person being blamed. And the end result is that everyone involved feels antagonistic. When has hostility and blame ever solved anything?" I asked. Then I concluded, "I need to discover methods that are going to flourish on their own. These methods must be created from the belief that there is no one to blame. That where we have been, and where we are, is exactly where we all had to be for the next step to happen, which is ... a movement of the heart."

The Thanksgiving Day Caper

By the time Thanksgiving Day arrived, I was starting to formulate a plan. It wasn't completely worked out, but I knew the foundation would be in developing some form of equitable partnership. But today was Thanksgiving, and it triggered all my old beliefs and expectations. I set my new thoughts concerning a "movement of the heart" aside to replicate the traditional holiday. Our 26-year-old son, David, and our 24-year-old daughter, Kristina, were home for the holiday. Along with the two of them, there would be ten other

CHAPTER 1

guests. Our children loved the holidays and always had high expectations — high expectations of me, that is. I did not want to disappoint them.

It was 10 A.M. Gary and I were standing around the kitchen island, stuffing a 25-pound turkey. It had been a horrendous week at work. Most of it was spent restoring the funding from a budget cut. I had worked long hours to get everything settled before the holiday. I wanted to be able to leave the stress behind and enjoy the long and "relaxing" weekend. However, that outside-of-the-home work stress wasn't even going to come close to the self-induced pressure and hard-core tension of hosting a dinner for fourteen.

Again, I found myself on a mission: I would make absolutely sure that this "relaxing and enjoyable" day was going to be just as special as Thanksgiving at my grandmother's was. No small task—those special dinners were filled with homemade everything, including the homegrown turkey. Of course, I don't remember my grandmother also working 45+ hours outside the home every week. But so what? I would not be daunted by trivia. I was intent on creating the magic my grandmother wrought.

As was our family tradition, Gary always was involved early on with the dinner. His philosophy was, "Organization is the best protector against stress," so we were organizing by dividing the tasks of cutting up onions, celery, chestnuts, and apples. As my organizing and obliging husband lifted the turkey, enabling me to scoop the perfectly made dressing into its cavity, he smiled contentedly and said, "Aren't you glad to have a husband who helps so much around the house?" I looked up into his dreamy brown eyes and noted how proud he was. "Yes, honey, I am truly blessed to have such a great helper."

"Just so you're aware," the Great Helper continued, "you have me all the way until noon. That's when the Lions kick off and, of course, I don't want to miss it. Then, after that game, there is another game. Do you believe it?"

"No. I can't believe it," I answered honestly.

"But I am all yours until noon," he continued. "Then I'm off to the games for the rest of the day." At that point he dropped the half-stuffed carcass onto the counter, threw his big arms around me, and proclaimed enthusiastically, "I just love Thanksgiving, don't you?"

Oh those dreaded football games. Grandma never had to contend with quarterbacks and touchdowns, I thought. All right, I can handle this. I need to accept the fact that when this magnificent dinner comes to its final diminuendo, I—or for that matter, any standing army—would not be able to drag Gary away from that repulsive football game, especially during the final two-minute warning (which I knew meant the game would go on another 30 minutes). "Accept it," I said to myself. "This is the reality. It's not going to change. Deal with it."

So, being a clever strategist, I took this fact into consideration and devised a plan. I would have everything synchronized perfectly. I would not be tricked by the two-minute warning. Cleverly, I would light the candles as the field-goal kicker ran out onto the field in the last four seconds of the game. If everything went according to plan, I knew I could pull this off. The only snag was if the game went into overtime by some sadistic field-goal kicker. If that happened, it would be too late for corrective action. By then, it wouldn't matter since I would already have been driven over the edge, with no return.

As it turned out, the game ended on time and the meal went off without too much of a hitch. Still, I was exhausted and stressed out by the time I sat down to eat.

A movement of the heart could not come fast enough.

Dear Abby...Do You Have a Solution?

Finally, it came—the final turning point.

A few weeks after Thanksgiving, I was having a morning cup of coffee at my kitchen island. As was my habit, I was browsing through the morning paper looking for the Dear Abby column, which had become a daily ritual long ago. After finding it, I sat back and read the following:

CHAPTER 1

Dear Abby:

We are two women who work together. I've been married for four years, and Jane has been married for 29 years. In spite of our age difference, we find the same thing waiting for us when we go home in the evening: not a husband who asks us how our day was, but a husband who asks, "When will supper be ready?"

While we cook, they read the newspaper, and after supper, while we clean up, they snooze. We keep our mouths shut because we realize there are worse things in marriage than this.

We would love to come home to husbands who contribute as much to a marriage as we do. We are interesting and attractive women. Does anyone have a solution, short of starting World War III? Please, no lectures on how some women would love to have a man to cook for after working 10 hours a day, or how much they miss the sound of his snoring on the couch.

Jill and Jane (not our real names)

Dear Abby responded:

Dear Jill and Jane,

There is more hope for you, Jill, than Jane. A 29-year-old habit is more difficult to break. Have you ever let your husband know that doing the job alone is more than you can handle or suggest that he set the table, whip the cream for the strawberry shortcake, or help with the dishes afterward? If you haven't, please do ... or don't complain.

Abby

Setting my coffee down, I walked over to the window and looked outside at the snow-covered bird feeder. Watching the chickadees'

The above letters are reprinted with permission from the Dear Abby column by Abigail Van Buren, ©1994 Universal Press Syndicate. All rights reserved.

tiny wings ruffle through the snow as they found their seeds made me smile. "Here we are again," I said to the little black-capped birds, "right back at the beginning—trying to find new ways to answer an old question, which is, how we are going to get the guys to *help out*?" But the more I thought about the letter, even the giddy chickadees didn't lift my feelings of doom.

It was not just Jill and Jane's situation that depressed me. I was also bothered with Abby's answer. After all, this was not just any old advice from just any old columnist. This was Dear Abby, a person whom readers, including myself, had come to recognize as a leader and champion of equality.

However, to me, she was much more than just another voice of wisdom. In my growing-up years after I had lost my mother, I had turned to her column for compassion and understanding. I found comfort in the fact that Abby wrote every day. After a while I not only trusted her, but I also depended on her to be there, and except for her two weeks of vacation, she always was. In a very real sense, she had become a surrogate mother.

Like most of her readers, I admired her ability to go straight to the core of an issue—to sift out her reader's emotional clutter so as to end up with what was really the problem. However, today I felt she had missed the boat. In that day's column, if I had read Abby's answer without reading the question, I might have assumed that her advice was given to a frustrated young mother trying to solicit help from her adolescent child.

"I guess," I told myself, "I should be relieved that she didn't advise Jill to promise little Johnny that if he does a nice job of whipping the cream, he gets to lick the bowl afterwards." But the frustration and gloom didn't go away. "Come on, Abby," I said out loud, "you can do better than this!"

The more I pondered the letter, the more I wished Abby had taken advantage of the moment to point out the continuing inequity in the working woman's household. I felt the letter could have served far more women if Abby had challenged Jill and Jane to re-examine their dinosaur belief systems—archaic beliefs that support

CHAPTER 1

the notion that women are responsible for what is still known as "woman's work," and "good" husbands should "help them out" once in a while.

"We are in big trouble." I said out loud to the chickadees. "Even my dear Abby, crusader of women's equity, views the man as the Great Helper."

As I continued to watch the busily feeding chickadees, I started thinking about beliefs again. "Why did Jill and Jane consider it *their* job to make the supper every night? Why was it *their* job to clean up? Why were they keeping quiet? Why did they consider it *their* job to keep the peace? Why were they made to feel they should be grateful because the worst has not happened? And finally, the biggest, why is it *their* job to get their husbands to help with the house?"

Hmm... Perhaps the Problem Is Not the Men, After All

On that fateful sunny winter morning, Dear Abby helped me realize something very central to the issue of women and housework. I realized exactly what was stopping me from having a fair and just household. And it was not a "what"; it was a "who." In the words of the cartoon character Pogo, "I have met the enemy and it is me." Like other "change opponents" over the past centuries, I had a greater fear of what I would lose than of what I would gain. In other words, it had to do with control. I thought back to the Thanksgiving Day caper. To avoid the feeling of losing something, I wanted to have control of the outcome for the Thanksgiving Day dinner. In today's New Age psychology, control has become a hated word. But there is no one, unless he or she is a complete noodle, who does not desire some control. Control of how it's done, I concluded, is not the enemy after all; it is the person's desired outcome that gets them in trouble.

"I get it," I said, as I stopped at a red light. It's probably true that most people would give up much of their control *if* they thought the person to whom they gave it to would create the same end result.

That raised an interesting thought about the Thanksgiving Day caper. As the light changed and I turned the corner, I thought more about the issue of control. Why did I want control of the meal?

I realized that because Gary doesn't have the same desired outcomes that I have around the ambiance of a special meal, I had fear about giving up the control. Even though I was not pleased with how much work I had to do to have it *my* way, I still preferred to keep the status quo rather than risk a change that might not bring about my desired outcome, which was a beautiful, scrumptious dinner with all the trimmings.

"Okay, Gary likes football," I told myself, "more than he likes fussy Thanksgiving dinners. But I like a fussy Thanksgiving dinner more than I like football. I believe what I want counts, but what Gary wants counts, too." So then, in the case of Thanksgiving, how do we both "get counted," since we both want different outcomes? More importantly, I began to ask, "Could understanding control and merging that thought with the belief that says, 'We both count,' revolutionize our household?"

I know this sounds like a long way around the barn to find simple answers for the mundane question of who does what, but along this journey I discovered a few things—like there were no enemies, and we were all just doing what we were taught to do—and I was beginning to ask the right questions.

CHAPTER 2

Our Lost Dreams

I was not looking for my dreams to interpret my life, but rather for my life to interpret my dreams.

— Susan Sontag, *The Benefactor* (1963)

When We Wish Upon a Star

"What are you going to be when you grow up?" Kathy had asked as we guided our raft down the winding Clinton River.

"The best sailor that ever lived," I said confidently. "I will be known around the world and at every port people will come out to greet me."

"Well, I want to be President of the United States," responded Kathy, "the best American president the world has ever had. And because of me, the world will be a better place for you to sail."

Like most children, we thought big. The future was in our hands, and just for the "wanting," our dreams would come true. Back then, I did not realize being born a girl would create such major barriers to my dreams—*if* I decided to get married and have a family, that is.

But few women I know have had their youthful dreams come true. Maybe it's because so many of our childhood dreams conflicted. For me, while rafting the Clinton, I dreamed of traveling the world, but I also dreamed of a career and family. I dreamed of adventure, but also of the house with the flower garden. I dreamed of the arts—of becoming an accomplished actress, musician, painter, or dancer—but I also dreamed of just being a wife and mother. I still dream. It is one of the more exciting attributes unique to humans.

Many anthropologists think the major difference between us and the animal kingdom is the human's ability to use tools. I think that the distinction is in the human's ability to make our dreams come true.

Why? Why do we all struggle so hard for our dreams? What do they represent? What do they say about us? Dreams, I have concluded, mirror our inner soul—our wants, our needs, our quests, the "what could have been" or "what might be." When all else fails, our dreams keep us going. They are always within us. No one can take them away. They are ours alone.

Validation

It was shortly after that infamous Thanksgiving holiday that The Woman's Network, which was part of a local chamber of commerce, brought together a panel of six women who had won their annual "Woman of Achievement" award. Since I was that year's winner, I was asked to be on the panel.

"We are asking the panelists," the coordinator said in her phone call to me, "to talk about the first time they found out they were 'girls.' So often we find that women are derailed early in childhood. Their dreams and aspirations concerning their future careers are dashed. Most were not encouraged the same way young boys were. Back then, gender roles were hard to break out of. Do you think you understand what I am referring to?" she asked.

"Perfectly," I responded enthusiastically. "I will have no problem addressing the topic." When I hung up the phone, I could feel more weight lifting off my shoulders. I was receiving outside validation for my new beliefs.

"It was when my seventh-grade biology teacher told me that girls make good nurses because they are *naturally* nurturing," said one of the women on the panel. "Doctors have to make quick decisions, which is easier for a guy to do since girls have a more difficult time making up their minds. It was a turning point for me," she said to an audience of nodding women.

It was my turn, and like the others I had prepared a short presentation. "I was about ten years old, watching my brothers play

CHAPTER 2

baseball in Little League. I loved baseball, too, and I was good at it. I desperately wanted to play on a real team, with *real* people watching." Then I recounted that eventful summer afternoon, running alongside my brother Allen as he headed for the ball field.

"Allen, I want to play too," I said.

"Play what?" he asked.

"Baseball, stupid. I want to play first base. Can I?"

"Of course not! Baseball is for boys," he said irritably.

"But why?" I asked. "I'm every bit as good as you are."

"Get real! You are not! Besides, no one wants you on their team. You're a girl, for God's sake. You think any of these guys wants a sissy girl on their team?"

Realizing how devastated I looked, he stopped running and looked down at me sympathetically. "Come on, Sis, there are no other girls out there. You know that. Besides, I need you in the grandstands rooting for me. You want me to win, don't you?"

I concluded my presentation by saying it was a profound moment. My realization about being a girl came just like it had for all the other women on the panel. It was when we were excluded. And the reason for the exclusion? "Girls just don't have what it takes."

Later that day in the Minneapolis skyway, I hurried to meet Gary for lunch. As I moved through the lunch rush, I thought back to my childhood and the baseball game. I started thinking of so many of the talented women that I had known over the years who, because of the demands of their family and household, never felt free to develop their own talents.

Those thoughts led me to develop the following metaphor:

Life Is Like a Baseball Game

Baseball is very much like real life. The players are on the field. The fans sit in the grandstands and root for the players. Most generally, the stands are filled with women. The playing field is filled with men. "Go, Hank, go! You can do it! I know you can! I'm with you! You're looking good, Hank!" a woman calls out to a young man on the field.

Since that woman is responsible for Hank's house, his kids, and his pets, the "game of life" can easily pass her by. Hank's fan's role, like many women's, is that of a bystander. Our *place* is reduced to sitting in the bleachers, waving pompoms, and cheering on the Hanks of the world.

Excuse Me—Is It My Turn to Play Yet?

But every now and then, when no one is looking, one of us sneaks out of her assigned seat and darts out onto the playing field. Nevertheless, make no mistake: right from the beginning, she is viewed as a *disadvantaged player*. Everyone knows immediately, if a woman plans on playing with the *big guys*, she's going to have a tough time. That's because the players are not equal. Therefore the game is not fair. The male players have the advantage, and it is an advantage so pronounced that it wipes out any chance of equity. Because they were there first, they have the best bats, the best shoes, and the best gloves. They are also stronger and can outrun us.

One would hope, with all their advantages, they would be satisfied, but they aren't. They have become greedy. They're no longer content with just winning. They want to control the game. If they control the game, they can also change the rules. If they can change the rules, they can always stay one step ahead of the game.

Now, every once in a while a woman "out of her league" hits a home run. Sitting up in the grandstand, cheering her on, some of the other women wonder how she did it. But then we remember our dreams and we know how she did it. Still, others will resent her. "Who does she think she is anyway, out there acting like a man?" one grandstander asks another. "Yeah, doesn't she know her place?" echoes the other grandstander.

"How dare she challenge her role!" screams a spectator. "There she goes!" someone else shouts. "Look at the infidel, running out there on the playing field! Taking the place of a man!" But the infidel doesn't hear. She only hears her own heartbeat, a heartbeat driven by a passionate desire—the desire to fulfill *her* dream.

When one woman fulfills her dream, she encourages others.

Watching her run onto the field, an open-minded spectator sits up. She takes notice. Something within her comes alive. Suddenly, she too is inspired and wants to play. "Go for it!" she screams. "I'm with you! You can do it—I know you can!"

But the infidel and the open-minded spectator are few and far between. Too many of us have become contented with sitting in the grandstand. We think that if we wait patiently, cheering for the players, we'll eventually get our turn to play. We think it's only fair. So we wait and we wait and we wait. Then, at long last, when we finally get our chance, the lights have been turned off and everyone has gone home, even the guy selling popcorn.

What about My Dreams?

Leaving the bleachers requires that we find a way to rekindle our dreams. And that is not an easy task. Sometimes it is easier to minimize them by telling ourselves, "Those were just silly old dreams anyway. I don't know what I was thinking of." We conclude they were nice to have but they weren't *that* important. Besides, there are too many barriers between them and us. One of the largest barriers, of course, is the expectation that we are to fulfill a *natural* role of supporter. It's the role our families have come to expect from us. It's no wonder so many of us feel defeated. Other people's expectations have controlled our life. And now that we've been shut out from playing for so long, we've lost more than our game plan—we've lost the desire to play.

I Guess That's Just the Way It Is

I continued thinking about this metaphor as I darted through the skyway. Even though numerous societal barriers have been overcome and young women have more opportunity today than when I grew up, many women still wait in the grandstands. The *largest* barrier is still there. Our deep-seated belief is that our very first responsibility is taking care of home and family, so that everyone else around us can play. We complain and gripe about it on a daily basis. We protest. We demand. We even go on strike, but to no avail. We still end up walking back into the stands, dragging our tattered pompoms and sighing, "I guess this is just the way it is."

The simple reality for the working woman is that she is working a double shift: one forty-hour shift *outside* the home, the other forty-hour shift *inside* the home. This double shift gives us no time to fulfill our own dreams. It gives us no time to become all we can be in the playing field. Just like Jill and Jane, who wrote to Dear Abby for answers, many of us have taken on this double shift with no prompting other than telling ourselves, "It just has to get done, and I am the only one who can do it." Or, "It's my job." Or, "That's how it has always been and no one is going to change it."

So — What Is a Partnership?

When I entered the restaurant that momentous day, I immediately spotted Gary standing and waving from a corner booth. "I ordered us a glass of merlot to celebrate," he said, smiling as I sat down.

"Celebrate?" I asked excitedly. "What's up?"

"Us," he said. "I've been thinking. From now on our life is going to be fifty-fifty."

"What does that mean?" I asked, confused.

"While I was driving to work this morning, I realized that what you have been saying for the last several weeks is true. I do see myself as a *helper* in the house, and it doesn't make sense. Since we both work equally outside the home, it's only reasonable that we should both work equally inside the home. It should be our *mutual* responsibility. So from now on we are partners," he said, lifting his glass. "I propose a toast to *us*. Here's to a long and equal partnership."

I remember thinking as I clicked his glass with mine that this would be a new beginning. Still, I was skeptical. Did Gary realize what he was saying? I decided I would test his sincerity by sharing my baseball metaphor. When I was through with my story about "life in the grandstands," Gary remained silent for a moment, thinking. He then asked, "Honey, what do you need from me to enable you to play in the game?"

I did not hesitate. "I need you to be a partner. Someone who

CHAPTER 2

will help me find a way to turn the lights back on. Someone who will take his turn sitting in the grandstands, waving the pompoms, while *I* play."

"Okay, Honey, go for it. You can do it ... I know you can!" He immediately caught himself. I could see that the light went on. "I mean ... I know *we* can!"

So that is how it all began, now ten years ago. I smile as I think back to that time and the question I was asking myself, which was, "Can a movement of the heart really transform into action?"

CHAPTER 3

The Woman's Household Personality

Character cannot be developed in ease and quiet. Only through experience of trial and suffering can the soul be strengthened, vision cleared, ambition inspired, and success achieved.

– Helen Keller, *Helen Keller's Journal* (1938)

Who Am I in My Home?

Over the next several months, I became a serious student of gender. In every home I walked into, every movie I saw, every TV show I watched, every book, magazine, and newspaper I read, I observed gender roles. I noticed our society has numerous expectations concerning its men and women. Some expectations are subtle and easily accommodated—for example, a woman in her hostess's kitchen, asking, "What can I do to help?"—to more glaring ones, like the waiter placing the check in front of the man.

I noted some of us are more comfortable with gender expectations than others. Who we are in our home is by far the best test in assessing our comfort level in adapting to our gender roles. How we are in our home reflects if we reject these roles or embrace them. Without realizing it, our home tells us—and others, as well—how we feel, what our values are, and what our beliefs are. It mirrors our conflicts and our peace. I have since come to identify all these messages that we send to ourselves and to others as one's "household personality." Basically, a household personality is simply a

CHAPTER 3

description of who we are at home. It might have nothing to do with who we are in the workplace.

For instance, I can delegate and act independently and assertively at work, but I suddenly transform into a caretaker and nursemaid as soon as I walk into my home. Similarly, a woman who is organized, efficient, and creative at work can become disorganized, inefficient, and non-creative at home. It is important to note that *there is no right household personality*. None is better, more clever, or more desirable than another. We simply are who we are.

I have collected all these individual traits, beliefs, and behaviors and categorized them into five personalities. By identifying your predominant household personality, you will have a greater understanding about the role you play within your home, and how and why you play it. It will reveal how rigid you are within this role and how adaptable you are to changing it. Your household personality will identify your charms, passions, and strengths, as well as your weaknesses. More importantly, your household personality will identify the personal barriers you will need to overcome to create a household partnership.

After you score the questionnaire, you may find you fit into more than one profile. However, most likely one will be dominant. As you contemplate the questions, answer the way you *feel*. Be careful not to answer the way you *think* you should feel, or according to things you *should* be doing or *should* like. Also, be careful not to answer the way you *wish* you were. To get an accurate look at who you *are*, you will want to answer the questions honestly. Take your time. Remember there are no right or wrong answers.

YOUR HOUSEHOLD PERSONALITY QUESTIONNAIRE

Please answer the questions with a number from 1 to 5 on the basis of how strongly you disagree or agree.

1: **strongly disagree**
2: **disagree**
3: **neither agree nor disagree**
4: **agree**
5: **strongly agree**

1. I couldn't care less if I am the only one doing the housework; I just want it done. _____

2. I have wonderful ideas, but I don't follow through on them. _____

3. While growing up, I thought more about my future career than the family I would have. _____

4. I agree with the statement, "Peace at any cost." _____

5. As a child I was a tomboy. _____

6. Nothing is more important than the freedom to do what I feel like. _____

7. I enjoy entertaining and making my guests feel special. _____

8. As a child, I did not enjoy playing with dolls. _____

9. A career was always my most important goal. _____

10. I feel I have a lot in common with children. _____

11. I adhere to the phrase, "Work first, play later." _____

12. I have fresh flowers in my home most of the time. _____

13. My laundry room usually looks like a disaster area. _____

14. As a little girl, I always talked about what great things I was going to do when I grow up. _____

15. I can easily put off an important house task until "tomorrow" for something fun to do today. _____

CHAPTER 3

16. I avoid discussing "hot" topics or having heated discussions. _____

17. I don't ever watch violent movies. _____

18. I always felt differently from my female friends, since my wants were more nontraditional. _____

19. I would rather barbecue and picnic outside than "fuss" inside. _____

20. I liked playing the games the boys played more than what girls played. _____

21. Having my own children has totally changed my career plans. _____

22. I do not back away from conflict. _____

23. I feel very connected to children because I feel like a child myself. _____

24. I think I have more "grown-up" than "child" within me. _____

25. I love fantasy. _____

26. I believe I am well informed on political issues and love debating the issues. _____

27. I am considered to have a successful career. _____

28. I don't like schedules. _____

29. I am slow to anger. _____

30. I find the concept of "women's work" contemptible. _____

31. I felt I had to "back off" from my career to raise my children. _____

32. I like every day to be different. _____

33. I called myself a feminist long before most of my friends. _____

34. Ecstasy is sitting by a roaring fire, sipping a warm drink with someone I love. _____

35. I'd rather just do the household work than argue about it. _____

36. I do not procrastinate. _____

37. I often feel guilty for neglecting the housework. _____

38. As an adult, I was an active (or verbal) supporter of civil rights issues. _____

39. I cook with fresh herbs as much as I can. _____

40. I need to be doing something all the time. _____

41. I knew early on that I had different goals from my female friends. _____

42. I have been told that I have radical views. _____

43. I enjoy academics. _____

44. I must have my house neat and tidy all the time. _____

45. I love, or would love, a flower garden. _____

46. I prefer to get "carry-out" food out rather than to cook it. _____

47. I love debating social issues, especially those involving women. _____

48. I am often working toward my goals while others are playing. _____

49. I think that people who live in a mess are lazy. _____

50. I go way out of my way to purchase fresh vegetables or fruit. _____

CHAPTER 3

51. I enjoy people in my home but I dislike formal entertaining. _____

52. Everywhere I look I see injustice. _____

53. My home is in good order but my career is more important than my house. _____

54. I prefer staying at a bed-and-breakfast inn in the country than at a resort. _____

55. I really can't rest until all the work is done. _____

56. I have been very involved in my community. _____

57. My closets, drawers, and cupboards are very disorganized. _____

58. I feel quite confident that I can have a career, raise a family, and take care of the home. _____

59. I am always buying candles. _____

60. It is all right that the home is my responsibility, because I want things done a certain way. _____

61. I enjoy people in my home and don't ever feel like I have to entertain them. _____

62. It seems like I am always arguing for what I believe in. _____

63. I am proud of my achievements. I would not change a whole lot. _____

64. I love buying little gifts and doing special things for my friends. _____

65. People who know me consider me mature. _____

66. I often find myself going crazy over the fact my family sees the household as my responsibility. _____

67. I often wish I were more of a "go-getter." _____

68. I much prefer working to not working. _____

69. I am grateful for any help I get within the home, because I feel it is my job. _____

70. It is important that I make my houseguests feel special. _____

71. I love bookstores and am an avid reader. _____

72. My friends know I am always available to "play." _____

73. I am angry a lot because I don't get enough help around the house. _____

74. My family and guests say that my home is warm and cozy. _____

75. I spend most of my weekends working around the house. _____

76. My mate never expects a clean house and dinner waiting for him at the end of a workday. _____

77. I like to feel appreciated about the special things I do. _____

78. I ask myself, "Why am I doing it all? Why is this my job?" _____

79. I have lots of friends and I like to keep in touch with them. _____

80. I usually don't like help when I am entertaining. _____

81. I tutor my children all the time. _____

82. It doesn't matter to me when guests "take over" in my kitchen. I prefer it. _____

CHAPTER 3

83. It infuriates me that my family does not do their share. _____

84. I often am the first person that friends call when they need emotional support. _____

85. I often neglect the house because it interferes with my community work. _____

86. I love being with teenagers. _____

87. I have been called compulsive or "overly responsible." _____

88. I would rather read to my kids than paint with them. _____

89. I prefer to use cloth napkins over paper even when eating pizza. _____

90. My closets are neat and organized. _____

91. I often prefer kids to adults. _____

92. I detest the term "housewife." _____

93. Candles, framed photos, oil lamps, flowers, and music fill my home. _____

94. I prefer museums to parks. _____

95. A great day for me is "forgetting" what needs to be done and taking the kids on a picnic. _____

96. I wish that I had more time for play. _____

97. I have lots of goals that I am working toward. _____

98. I like setting a mood in my home even when I am alone. _____

99. I can make convincing arguments and often win people over. _____

100. I usually find a pretty good reason for not getting something done. _____

THE WOMAN'S HOUSEHOLD PERSONALITY

101. I like having "to-do lists" and will follow them. _____
102. I can't really rest if there is work to be done. _____
103. I have music on much more than TV. _____
104. I am always asked to be on committees. _____
105. Money is not within my top five priorities. _____
106. If I get angry, I usually try to settle it within myself. _____
107. I am considered an overachiever. _____
108. I enjoy creating a lovely event. _____
109. I think people get too consumed with how their homes look. _____
110. I'm a rebel. I never will fit into the "woman's role." _____
111. I willingly make hard sacrifices in seeking my goals. _____
112. I would drop everything to play in the first snowfall. _____
113. I have lots of willpower. _____
114. I love holidays and look forward to them. _____
115. Because I work so hard, I often am taken advantage of. _____
116. I am usually involved (actively or verbally) in some kind of protest. _____
117. I liked playing "dress-up" when I was little. _____
118. I like to have control of both my home and workplace. _____
119. I am considered a leader within my community/church. _____
120. I must have goals to work toward and fulfill. _____

CHAPTER 3

121. I always send sentimental birthday cards. _____

122. I am frugal and do not waste money on foolishness. _____

123. I spend time painting, photography, gardening, cooking, writing, and sewing. _____

124. If the choice is sharing the work or doing it my way, I prefer not to share it. _____

125. I think I am very assertive. _____

How to Determine Your Household Personality

You have now completed the questionnaire. Refer to the following guide for instructions on how to score your answers.

Scoring the Household Personality Questionnaire

To score your answers, note the groups below, marked A–E. Under each of the groups are the numbers assigned to the questions you have just answered, all 125 of them. Record the numerical response you gave to each question in the space provided. For example, under column A, the first number shown is 5, which represents question number 5. Whatever numerical response (1, 2, 3, 4, or 5) you gave to question number 5 should be written on the line next to that number. Continue on with all the questions, writing down the numerical response you gave to each of the 125 questions. When you have finished writing in all of your responses, add up the numbers in each group to determine the total for that group. Then write the totals for each group in the section following the groups. Each group is shown with its corresponding profile. The higher the number, the stronger you are in that profile. The highest number you could score in any of the profiles is 125.

Dual Profiles: If you have two groups whose scores are less than eight points apart, you fall into a large category of women who have dual profiles. You will want to read both profiles and combine them. Be sure to read all of the profiles, for you will learn just as much about yourself from who you are *not* as from who you *are*.

Group A	Group B	Group C	Group D	Group E
5 ____	1 ____	2 ____	7 ____	3 ____
8 ____	4 ____	6 ____	12 ____	9 ____
20 ____	11 ____	10 ____	17 ____	14 ____
22 ____	16 ____	13 ____	25 ____	18 ____
26 ____	24 ____	15 ____	34 ____	21 ____
30 ____	29 ____	19 ____	39 ____	27 ____
33 ____	35 ____	23 ____	45 ____	31 ____
38 ____	40 ____	28 ____	50 ____	36 ____
42 ____	44 ____	32 ____	54 ____	41 ____
47 ____	49 ____	37 ____	59 ____	43 ____
52 ____	55 ____	46 ____	64 ____	48 ____
56 ____	60 ____	51 ____	70 ____	53 ____
62 ____	65 ____	57 ____	74 ____	58 ____
66 ____	69 ____	61 ____	77 ____	63 ____
73 ____	75 ____	67 ____	79 ____	68 ____
78 ____	80 ____	72 ____	84 ____	71 ____
83 ____	87 ____	76 ____	89 ____	81 ____
85 ____	90 ____	82 ____	93 ____	88 ____
92 ____	96 ____	86 ____	98 ____	94 ____
99 ____	102 ____	91 ____	103 ____	97 ____
104 ____	106 ____	95 ____	108 ____	101 ____
110 ____	115 ____	100 ____	114 ____	107 ____
116 ____	118 ____	105 ____	117 ____	111 ____
119 ____	122 ____	109 ____	121 ____	113 ____
125 ____	124 ____	112 ____	123 ____	120 ____
Total ____	Total ____	Total ____	Total ____	Total ____

WRITE IN YOUR TOTALS FROM EACH COLUMN.

Group A _____ The Rebel
Group B _____ The HoneyBee
Group C _____ The Sojourner
Group D _____ The Stargazer
Group E _____ The Tigress

CHAPTER 3

EVALUATING YOUR SCORE

90 Points or More

Since you have the majority of the characteristics in this profile, you will find in her your strongest identity. You not only share her likes and dislikes, but she also represents your *inner* desires and needs.

80 – 89 Points

You share a great many characteristics with this profile and have a good deal of understanding for her. You will find in her a great deal of your *external* self, the "self" that others might see you to be.

70 –79 Points

You have enough characteristics in this profile to understand and enjoy her. You will most likely find that your closest friends fall into this profile, but you have a *different lifestyle* and *several habits* that differ from those of this profile.

60 – 69 Points

You have enough characteristics of this profile to have *some* understanding of her. You also share some of her likes and dislikes, but your lifestyle and habits are *very* different from those of the profile.

Depending on how high or low you are in this score, you will probably find that you have some strong disapproval of her lifestyle.

Below 60 Points

You have so little in common with this profile that you will have difficulty in relating to or understanding her. (This is someone you might want to get to know; being opposites, you have a lot to teach each other.)

The following chapter will provide you with a description of your household personality.

CHAPTER 4

It's No Wonder I Do What I Do

One is not born, but rather becomes, a woman.
— Simone de Beauvoir, *The Second Sex* (1949)

The Rebel, the HoneyBee, the Sojourner, the Stargazer, or the Tigress?

By now you have discovered the name of your household personality. Most likely you also discovered you are not just one profile, but like me and many others, you are a combination of all of them. However, one is predominant (a score of 80 or more). If not, go back and verify your answers on the questions to which you gave a response of 1 or 5, just to ensure their accuracy.

The Rebel

Chances are, if you are a Rebel, from the time you were little you never saw a need for gender roles. You could shimmy up a tree and throw a football as well as any other boy on the block. You detested ribbons, bows, and anything with lace, preferring instead to have your hair pulled back in a ponytail and to wear jeans. It wasn't so much that you didn't see "girl stuff" as cute, it's just that it got in the way of things—things like building treehouses or fishing.

Your girlfriends could not bring Barbie and Ken up for a visit; you were too busy writing your acceptance speech for president of the treehouse association. You had no time for drinking tea or other Barbie-doll foolishness. *Ugh*.

You probably even remember your emotional trauma when, at age ten, you first discovered a deep chasm separated you from males.

CHAPTER 4

You found out boys were endowed with a series of birthrights—rights like voting and such, which girls only acquired within the last century. When you first learned of these facts from your history teacher, you were certain she had misspoken, was in the sauce again, or was really talking about Martians. Up 'til then, the only difference between the genders you knew of was that Jimmy couldn't shoot a BB gun as straight as you and Scott was always a sucker for a fastball, low, hard, and away. You never did too well at accepting things that did not measure up to the way you thought things should be. So in order to cope, early on you perfected the defense mechanism of denial. This defense served you so well that you brought it with you into adulthood.

Rebels knew they were feminists long before it became politically correct. Consequently, you always felt a bit out of step with traditional thinking. To you, the idea that women belong in the kitchen is just as nonsensical as the notion that a man's home is his castle. Logic is one of your strengths. You are able to identify faulty concepts faster than most. And societal roles based on gender are one of those faulty concepts that you discovered by age three.

As a Rebel, you may recall the time you and your best pal (Rebels' best pals are also Rebels) stood ramrod tall in your high school sociology class and (to the dismay of all in earshot) assertively proclaimed, "We are sure this institution of marriage is some evil fascist conspiracy to assure the continual oppression of women. We don't know about the rest of you, but hell no, we won't go." True to your rebellious nature, you were just as amused by the gaping mouths of the girls around you as you were by the boys' critical sneers.

Gutsy little Rebels could care less who they please, or who they offend with their "radical" views. You are as irritated with the "submissive little females" as you are with the men who seek them. Later, on the college campus, you were likely carrying signs protesting U.S. imperialism or the abuse of animal rights in the science lab. Wherever there is oppression of people, animals, or ideas, Rebels are there, speaking up for the underdog. Yes... you thought you could change the world. (Again, denial worked for you.)

Over the years, you have become very aware that inequality exists, not only in the world, but also in your home. You are frustrated because even though you recognize the injustice, you have somehow lost sight of how to change it. The world, for some reason, seems to be an easier battleground to "right the wrongs" than your own home does. And even though this home is important to you, it often feels like a "den of inequity," one you dream of escaping from.

You, more than any other household personality, are frustrated that your family ignores your pleas for help. You will regress to shouting, screaming, and complaining as a means of protest. You might have even been known to go on strike within your own home for weeks on end, just to make a point. If they still aren't listening, you've even resorted to guerrilla tactics, like building a campfire in the backyard and ceremoniously burning all the clothes you have found strewn around the house. Still, to your dismay, these antics have been unsuccessful. In fact, they are met with passive tolerance ("Oh, you know how Mom is!"), which only infuriates you more. Rebels can tolerate being ignored, but not patronized.

You are the most perplexing of all the household personalities concerning your home. That is because you are just not sure how you feel about it. Some days your home feels like a peaceful haven, while on other days it feels like a prison. On the days it is your prison, you will neglect it as a means of demonstration. Because you are acutely aware of the gender inequity within it, you will be damned if you are going to reinforce those ugly stereotypes by cleaning up after everyone, so you don't. And since the art of compromising is not your greatest strengths, you aren't going to spend one more moment of your precious time getting other family members to see what should be obvious. So you try passive manipulation. "If they don't care, then neither do I." But it still doesn't work. And your frustration grows and grows and grows.

Outside the home, Rebels often excel. Since you are continually calling for the abandonment of archaic belief systems, you seek new avenues to institute change. Therefore, you are the first to flee the nest to find other outlets for your causes. Of course, you don't have

CHAPTER 4

to go far. You are a natural-born leader, a sought-after committee member, task-force leader, or campaign manager. You are also a great orator. If there is a speech to be made or a charge to be led, the animated Rebel will be the first to leap on top of the soapbox or lead the march to Washington.

As a Rebel, you are a breath of fresh air to many of the women in your life. The men are fascinated with your "assertiveness" as well. No need to seek out male companions. The males are always homing in on you. They enjoy your thought-provoking conversations, inspiration, and snappy comebacks. They see you either as a challenge or someone to bait. Most of it is in fun, which you enjoy and are comfortable with. In fact, Rebels often prefer the company of men to women.

Your humor is one of your most endearing qualities. It is quick, subtle, and dry. Even when angry, humor can disarm you. That's because you react to it as a form of intimacy. Though you take life thoughtfully, wit and laughter always take priority. This humor also gives you an edge with children, especially teenagers, at least the ones who don't take themselves too seriously. The neighborhood kids begin drifting in about 9:00 P.M., knowing that the welcome mat at your household is out twenty-four hours a day. They love to sit at your feet while you candidly reveal the shocking antics of your youth. You all howl with laughter into the wee hours of the morning, while you embellish on stories of your youth. Needless to say, the teenagers keep coming back. They also bring their pals.

Your troubled friends will seek you out as well. Rebels are always there when needed. You have never understood the concept of "fight your own battles." If you believe in the cause, you will fight anyone's battles. Like Scarlett O'Hara in *Gone with the Wind*, Rebels can be relentless, shrewd, and daring when fighting for justice. And because they are so tenacious, few people are brave enough to face off against them. Rebels can easily draw a crowd, lead a mob, or be a lone voice crying in the wilderness to right a wrong, but sadly, your fair, compassionate world does not yet exist. (Once again your denial helps.)

Because you are among the most discouraged to find yourself still alone in the kitchen, you are one of the most receptive of the females to creating a household partnership. Your intellect tells you that you have everything to gain (which is more freedom to do what you really enjoy) and nothing to lose, but even more important, you will have "righted a wrong."

The HoneyBee

If you are a HoneyBee, your mate considers himself extremely fortunate. HoneyBees are not only rare, they are the easiest people on the face of the earth to live with. You love harmony, order, and routine, and your home reflects all of these attributes. You also desire peace at all costs, usually your own. But no matter, you are extremely generous with your goodwill and generally take the high road to avoid conflict. Beware, you can sting if stepped on. The problem is, one never knows until it is too late. You don't give off a lot of signs before your deed. It's usually a sneak attack. But that's because it takes an awful lot to get you to the stinging stage. Even you are surprised when it happens. It's because you're the most rational and non-emotional of all female household personalities. To put it simply, you are all grown-up. For example, you probably refuse to ruin too many of your days squabbling over who didn't replace the toilet paper, or whose turn it is to wash the dishes. Quite frankly, you find it beneath you.

This does not mean you don't notice. Far from it. In fact, you are quite judgmental of people who do not share your work ethic, probably viewing them as lazy. It's just that you feel above it all, and if your family doesn't notice what needs to be done, well, you are not going to start "buzzing around" about it and ruin your busy day.

Consistent with your nature, you refuse to condemn others, publicly or privately. Since you feel fairly confident of who you are, there is no need. You have no desire to get into a "one-up" or "I am better than most" mode. HoneyBees also are not in the habit of making family members feel guilty for not pitching in. Of all the

CHAPTER 4

personalities, you truly believe that taking care of the home is your sole responsibility, and you regard any "help" as a personal gift. This is a dangerous belief. It has set you up to be profusely thankful for any pittance thrown your way. "I'm the only one that can do it" thinking has rubbed off on your family. They have come to believe that any help they provide toward maintaining the "hive" should be rewarded. After all, it really is *your* job!

To say the least, you are a bit compulsive about organization. Your favorite saying is, "There is a place for everything, and everything has its place." Your closets are meticulously tidy. If you find them otherwise, no matter: you will put everything back the way it should be, and you do it without complaining to the person who made the mess. This is because your pragmatic mind says that others can't change, so what's the use? Therefore, you find it is easier and less stressful to just do it yourself. Besides, you are way too busy to deal with another's irresponsibility.

The truth is, you feel better about yourself when you're working. It gives you a sense of purpose and fulfills your inner desire to be needed. The problem is you are often taken advantage of. You're growing resentful, if you aren't there already. Because you do much more than your fair share, you continue to balance those *ugly* resentful feelings with the good feelings that come from being needed and productive. And with optimistic, sunny HoneyBees, the good feelings usually win out.

HoneyBees have an extremely well-developed set of values. They are loyal employees, great friends, loving partners, and devoted mothers. However, there is a gnawing problem you cannot help but be aware of. You are not having as much fun as others do. While everyone else is having a "grand ol' hootenanny" time, HoneyBees are on the sidelines doing all the work. The adage "work first, play later" is your personal motto. The problem comes, however, when this "play later" almost never arrives. This can be a great loss for those around them, since HoneyBees make events and gatherings more special. They are always much more fun than they think they are, and are greatly missed when their family tells the waiting party that the HoneyBee is just too busy to come out to play.

As a busy little Bee, you consider your home to be your own personal hive and you take tremendous pride in maintaining it. You have no issue with mowing the lawn, painting the eaves, and washing the clothes all at the same time. Even though you relish the control you have in your home, you would relinquish *some* of the work if you could be assured it would be done to your satisfaction. The dilemma is that your family does not "assure" you, especially in the meticulous way you want it done.

HoneyBees need to be warned that they are susceptible to the physical effects of anxiety and stress that they place upon themselves. It is understandable. Your quest for perfection is unrealistic and you are often overwhelmed. No wonder, for you operate from a framework that says, "I am the only one who can get the job done to my satisfaction."

HoneyBees can easily identify with the Rebel's wrath. The difference is, however, you have a tendency to turn your anger inward whereas the Rebel turns it outward. There is no mystery as to why you choose to hold onto your anger. It's because you believe you have more control over your life if the problem lies within you. You react to your anger and frustration by telling yourself, "I simply must find a better way!" Then you fly off to pollinate another purple cone. After all, there is work to be done and there is no time for silly sulking.

You are also susceptible to the same problems at work that you encounter at home. Because you are so responsible and conscientious, you are a highly respected employee. Your employer can always count on you to go the extra mile and do what needs to be done to get the job done. Still, the need for perfection produces far too much stress and ultimately brings on pollinating fatigue (a unique condition known only to affect HoneyBees). This fatigue often hampers your ability to buzz and you may find yourself responding to most invitations to play with, "I'm just too tired."

For the HoneyBee, children and other family members come first. You want everyone to have the things they need and you will go to major extremes making sure they have them. The rule is that whatever it takes to finish the job will be done. Period. It's not that

CHAPTER 4

you can't depend at all on your mate, but since you are overly responsible you feel the family's emotional and physical well-being is *your* job. In fact, some HoneyBees produce the bulk of the household income.

You usually have an obsessive need for perfection, but if you are a typical HoneyBee, you will not admit it. That's because you view a perfectionist as imperfect. You believe people who seek perfection are odd, deranged, and perhaps even a bit evil. No wonder you are slow to admit to this nefarious shortcoming. As long as you judge perfectionists as overcompensating, controlling, and judgmental, you are going to hide in the daffodils, thinking your own perfectionist nature is your secret. But since HoneyBees are never really good at sneaking around, you don't fool anyone.

Given the choice between being in the kitchen alone or having your house in shambles, you may decide to forego the household partnership, thank you very much. It's a logical decision. You have the most to risk in developing an equitable household. It entails a loss of control over the home, the ultimate sacrifice to all self-respecting HoneyBees. Consequently, you are the hardest to convince that by letting go and developing a partnership, everything won't fall apart. That's because it probably will, at least for a while. Over time, however, you will come to realize that *perfect* pollination isn't everything, and "good enough" is often good enough. If you can let go of some of your desired outcomes, you will find that a household partnership provides you with many more benefits than you give up. And just think—there will actually be time to stop and *smell* all those purple cones you have been pollinating!

The Sojourner

If you are a Sojourner, you have (more than any other household personality) a desire to be unfettered by rules and responsibilities. Unleashed freedom is where it's at for the roaming and uncommitted Sojourner. This lack of commitment does make for some problems. For instance, you have countless projects on your "to-do" list—if you could only find the list. And whether you find it or not is

IT'S NO WONDER I DO WHAT I DO

irrelevant. You will only refer to it if the mood strikes. God forbid it would obligate you to have to do something! Freedom and the ability to do what you want, when you choose, and with whom is your greatest desire. Needless to say, dear Sojourner, keeping your home looking immaculate is not your number one priority, and ... well ... it sort of looks that way.

But not to fret, there are other priorities, like being adored by your children, or any child for that matter. You have much more in common with their play, and frankly, you like doing what they like doing. For example, you don't understand why anyone would object to kids milling about in the kitchen at midnight making chocolate chip cookies. Midnight, in fact, is your favorite time. After you all polish off a dozen chocolate chip cookies, it's too late to clean up the mess. Besides, the sound of scrubbing pots and pans would only wake up the rest of the household. So you go to bed with a clear conscience.

But Sojourners pay for their fun. The next morning you don't hear the alarm and you miss the kids' school bus. By the time you drop them off, you are late for work. It's at this point you tell yourself, "With so little sleep, how could I possibly put in a good day of work? Oh, well—I'll just go home and clean up the kitchen." On the way home you begin thinking, "Maybe my husband will clean it up. After all, I can't be expected to do it all!" So you divert your car to the movie theater. The problem is you forgot your wallet.

Still and all, Sojourners are known for their fun. That's why every kid on the block wants to move in. You are just way too cool. There is always junk food to eat (your favorite), or somewhere to go (doesn't matter where), or someone to talk with or play with. Nothing is ever too serious or so important that it can't wait, be put off, rescheduled, or, for that matter, simply forgotten. Your friends find your outward, devil-may-care attitude delightful, but they know you come with a price, for you are always late, not showing up, or canceling engagements. Your excuse, "Are you sure we scheduled that? I don't have it on my calendar," can wear them out. (They already are aware that you don't keep a personal calendar.)

CHAPTER 4

Consequently, this noncommitted lifestyle of the Sojourner causes you some guilt. Try as you might, you have not been able to shake those despicable "shoulds" and "should nots" that society shoulders you with. An inner voice keeps saying, "You should have a cleaner house, a checkbook that balances, a clothes dryer that doesn't double for your computer desk, a refrigerator that stores food instead of overflowing with pottery clay, and a meal that is cooked instead of bagged." And it's not just society. You, too, tell yourself you *should* be able to do the household chores, notwithstanding your forty-hour work week. After all, others do. You know of them. They are those boring people who confront procrastination and responsibility head on. In fact, they actually end up attacking some of those "they can wait until tomorrow" chores today. These people are not your friends—they lack spontaneity and creativity.

No need to worry too much about the Sojourner's guilt. They are the most resourceful of all the female household personalities and employ very interesting techniques to deal with their procrastination. When all those chores start to pile up (bills, clothes, dishes, garbage), they inconveniently coincide with the Sojourner's discovery of the greatest American novel ever written. What a travesty if mundane household chores would come between you and such a wonder of literary work! Or, perhaps, it is *finally* the right moment to take up the flute. After all, you've always intended to do it before, but never found the time. Sojourners have perfected the ability to combine procrastination and rationalization until it rises to an art form. Before you applaud too loud, however, they also suffer the consequences of a disorganized life.

But again, we return to their priorities. Sojourners are more interested in people than things. Therefore, they never want for company. Your many friends are always dropping by because your home is the most comfortable place in town. Primarily because you feel so relaxed (after all, no need to fuss over company!), your friends feel at home. They just kick back and snuggle in. "Oh, don't worry about the mess!" you say. "It can wait until morning." Your friends love sitting barefoot in your overstuffed chair (toes all tucked into that snuggy little tear in the back cushion), and will budge only to put another log on the fire. They might even split it for you, since they are pretty sure you won't. They sip wine (from the bottle — no glasses!) and philosophize with you into the wee hours of the morning on why there need to be more women in the United States Senate.

Another charming quality, absolutely unique to Sojourners, is your total lack of ownership regarding your possessions. The friend who complains about her mother-in-law who comes in and takes over the kitchen has you completely baffled. For you, that would be Nirvana. Anyone with a detectable pulse is welcomed in your kitchen — to clean it, mess it up, rearrange it, or complain about it. You would welcome any stranger in for dinner if he or she is willing to cook it, even if your kitchen is rearranged in the process. However, it's not just your kitchen that reveals your generosity. Anyone can borrow, or sometimes have, anything you own.

As a Sojourner, your career tends to interfere with your personal desires. After all, employers ask an awful lot. For example they want you to show up. They then expect an entire five days of work out of the week's seven. "For the love of God!" you cry in silent desperation. "They want my blood!" When you realize that the only thing in this for you is money, you are ready to move on. Sojourners will only excel at their place of employment when given a great deal of leeway. But in the *right* career you have a happy employer since you are a team player and are known not to make waves. (Basically, you don't care enough.) Because of the freedom it provides, many Sojourners are self-employed — perhaps not successfully, but happily.

Sojourners need a great deal of "alone time," and are often found retreating to places where no one knows them. Mountaintops, Katmandu, sailboats, out-of-the-way beaches — all serve well, along with a good book and a box of chocolates. You need this time to ponder about the great adventure that you soon will undertake. Just as long as this adventure does not require you to change a whole lot, that is, or commit you in a major way, or ask something of you.

CHAPTER 4

This last requirement is important. Because of your complete rejection of a double standard, you are one of the "nicest" mothers. Since you feel turnabout is fair play, you won't ask something of your children that you won't do yourself. For example, you don't waste too much time rallying the home troops to begin a home improvement project which you aren't that big on doing yourself. You would rather spend time watching a sunset with the kids, playing in the snow, or running down to the Latin quarter where you can discuss the importance of *carpe diem*, and you assume it's the same for your kids.

Even though no one's in a Sojourner's kitchen, including the Sojourner, it's not necessarily the way you want it, or even like it. Therefore, you are fairly easy to convince that equity in your home would give you a much more organized life, less guilt, and a great deal more permission to have the life you wish. Why procrastinate on getting rid of the guilt of procrastination? It is not your job to see that everything gets done. A household partnership would share those haunting "shoulds" with your mate. But more critical to a Sojourner in gaining an equitable household is the freedom to do more of what she wants to do—whatever that is.

The Stargazer

"*Star bright, star light, first star I've seen tonight. I wish I may, I wish I might, have the wish I made tonight.*" Little Stargazers could always be heard reciting poetry and humming melancholy songs while they prepared tea parties under the drooping willow tree in their backyard. Even then, they were the most gracious of hostesses. Their guests included Winnie the Pooh and his friend Christopher Robin, and, of course, Daisy Doll, along with Mickey and Minnie (they make such a nice couple).

Little Stargazer prepared the table beautifully, using wild violets and dandelions arranged to perfection in a discarded but now painted Campbell's soup can (one she designed especially for the occasion). Even the beauty of a Chinese Ming vase would fade in comparison to the floral arrangement she would create from a tin can. After everything was prepared, she would dress in her most elegant pinafore, braid her hair, sit down, and pour tea for her guests. Yes, she was convinced that it was in her power, or anyone else's for that matter, to capture a fanciful life filled with Winnie the Poohs, Christopher Robins, and tea parties. From being a gracious hostess, grown-up Stargazers have changed very little since "tea time under the willows."

If you are a Stargazer, you were born to enjoy the finery in life. Finery should not be confused with "expensive." Stargazers are able to create exquisite surroundings without so much as a penny in their pocket. You give new meaning to the concept of making lemonade from rotten lemons—or rotten apples—for that matter. Your house can be a tent or a mansion—no matter, you will make it "a thing of wonder."

Whatever the world throws your way turns out somehow to be a blessing. Money helps, but you can find beauty all around you even without it. It shows up in the gardens you grow, the music you play, the pictures you paint, the pillows you fluff, and the meals you cook. No other household personality is more sensitive to their external environment than the Stargazer's, and your home shows it.

Stargazer's homes are like charming cozy bed-and-breakfast inns. There are always flowers on the table, music in the background, a fire in the fireplace, and specialty coffees brewing. Even when you're home alone, there are oil lamps burning, a piano playing, and a gourmet meal elaborately spread out on a table set for one. For others these preparations are reserved for a special occasion, but for you it's a natural state that you need for your emotional peace. You know no other way. Setting a serene mood is as important as breathing and you do it with the same ease. When you do go out of your way to create an extra-special evening, you have very lucky recipients. This is not about being garish. You simply enjoy the feeling of making others feel special, primarily because it comes so easily.

Stargazers write most of the creative household decorating, entertaining, and cooking magazines found in the bookstores. They

CHAPTER 4

not only have a knack for it, but they also have the "eye." I've observed a Stargazer change a dismal and uninviting den by simply moving a couch from the wall into the center of the room. She then places a round braided rug in front of it, and salvages an old chest from the basement for a coffee table. While rummaging through kitchen cupboards she comes up with just the "right" basket and fills it with dry weeds collected from the yard. She cleverly turns a hollow branch into a candleholder and finds an antique picture of Grandmother's farm in the old chest. She arranges the basket, the candleholder, and the antique picture upon the chest with the skill of a sculptor. For her final touch, she finds a colorful afghan stuffed in a closet and drapes it over the back of the couch. Bingo! She has turned mundane into charming in less than a few hours.

Even though Stargazers are one of the most giving of the household personalities, they do not like to be taken for granted. Consequently, neglecting a Stargazer is a bad idea. Family members of a Stargazer only forget a wedding anniversary or Mother's Day once. In short, Stargazers do not respond well if they feel they are the only ones giving.

It's not that you keep score, but you do not survive well in an atmosphere where you are being taken advantage of. Stargazers, like their sister Rebel, have a keen sense of justice and fairness. No one, except the HoneyBee, operates from the Golden Rule as much as the Stargazer does. Therefore, your expectation is that you be treated as well as you treat others. Generally you are, for you are careful about placing yourself in harm's way. Stargazers tend to surround themselves with friends that are nurturing and caring. They usually will not be treated poorly by someone more than once. Seldom do they keep a friend who is insensitive to their needs. In other words, mistreat a Stargazer, and you are off her guest list.

Because of your unique ability to empathize with others, you and the HoneyBee are the most nurturing of the profiles. This trait comes naturally for you. Stargazers have spent a lifetime caring for someone, beginning way back with Pooh Bear and Daisy Dolls. Therefore, their fortunate children seldom lack for attention.

You can always spot a Stargazer's child. They are the ones who say "please" and "thank you," shake hands, and respond with "Nice to meet you." These kids also have table manners that would shame most adults. Consequently, their children are welcome guests in the homes, or even formal affairs, of friends and family. One doesn't ever have to speculate. If their gift was received by a Stargazer's child, a handwritten thank-you note will be in the mail the following week. Stargazers simply don't tolerate insensitive or unappreciative behavior, especially from their children.

At the workplace, a Stargazer is either biding her time or setting the world on fire. As discussed, you are one of the most creative of the household personalities. Therefore, you will excel in a work environment that taps into these attributes and will fail miserably if you are stifled or become bored. No need to worry, however. You won't stay in any environment that does not appreciate or nurture you. You will soon be off to find an appropriate outlet for your creative energies. This often is the home. A home office is ideal for the Stargazer. It is here where your works of artistry are most apt to take shape.

Even with all your talent and energy, you are only human, and for some reason Stargazers tire faster than any other of the household personalities. Because they are so sensitive to their external environment, they can be affected physically if they are living in an unappreciative and non-nurturing home. With insensitive friends, you can walk away, but you can be stuck with an ungrateful family.

It might help to realize that it is human nature for others to take for granted what is always there. It may be too much to ask for compliments at each of your gourmet meals, for each beautifully packaged gift, or for each elegantly prepared flower arrangement. The truth is your family has come to expect gracious living and will only notice when the flowers are wilting. But it doesn't matter—when you feel taken for granted, the tea party is over.

So as a Stargazer, you just might be ready for a change. Your belief that you can keep your home beautiful, your family happy, and your employer grateful all at the same time is based upon a

CHAPTER 4

societal myth—probably one you picked up by hanging around with Winnie the Pooh and Daisy Doll too long. Stargazers have to eventually realize the tea party does not last forever.

By developing an equitable household that has a partnership at the helm instead of a fairy godmother, you will have more opportunities to create all the wonders you so dearly love. Stargazers deserve to have someone next to them in their cozy kitchens preparing tea parties. Perhaps these parties will be somewhat less frequent, but they will be much more appreciated.

The Tigress

If you are one of those interesting, daring, and confident Tigresses, growing up, getting married, and having children was never in one of your little Tigress dreams. "No way," growls the young Tigress. "I have other plans—big plans—and they involve prowling the jungle, swinging through the vines, stalking prey, and discovering new hunting grounds. You won't find me at home, stuck in some dumb old den, taking care of cubs."

Sound familiar? Well, it does if you are a Tigress. And, if you are one, you have known most of your life that you march to the beat of a different jungle drum.

You saw your childhood as a waiting room, something to get through quickly on your way to the operating room, courtroom, editing room, college classroom, board room, Wall Street, or perhaps the White House. Now, that's not to say your childhood was uneventful—far from it. But let's face it. You were considered a *tad* strange. Unlike many of your friends, you didn't have a great deal of time, or patience, for "monkey business." Your youthful years had to be spent in more meaningful endeavors. Your peers watched you do strange things like reading classics or skipping Sloppy Joe lunches to be in the science lab. You probably collected stamps or figurines while your friends collected marbles. And you ran five miles a day (or at least you thought about it). These behaviors, of course, set you apart from the other girls. But now you are all grown up, and you no doubt have a successful career or are headed for one.

When asked what you contribute this success to, you usually respond about some inner vision or willpower, but the truth is, you simply listened to the call of the jungle drums—drums that beat deep within you, driving you to fulfill your dreams. As long as the drums keep sounding out the messages like "I know I can—I know I can—I know I can," you are out there conquering jungles at breakneck speed.

But there might be some trouble in the jungle. Something completely unplanned happened along the way. If you are a Tigress and you are reading this book, chances are you stepped off your chosen path long enough to acquire a family and a household—maybe not children, but a mate, probably a cat, or possibly a parakeet. It's a strange turn of events for the Tigress, for these "happenings" were not in your initial plans. At some time during your hunt, you were forced into discovering (even though you are independent, strong, and self-reliant) that you had a weakness—at least you thought it was a weakness. This "weakness" is that you get lonely. Acquiring a mate eased those feelings, but it also translated into a household—something a prowling, self-reliant Tigress of the jungle never thought she was going to have to contend with.

Another problem: You will have trouble forming household partnerships. Tigresses are leaders, and they tend to exert control of the home through "to-do" lists, order forms, and those dreaded house meetings. But, inside your den, your leadership capabilities often fall flat. In most homes, family members are not as impressed with the Tigress's great achievements as she is, so certain strategies are not working for you, like trying to control the house. The more you try to control the home the way you control your life out in the jungle, the more you reinforce the concept that the home really is *your* responsibility. After all, you are so competent!

But there is a limit to your competence. The "can do" Tigress simply *cannot* do it all, and it is showing. Yes, you have a natural ability to protect your own from outside prey and all, but being in the jungle all day has given your predators the advantage and they are gaining ground—predators such as your mate's needs, house-

CHAPTER 4

hold duties, the demands of the extended family, finances, entertaining, and community work. The drums are beating louder and louder, and even though you are a ferocious and resourceful Tigress, responding to the beat of all those jungle drums each day is beginning to drive you up the banana tree.

But you will not be daunted. Most Tigresses, like the Honey-Bees, are pragmatic, and no doubt believe they can find a way out of this dilemma of balancing den and jungle. You are fortunate, though, because you are already aware something does not seem quite fair. And, like the Rebel, you will fight to the death to change what you believe is unjust. Also, like the Rebel, you have never embraced gender roles, have never seen the logic in them, and have never planned to have your household controlled by them. Still, with all this effort, you may have become a victim to the concept of "woman's work."

It gets worse. There is one situation that makes the jungle drums beat off the scale, a situation that drives the Tigress into a crazy tail-chasing behavioral fit, and it will come as no surprise. It is motherhood. If you are a Tigress with cubs, you have fallen prey to an all-consuming obsession. Nothing brings out your no-holds barred, "all or nothing" characteristic quicker than undertaking the role of motherhood. More than likely, it will be ALL rather than nothing. In fact, a Tigress is often willing to give up everything she has conquered for the sake of her cubs. And to the surprise—nay, the shock—of those around you, many Tigresses have done just that.

If you are a Tigress who has been derailed (or fulfilled) by motherhood (whichever fits), those around you might not even recognize you as a Tigress. But have no fear; you have not lost your *tigerhood*. You are simply lying in the weeds, waiting for the cubs to be weaned. "That's all right," smirks the Tigress. "I will hunt later. My time will come." (Grandma Moses, no doubt, was a Tigress lurking in the weeds, waiting for a "later.")

But if you are the Tigress who did not derail with motherhood, and are still balancing jungle and den and trying to do it all ... well ... you're "going bananas." The Tigress who remains out in the jungle after the birth of her cubs also has to contend with the guilt she feels. (This feeling increases her stress.) You feel guilty when you can't give everything you have to your career, and you feel guilty when you can't give your all to the cubs.

No wonder so many Tigresses wander off the jungle path! For there seems to be no answer: no matter which way you choose, you will feel guilty that your destiny remains unfulfilled, but which destiny — den or jungle? This paradox is creating heavy stress. Unfortunately, no one around you has a clue about this "going berserk" thing until one day your family finds you screaming like a banshee from the top of a banana tree. Granted, because of your quest for excellence, much of that pressure is self-induced, but nevertheless, it is big-time pressure.

Is there no solution for the inner-driven Tigress? Yes — developing a household partnership for the Tigress makes all the sense in the world. A partnership would not only remove much of your stress, but it also addresses why you are wearing tiger earmuffs. For anyone who does not know what tiger earmuffs are, let me explain. These particular earmuffs drown out the sounds of the jungle drums that the Tigress loves but, because of her cubs, can no longer respond to. If these muffs are not eventually removed, haunting loneliness grabs the caged Tigress and a great sadness can descend upon her regal head. This sadness makes her feel like no one understands her or realizes how hard her sacrifice has been. These are dangerous times for the Tigress and for those around her, for there will be a tendency to respond to this sadness by roaring and gobbling up everyone in sight.

But a household partnership allows you to remove the tiger earmuffs and get back into the jungle. The reason is that your mate will equally share the cubs. You no longer need to be in the den's kitchen alone, for you are a Tigress and you have the resources to make changes. Consequently, you are one of the most likely to succeed in implementing a household partnership. It will be a partnership that provides you with the ability to stay in the jungle, and to also have a happy and contented den life.

CHAPTER 5

I'm Running As Fast As I Can

Men weren't really the enemy—they were fellow victims suffering from an outmoded masculine mystique that made them feel unnecessarily inadequate when there were no bears to kill.

– Betty Friedan, in *Christian Science Monitor* (1974)

The Thou Shalts

Several months after Gary and I started operating as partners, I remember knowing that there would be no turning back. Both of our lives had changed considerably. The house was running more smoothly than ever before, my resentment was gone, and I was more content than I had ever been. No longer did I feel as if I had two jobs. The responsibilities had *mostly* been split in half. Then came more validation.

It was a warm evening in July. Gary had made dinner and I had cleaned up. We decided to relax on our porch with a cold drink. As the blades of the ceiling fan sliced the air above us, Gary looked at me and said, "You know, this arrangement works as well for me as it does for you."

"Really?" I said with excitement. "Tell me why."

"Well, now that I am more involved with what has been traditionally called 'women's work,' " he said, "I have a greater sense that you are in for the long haul in what has traditionally been known as 'men's work.' "

"That's interesting, but I'm a bit confused. What do you mean by 'the long haul'?"

"It's sort of hard to explain," said Gary, "but I'll give it a shot. You see, even though you have a meaningful career and enjoy your work, from the day we got married I have felt that any time you wanted to leave your job, it was your option. I felt I would have little to say, since I believe that it is really *my* job to provide the financial support for the household. I know it doesn't make sense, but deep down inside my soul, I've always thought that *I'm supposed to be the breadwinner*."

"I assume it's a man thing," I said, trying to understand.

"Yes, just like you feel taking care of the home and family is a woman's thing. But with our new partnership and mutual responsibility, I feel a lifting in this overall burden of the 'man's job.' Just as I am your partner in the home, I feel you are also my partner outside the home in the working world. I guess what I'm saying is that this concept of partnership has been a good idea."

Gary and I talked late into the evening that night. Many issues came up that indicated that we *both* felt responsible for the roles society had placed on us, but since we had formed our household partnership, we felt free from the expectations that were solely related to gender. An unexpected by-product of our sharing was a new vision of equality—equality that did not just affect my household workload; it affected our intimacy as a couple, as well.

"I no longer feel tied to a role that was given to me at birth, a role that has just as many prerequisites as the woman's role," Gary said.

"Prerequisites? And what would they be?" I asked inquisitively.

Gary stood up to make his point. "To all the men on the face of the earth ... listen up! To be a real man thou shalt achieve the following." As if he were Moses on Mt. Sinai calling the Ten Commandments down to his followers, Gary bellowed, "Thou shalt triumph over all peers! Thou shalt be braver than your peers! Thou shalt be stronger and swifter than your peers! Thou shalt be wealthier than your peers! Thou shalt be taller than your peers! Thou shalt be more powerful than your peers! Thou shalt command more fear and respect than your peers! Thou shalt acquire more things than

CHAPTER 5

your peers! Thou shalt display no feelings except *manly* feelings, so as not to appear weaker than your peers! Thou shalt have more beautiful women at your side than your peers!"

I applauded his list. "Very good!" I exclaimed. "Excellent!"

Encouraged, Gary continued. "We are told," he stabbed the air with his finger to make his point, "that if we keep and follow these commandments, we're destined—barring unforeseen disaster—to reach the top. Once there," he paused to think, then his tone changed to a question, "I don't know... I guess we look down?"

Gary fell back into his chair, appearing exhausted from the sheer magnitude and drama of the perceived expectations. He then said to me, "Now, just as we have adapted to the above commandments, you women have come up with more. We now must be much better fathers, more intimate partners, and share equally in the household work. Some men will say, 'enough is enough,' without realizing that as they become equal partners in their homes, their own archaic male roles will also erode away. Which is every bit as good for us as it is for you women." He winked at me and concluded, "We could be on to something. This household partnership thing could be a beginning to an end."

I smiled, and applauded again. "We've come a long way, baby."

Who Has It Worse?

While driving to work the next morning, I remember thinking how much had changed. In the past, every time Gary and I got into a "Who has it worse—men or women?" conversation, we always ended up in the same place—the place where everything breaks down. We would then call a truce, reluctantly agree to a conciliatory handshake, and mumble, "Yeah, I guess neither one of us has it *exactly* the way we want it." Begrudgingly, we'd give each other a faint smile and walk away. As we each turned our backs on the other, I walked away feeling frustrated and hurt. Gary walked away feeling frustrated and angry. As the distance between us widened, each of us thought the same thing: "He (or she) just doesn't get it." No doubt, many couples share the same dynamic in their relationship.

On Your Mark, Get Set, Go!

As men and women turn and walk away from each other, initially we look pretty much the same — heads down, feet shuffling, clenched fists stuffed away in our pockets — but it's *where* we walk that reveals our most intrinsic difference. We women walk to *someone* — a friend, a confidante — to process our feelings. Men tend to walk to *something* — a book, the TV set, the reports brought home from the office, or a project like the dissembled alternator on the work bench. This *something* becomes a long lonely path where, instead of processing their feelings, men try to shake the unrest. Once on this path, many men do the only thing they know, the thing they have learned from the beginning. They start to run. Their life's race is on. They are off to reach the top, by conquering all those *thou shalts*.

Right from the starting gate, which is often his marriage, he leaps out. At first, the man's steps are steady and his stride comes easy and smooth. He's feeling good. He's enjoying the warm breeze playing in his hair, the rhythm of gravel scrunching beneath his feet. "Yes ..." he says, "this is the life." He feels free, independent, and confident. He relishes in this good, "manly" feeling. "Ah ... if only it could last forever."

But it doesn't. The gravel becomes stonier. The level track begins climbing skyward, and before too long it becomes a wilderness trail. It wears on him. Obstacles appear and must be skirted or overcome, obstacles such as arguments with his mate concerning what he *didn't* do.

As he continues to run, the conversation he had earlier with his mate becomes a gnawing annoyance. Most of the time the running pushes his feelings deep inside, but this time he can't shake them. More and more he senses he's not appreciated. That's why he is in the race again. He wants to show his mate how wrong she is. "I'm a good guy," he tells himself. "She's fortunate to have me." Now he's out to prove he's a winner. He is not only running for himself, he wants to prove something to *her*. So he runs and runs and runs.

Time passes and eventually he stops and steps off the stony

CHAPTER 5

trail. He tries to remember what the race is about. If he's lucky, nothing comes to mind. Birds sing while white clouds billow in the blue skies above him. He notices this—perhaps for the first time. Life is good. *He* is good. Everything is right. "Ah . . . if only it could last forever."

But it doesn't. When he looks back, he remembers instantly why he is running. He must reach the top before someone else does. And now his worst fear is upon him. Someone is behind him, and he's catching up. *"Damn!"* he shouts. He despises the feeling of a rival breathing down his neck. But he has been in this situation many times before and knows exactly what to do. He must run faster. So he runs and runs and runs.

Sometimes it works. The approaching runner drops back, never to challenge him again. But other times the challenger gains. It's an awful feeling. Inch by inch the approaching runner starts closing the distance. Soon, he and his challenger are pounding along the trail neck and neck. Sweat begins to drip, then runs in rivulets from his body as his challenger slowly pulls ahead. He observes his rival's newer shoes, his more muscular calves, his longer strides. The runner's feelings of impending loss deepen.

Thou Shalt Run . . . Always

It's difficult to concede. Now exhausted, he returns to his previous pace. Painfully, he accepts the fact that the "better man" won because he was swifter, stronger, and more powerful. It eventually sinks in that he won't be able to keep up with him. He remembers that in the past the battles went on longer. The thrill of the victory has great memories. But more and more, he finds his heart is not in it. "You lucky slob," he says, as he watches his challenger turn the corner. "If I had those shoes, it would be a different story. Let him have it. See if I care."

But he does care. That's the problem. It's because those *thou shalts* still haunt him. So he increases his pace again. And he runs and he runs and he runs.

A Running Partner

But it gets lonely. At times it gets so lonely that he'd give anything for someone to talk to. Not *deep* talk, mind you, but someone to ask, "Hey, how's it going? What did you think about that last hill? Do you need a rest?" In fact, he's been known to slow down for the runner behind him, just so he could feel the presence of *someone*—even if it is his competitor.

This is where partnership comes in. Partnership is about having the runner's mate join him as a running partner. She is not his coach, who tells him how to do it better. Nor is she someone racing behind him to help keep his pace up, nor is she running in front to keep his adrenaline pumping. Partners run side by side, reveling in each other's victories and supporting each other in defeat. It gets better. This running partner will ignore the guys running past him. They don't matter. She is running with *him*.

With this partner, the man now gains a second wind. After his exhausting day, and still "miles to go before he sleeps," he'll be amazed at the extra boost of energy that billows up from within, just knowing his partner is keeping pace with him.

The conversations have long faded, leaving only the sound of her breathing, or the occasional touch from her hand, but he knows she's there. He smiles at her touch. He has come to understand it's her way of telling him how much she appreciates him. He grows confident that she understands his internal struggles. This confidence fuels more energy to do what has to be done. There's no longer the need to talk. The silence, broken only by his exhalations, peacefully envelops him. He is content. He loves having a running partner. And now, *they* run and *they* run and *they* run.

What's in It for Him?

"*They*" is not an overnight happening. And your mate may not immediately want to start running with a partner. He will need to warm up, get used to the idea—stretch, reach, and tap into a new way of thinking. Remember that our lives have changed drastically,

CHAPTER 5

as well. Today's working women are also expected to be marathon runners. They're grappling with new commandments, just like the guys are. We're all struggling to find answers about how *we* can create homes we *both* want to come home to.

CHAPTER 6

The Man's Household Personality

Our humanity rests upon a series of learned behaviors, woven together into patterns that are infinitely fragile and never directly inherited.

– Margaret Mead, *Male and Female* (1949)

Who Am I in My Home?

Of course, not every man is ready to become a partner. A lot depends on the man's attitude. How does he see the world? What does he feel about his home? What are his opinions about gender? How does he view his household role? These are all-important questions that need to be answered before a partnership can develop.

Obviously, men also have a household personality that is predominant. Identifying this profile will help him to recognize why he does what he does within the home. By understanding the man's predominant household personality, you as a couple will gain greater insight into the barriers you need to overcome in order to initiate a household partnership.

Now, to the male answering the questions: Answer the way you actually *feel*, whether positively or negatively. Be sure you avoid answering the way you think you *should be feeling* or what you *should be doing*. Also, don't answer in ways you *wish* you could feel or act. To get an accurate view of who you are, answer the questions as frankly and honestly as possible. Remember that there are no right or wrong answers.

CHAPTER 6

YOUR HOUSEHOLD PERSONALITY QUESTIONNAIRE

Please answer the questions with a number from 1 to 5 on the basis of how strongly you disagree or agree.

1: **strongly disagree**
2: **disagree**
3: **neither agree nor disagree**
4: **agree**
5: **strongly agree**

1. I don't get upset if the house is not in perfect order. _____

2. I believe household jobs should be divided by what's fair, not by gender. _____

3. I don't think housework is really my job, but I still help out more than most men. _____

4. I do the outside work; my mate does the inside work. _____

5. I do not think I am "helping out" in the home; it is just as much my job as my mate's. _____

6. I was taught (or believe) that housework should be equally shared between men and women. _____

7. One of my greatest enjoyments is working on a home-improvement project. _____

8. Even though I participate a lot in parenting, it's less than what my mate does. _____

9. I'm considered quite the "go-getter" at work. _____

10. When it comes to doing home chores, I procrastinate. _____

11. I'm not someone who's known to confront issues. _____

12. I have made my share of enemies at work. _____

13. I do at least half of the grocery shopping, but my mate needs to tell me what to buy. _____

14. I have most of the household tools required for any home repair project. _____

15. I believe I am responsible for one-half of the housework. _____
16. I will spend a whole weekend on a household project. _____
17. I am disappointed/hurt when the kids go to their mother for comfort instead of me. _____
18. I do not run away from conflict—in fact, I rather enjoy it. _____
19. When winter sets in, relaxing with nothing to do is my idea of a great weekend. _____
20. I love competitive games. _____
21. I like competing with my male friends more than I like talking with them. _____
22. I often don't feel appreciated for all the housework I do. _____
23. If it needs painting, I paint it. If it needs fixing, I fix it. _____
24. There is no doubt that I do (or I believe men should do) 50 percent of the parenting. _____
25. I work just as hard around the house as my mate does, but I don't do "women's work." _____
26. I teach my boys (or believe boys should be taught) to do cooking and cleaning. _____
27. I agree with the statement, "A man should be the boss of his home." _____
28. I don't enjoy conversations in which there is a lot of emotion. _____
29. I do a lot of the cooking but I probably don't always clean up really well. _____

CHAPTER 6

30. When it comes to the housework, I often feel like my mate bosses me around. _____

31. I hate sitting still. I need to be doing something around the house. _____

32. I wait on my mate as much as she waits on me. _____

33. My neighbors and friends call me if they want help on a "fix-it project." _____

34. I find it irritating when my mate tells me how to clean. _____

35. It's important for a woman to know how to make her man feel like a man. _____

36. I do not view housework as "women's work." _____

37. A woman's natural place is in the home, taking care of her family. _____

38. I clean the bathrooms as often as my mate does. _____

39. My mate sometimes feels neglected because I'm so involved in house projects. _____

40. If there is work to do around the house, I can't stop until it's done. _____

41. I don't have to be asked to pick up groceries or household supplies. I stop at the store on my own. _____

42. Men should take care of bringing home the money, so that the women can take care of the kids. _____

43. No matter how much I help, it seems my mate is always doing more than me. _____

44. My major goal is to be successful within my job. _____

45. I don't like feminists. _____

46. I'm somewhat amazed how people get so upset over the smallest incidents. _____

47. It's my job to take care of my family. _____

48. I'm irritated when my mate goes behind me, redoing a housecleaning job that I just did. _____

49. I never resent doing my share around the house; it's my responsibility. _____

50. My mate and I divide the housework equally. _____

51. My mate would like me to be more intimate. _____

52. You won't find me watching TV when there is work to be done. _____

53. I do a lot more housework than my mate gives me credit for. _____

54. Most people see me as a very easygoing guy. _____

55. I don't know how to do housework and I have no desire to learn. _____

56. I hate being dragged into someone else's conflict. _____

57. I think it is ridiculous for a woman to work all day and then do all the housework at home. _____

58. Sometimes my mate and I argue about how chores ought to be done. _____

59. The burden of finances should be shared equally. _____

60. I am always noticing flaws within the home that need to be fixed. _____

61. I demand respect. _____

62. The little things in life never bother me. _____

CHAPTER 6

63. When I come home from work, I don't want to hear about problems. _____

64. My mate has her way of doing chores and I have my way. _____

65. I am always thinking about how I can make something better. _____

66. My mate and I are very satisfied with the level of intimacy we have. _____

67. One of my favorite expressions is, "If there is a will, there is a way." _____

68. When I am cooking, I prefer that my mate stay out of the kitchen. _____

69. My mate should handle most of the day-to-day management of the home. _____

70. My family seldom sees me flare up. _____

71. When I'm in the car, I'm pretty easygoing, seldom driving fast or swearing at another driver. _____

72. Women probably think I'm macho. _____

73. I have my way of doing things in the house, and often it's not the way my mate likes it done. _____

74. I love problem-solving. I find it invigorating. _____

75. I have no problem sharing my feelings with my mate. _____

76. I consider myself a very creative person. _____

77. I feel like I do a lot around the house, but my mate would no doubt disagree. _____

78. I live hard, drive fast, and have lots of stress in my life. _____

THE MAN'S HOUSEHOLD PERSONALITY

79. I think about compliments for my mate, but for some reason I don't tell her. _____

80. Let's face it. Most women want a man to take care of them. _____

81. I do laundry, but my mate folds it and puts it away. _____

82. I have a great deal of confidence in myself that I can either "fix it" or find a way. _____

83. I view my mate as an equal partner. _____

84. I don't expect my mate to cook or clean up after me. _____

85. The kind of work I do around the house is much more suited for men. _____

86. I know I do more around the house than most men, and my mate needs to recognize that more. _____

87. I can't stand weak men. _____

88. I wish I told my family "I love you" more than I do. _____

89. I would rather talk about work issues than house issues. _____

90. I am a contented guy who doesn't have to set the world on fire. _____

91. My mate is always calling me to pick things up on the way home from work. _____

92. I can get extremely frustrated while working on a project, but I never give up. _____

93. I cook, do laundry, iron, write grocery lists, change beds, and clean bathrooms. _____

94. I love to be active most of the time. _____

CHAPTER 6

95. When it comes to sharing the housework, if 10 is the highest, I'm an 8. _____

96. Outside of sleeping, I need three or four hours each day by myself. _____

97. I find great enjoyment in the early morning's quiet and in the evening's peace. _____

98. I know where everything is; I do not ask my mate where items in the house are stored. _____

99. I enjoy the lighter side of life. _____

100. I prefer to have my mate at home taking care of the family and me. _____

101. It doesn't really bother me if I come home to a house full of kids and chaos. _____

102. I have no doubt that I share equally in the parenting of our children. _____

103. You are not going to find me doing housework on a regular basis. _____

104. If I were rated about how I feel about feminism, 10 being the most supportive, I'm a 7 or 8. _____

105. I should help my mate around the house more. _____

106. If I were rated on how much parenting I do, 10 being the highest, I'm a 7 or 8. _____

107. I can't understand why so many people make such mountains out of molehills. _____

108. The so-called women's movement has caused nothing but problems. _____

109. My mate often says to me, "Relax—why do you always have to be doing something?" _____

110. When traveling, I do my own packing and my share of the children's packing. _____

111. I don't usually feel in a hurry to get something done. _____

112. I will do whatever it takes to get ahead. _____

113. Overall, I do about 40–45 percent of all the household chores, probably no more. _____

114. Doing a project around the house is relaxing. _____

115. When things need to be done (i.e., windows washed), I just do them. _____

116. I am the first to pitch in with the housework, but my mate compiles the "to-do" list. _____

117. I don't ask my mate to help me with my projects and she shouldn't ask me for help with hers. _____

118. I'm a perfectionist. _____

119. I sometimes feel guilty that I'm not more involved in raising the children. _____

120. My mate complains about me not picking up after myself. _____

121. I do not believe in a double standard; what I do, so should my mate. _____

122. I'm happiest when I'm in control of my home. _____

123. I participate equally in the planning of vacations, entertaining, holidays, and birthday parties. _____

124. I have an awful lot of things I "should" do. _____

125. It would be rare for my mate to have to say to me, "Why don't you help me?" _____

CHAPTER 6

How to Determine Your Household Personality

You have completed the questionnaire. Now refer to the following guide for instructions on how to determine your household personality.

The Male's Household Personality Score Sheet

To score your answers, note the groups below, marked A–E. Under each of the groups are the numbers assigned to the questions you have just answered, all 125 of them. Record the numerical response you gave to each question in the space provided. For example, under column A, the first number shown is 9, which represents question number 9. Whatever numerical response (1, 2, 3, 4, or 5) you gave to question number 5 should be written on the line next to that number. Continue on with all the questions, writing down the numerical response you gave to each of the 125 questions. When you have finished writing in all of your responses, add up the numbers in each group to determine the total for that group. Then write the totals for each group in the section following the groups. Each group is shown with its corresponding profile. The higher the number, the stronger you are in that profile. The highest number you could score in any of the profiles is 125.

Dual Profiles: If you have two groups whose scores are less than eight points apart, you fall into a large category of men who have dual profiles. You will want to read both profiles and combine them. Be sure to read all of the profiles, for you will learn just as much about yourself from who you are *not* as from who you *are*.

THE MAN'S HOUSEHOLD PERSONALITY

GROUP A	GROUP B	GROUP C	GROUP D	GROUP E
9 ____	1 ____	3 ____	4 ____	2 ____
12 ____	10 ____	8 ____	7 ____	5 ____
18 ____	11 ____	13 ____	14 ____	6 ____
20 ____	19 ____	17 ____	16 ____	15 ____
21 ____	28 ____	22 ____	23 ____	24 ____
27 ____	46 ____	29 ____	25 ____	26 ____
35 ____	51 ____	30 ____	31 ____	32 ____
37 ____	54 ____	34 ____	33 ____	36 ____
44 ____	56 ____	38 ____	39 ____	41 ____
45 ____	62 ____	43 ____	40 ____	49 ____
47 ____	70 ____	48 ____	42 ____	50 ____
55 ____	71 ____	53 ____	52 ____	57 ____
61 ____	79 ____	58 ____	60 ____	59 ____
63 ____	88 ____	64 ____	65 ____	66 ____
69 ____	90 ____	68 ____	67 ____	75 ____
72 ____	96 ____	73 ____	74 ____	83 ____
78 ____	97 ____	77 ____	76 ____	84 ____
80 ____	99 ____	81 ____	82 ____	93 ____
87 ____	101 ____	86 ____	85 ____	98 ____
89 ____	105 ____	91 ____	92 ____	102 ____
100 ____	107 ____	95 ____	94 ____	110 ____
103 ____	111 ____	104 ____	109 ____	115 ____
108 ____	119 ____	106 ____	114 ____	121 ____
112 ____	120 ____	113 ____	117 ____	123 ____
122 ____	124 ____	116 ____	118 ____	125 ____
Total ____	Total ____	Total ____	Total ____	Total ____

WRITE IN YOUR TOTALS FROM EACH COLUMN.

Group A ____ The Emperor
Group B ____ The Philosopher
Group C ____ The Dapper
Group D ____ The Hunter
Group E ____ The Partner

CHAPTER 6

EVALUATING YOUR SCORE

90 Points or More

Since you have the majority of the characteristics in this profile, you will find in him your strongest identity. You not only share his likes and dislikes, but he also represents your *inner* desires and needs.

80 – 89 Points

You share a great many characteristics with this profile and have a good deal of understanding for him. You will find in him a great deal of your *external* self, the "self" that others might see you to be.

70 – 79 Points

You have enough characteristics in this profile to understand and enjoy him. You will most likely find that your closest friends fall into this profile, but you have a *different lifestyle* and *several different habits* from those of the profile.

60 – 69 Points

You have enough of the characteristics of this profile to have *some* understanding of him. You also share some of his likes and dislikes, but your lifestyle and habits are *very* different.

Depending on how high or low you are in this score, you might find that you have some strong disapproval of his lifestyle.

Below 60 Points

You have very little in common with this profile and will have difficulty relating to or understanding him. (This is someone you might want to get to know. Since you have opposite lifestyles, you have a lot to teach each other.)

The following chapter provides you with a description of your houschold personality.

CHAPTER 7

One Man's "Castle" is Another's "Home on the Range"

It's not the men in my life that count, it's the life in my men.

– Mae West, in *Belle of the Nineties* (1934)

The Emperor, the Philosopher, the Hunter, the Dapper, and the Partner

Now that the male has completed and scored his questionnaire, he too has a name for his household personality. Like the woman, he probably is a combination of all five. However, one or two personality types are predominant. Gary was a Dapper before he became a Partner. The same scenario can be yours. Each one of these personalities can become a Partner. It's just that some will have further to go than others.

The Emperor

As the Emperor drives into his driveway, he already envisions his homecoming. "How thrilled they will be," he tells himself. Even though he has only been gone for ten hours he expects a hero's welcome. "Hey ... I'm home, everyone!" the Emperor shouts as he steps into his castle. He stands just inside the front door and waits for everyone to halt what they are doing and come running. He confidently expects to be greeted by cheers, lots of hugs, kisses, and wonderful cooking aromas rolling in from the kitchen. After all, he *is* the Emperor, and he *has* arrived.

CHAPTER 7

For the most part, an Emperor will not be disappointed. His subjects have learned that giving attention to the Emperor is a smart move. Their rewards will be great. To adore the Emperor is to ensure that the world's treasures will be bestowed for the asking. And since Emperors are suckers for praise, there's nothing a beloved Emperor won't give to his grateful subjects. But take him for granted, ignore his ego, and you have an acrimonious and indignant majesty. His subjects are keenly aware of these traits. They know if they do not pay homage to his Majesty, they will evoke resentment and be removed from his benevolence. He is easy to read.

If a woman's mate is this all-powerful Emperor, she finds him chivalrous, ambitious, passionate, and a fearless competitor. It is those traits that attracted her. And, no doubt, they're the same traits that exasperate her. Endowed with these fiery characteristics, an Emperor's life is a demanding, fast-paced rat race, which takes a good deal of machismo spirit to fuel. But he loves it. He would change very little. He likes the pace. He likes the game. He loves the excitement. Simply put—it's good to be the Emperor.

This lifestyle keeps him in touch with other Emperors, his favorite people. Therefore, he's known as "a man's man," and a fellow Emperor is his kind of man. They understand each other, and maintain strong bonds, just as long as they stay out of each other's domain. If one dares to trespass on the territory of another, he makes an implacable enemy. I suspect most of the major world conflicts involved a trespassing Emperor or two.

But world conflicts are not entirely his fault. They are an unavoidable by-product of his unquenchable quest for power. This mortal quest has forged him into a role of conqueror and strategist, the two critical skills that he believes are needed to keep his kingdom intact. He discovered early on that the strategy of "divide and conquer" is his most effective method for gaining and holding on to power. Emperors have discovered something else. This "divide and conquer" strategy works best when he categorizes his life into three distinct activities: work, play, and home (synonymous with "castle"). His success at keeping things under control depends on how well he is able to keep these three areas of his life from spilling over into the other.

First, let's talk about his work. Since he loves to have fun, he works hard to make his job a game. Because he plays the game well, he is used to winning. Being liked is not his goal. Winning, or better yet, conquering is where it's at for the Emperor. He knows what it takes to get the job done, and if someone is blocking it from happening, they'd better be fast on their feet because Emperors do not take survivors. They are more known for the body count they leave behind.

Play is no different. He throws the same passion into his sports as he does his work. Consequently, he is not too intrigued by athletics or hobbies in which he doesn't have a chance to win. Reading a Shakespearean play, painting a canvas, attending an opera, or writing a love poem are probably not his favorite pastimes — that is, if there is no competition involved. He prefers to play on a field of equals, his equal being another Emperor. Therefore, work *and* play keep him away from the castle a large amount of time. Some mates tolerate his absence quite well, while others want his playtime. A good Emperor will usually acquiesce to his family needs, if for no other reason than to avoid conflict. As an Emperor he relishes the conflict at work or play, but he detests it within his castle.

That brings us to his castle, which must be a dwelling of peace, a place where he goes when he no longer wants to compete. That is why he abhors any disharmony within its hallowed walls. Since conflict is something he must win at, and because he doesn't enjoy competing at home, he does something quite foolish. He tries to control his castle. He thinks it will ensure him a peaceful paradise. He is under the mistaken belief that if he rules the people living within his domain, there will be no conflict. Therefore, he will live happily ever after as a blissful Emperor. Emperor Blissful denies or minimizes the fact that *no one* is actually able to control all things at all times. Consequently, Emperors Blissful have a slightly exaggerated sense of what they are capable of implementing, but they

CHAPTER 7

are the Emperor, and this supreme confidence in their power to control comes with the throne.

As far as his involvement and sharing of the household chores, he considers this ... well ... beneath him. Of all the personalities, he is the most invested in keeping the status quo that says, "Men do men's work and women do women's work." Men's work to him is defined as everything away from the house. Yes, even the traditional man's job of taking out the garbage is usually delegated to someone else. He can't be bothered by insignificant household duties.

Emperors actually think the world would be better off if everyone did exactly what nature intended for them to do. Translation? He believes the woman is best suited within the home. It is here that she does what she does best: nurture and take care of things — things like him, for instance. And if his mate has done something silly like getting a job, he will probably say, "Well, if you must. Just as long as it doesn't interfere with your real responsibility, which is keeping the home peaceful." Strangely, it doesn't matter if she is making a CEO's salary or minimum wage. He'll think her first job is having dinner on the table. And since few women today agree with this arrangement, this can get ugly — quickly.

Try as she might, we know it is impossible for the woman working outside the home to do it all. Therefore, many castles have an unpleasant revolt going on that is designed to overthrow the Emperor's rigid decrees (which he believes are still nailed to the castle door). But, since his traditional beliefs about women keeping the "castle fires burning" are sacred, it becomes nearly impossible for his Majesty to adjust when the Queen decides to leave the castle and return to the workplace. In fact, some Emperors become so distraught when required to make sacrifices (for instance, they might have to find their misplaced crown all by themselves or occasionally fluff their own robes), they begin to plot a form of espionage — which means they try to make it as difficult as possible for their Queen to do both jobs, even though she tries valiantly. If the Queen stands firm and refuses to return to the "good ol' days," the battles will ebb and flow for years.

The major criterion behind the "castle mood" depends on what type of Emperor he is. There are three types. The first is Emperor Blissful. Emperor Blissful, as mentioned before, is out of touch. This Emperor believes he is in control. Consequently, he is blissfully contented though misguided. But so what? Unless his angry subjects rise up against him, nothing will change. He will continue to stay in his blissful but unenlightened state. There is little hope of change in this castle. Basically, no one wants change, or they do not want to pay the price to get it.

The second type of Emperor is the result of deception. The Emperor who lives in this state is called Emperor Head-in-the-Moat. This Emperor is completely unaware that his subjects are just letting him think he is in control of the castle, when all along they are the ones who are actually making the decisions. They know that when he feels he is not in control, he becomes moody and pouts. Being a clever lot, his subjects know how to conceal who has the real power. There is little hope of change in this castle. Again, no one wants it.

The third type is Emperor Deflated. This is an *unhappy* state for an Emperor. Emperor Deflated has a couple of things going on. Due to unfortunate circumstances, work is probably falling apart, no doubt caused by another Emperor's trespassing or because Emperor Deflated has misjudged one of his enemies. Or there is "trouble in paradise" and he finds his castle is falling apart. When a crisis occurs at work, it spills over into his castle. And in the same vein, if a crisis occurs in the castle, it can't help but spill over into his work. This is a nasty situation. The Emperor strives to keep his three worlds neatly separated. However, in a calamity, it becomes impossible to keep work, play, and castle apart. When this occurs, he feels out of control. This loss of power produces anxiety for him, as well as a sense of failure. What strategy Emperor Deflated elects to use in addressing these troubled castle times will determine how successful he is in resolving them. If he tries to grasp tighter, he will do greater damage to his relationship. If he leans back, assesses, and reaches out to his family for support, something magical could occur. There is lots of hope for change in this castle. The Emperor and his

CHAPTER 7

family don't realize it as yet, but when change arrives they will all come to love it.

Emperor Deflated could find out that there is not, nor ever was, any need for him to "go it alone." When he reaches out for help and support from his subjects, most Emperors Deflated find very competent and able family members, family members who are quite capable of running their lives as well as supporting his. When this is discovered, magic happens. And this magic can move him into a higher level of consciousness and into a life that consists of give and take, compromise, and gifts for all—even for him. Through the power of compromise, Emperor Deflated is able to realize he no longer needs to control *all* the decisions that come down the pike. He learns that a happy castle is one where others count, too. Once this is learned, his subjects (if they are still around) have access to his sensitivity, perhaps even his soul. It is here that they find a "kinder, gentler" Emperor.

If, per chance, this miracle has happened to the Emperor in your life, he is probably wiser and has matured. He has survived many battles to get where he is. Therefore, he is in a better place than Emperor Blissful or Emperor Head-in-the-Moat to take the next step, a step that would eventually lead him into sharing the control of the castle *equally*. This is where your household partnership comes in. It might be difficult to grasp at first, but of all the male personalities, Emperors have the most to gain. A household partnership would lift a huge burden of responsibility off his shoulders. He would quickly learn there is a much greater benefit in sharing the load than in shouldering it himself. The result of this sharing is intimacy. When these two happenings occur, the Emperor can be converted into the most wonderful Partner. Remember that those who have the furthest to travel appreciate the journey's end the most!

The Philosopher

"Why does life have to be so combative? I just don't understand why people can't be more accepting of one another. Haven't they ever heard of 'live and let live'?" says the Philosopher as he gets into his

ONE MAN'S "CASTLE" IS ANOTHER'S "HOME ON THE RANGE"

car and heads for home. Today, the boss was all over him. It was the usual complaint. "Why didn't you follow through on this assignment?" he asked him. The Philosopher explained he thought it was a low priority, but as he came to find out, it was the boss's highest priority. This isn't the first time the boss has come down on him for missing a deadline. "I don't get it," the Philosopher says. "Why does he make such mountains out of molehills?"

As the Philosopher approaches his home, he hardly notices the neighbor's bicycles abandoned in his driveway. He simply pulls his car around them. He also doesn't become flustered because his teenager's car is parked in front of his garage stall. No problem. The Philosopher parks on the other side. "I'll put the car in the garage later," he says, as he maneuvers through the baseballs and other toys left by the kids, on the way to the front door.

Thinking back to his boss, the Philosopher continues his reflections. "Hey, it's not like someone's going to have cardiac arrest over one stupid incomplete assignment, are they? God, why doesn't he get a grip?" As he glances back to the garage, he notices that the kids forgot to take the garbage out. "Oh well, they'll get it next week," he says opening the screen door. It is then that he remembers the hinge is still loose. He opens it carefully so it doesn't fall off the door frame. It has been five months since the hinge's screws worked loose. "Hmm ... got to fix that hinge this weekend," he says as he wanders into the house.

If your mate is the Philosopher, his heavy thoughts of the day lift as he finds himself inside the home. "Ah ... home at last," he sighs. His burdens fade away as he heads for his "cave." What constitutes the cave varies according to the interests of individual Philosophers. There are TVs, workshops, gardens, lawns, jogging paths, walking the dog, or a home hobby. His cave is the place where he goes for his quiet time, a place where no one is upset with him and no one makes demands. This Philosopher is lucky. His family is sensitive to this quirk and leaves him alone. They know he only needs a minimal "time out." It won't be long before he emerges from his hibernation like a contented bear, refreshed and happy.

CHAPTER 7

He is now ready for family time, and because his children adore him, his arrival is warmly welcomed.

A Philosopher's ideal life is one of minimal strife. His belief is that nothing is really so important that it ruins one's peace of mind. This attribute makes him very attractive to women looking for a "nice guy." When women are "looking," they love the laid-back, easygoing, contented, "happy-go-lucky" Philosophers. A family man—the man of every woman's dreams. It is almost unfair that these same admired traits become the very ones their mates want to change.

Initially, living with him is "a piece of cake." If his house is not in perfect order, if the kids are not exactly setting the world on fire, or if his boss has just passed him over for a promotion a third time, well, he might not be happy about it, but he won't go ballistic. For Philosophers, there are far more important things in life than "sweating the small stuff" or pressuring others.

"What are those 'more important things'?" his family asks. Well, lots of things. The Philosopher enjoys a windy day, a sunset over the lake, a picnic basket, or a cozy place on the couch, a fire in the fireplace and a bowl of popcorn. He is the least demanding and most relaxed of all the male profiles. He is also one of the most gentle. And, when it comes to gender roles, he is not locked into traditional thinking. He can iron his own shirt, wash his own socks, or be content to wear his dirty ones. But there is a problem. He's just a bit *too* relaxed.

To the contented Philosopher, this "too relaxed" stuff causes some major problems with his family. As his mate, you would dearly love to see a reaction from him, which would give an indication that he cares. You know the situations. You want a feeling—a "connection"—when you tell him that your boss just fired you and you feel unfairly treated. Or your teenage daughter wants more than a sad look when she tells him her boyfriend just broke up with her and life as she knows it is over. You all want more from him than his typical comment, "Oh, don't worry. It'll be okay," or a pat on the head and his let's-move-on question of, "By the way, has anyone seen today's newspaper?" Your major frustration is his perceived apathy. He doesn't appear to think that much of anything is a big deal, even if it is a very big deal to you. To put it simply, Philosopher's laid-back "life-is-no-big-deal" attitude can drive those around him right into the loony bin.

To his credit, he's not a hypocrite. He doesn't ask from others what he doesn't ask of himself. Since he sort of likes to keep his thoughts and problems inside, wouldn't the world be a nicer place to live if everybody else felt the same way? "Gee ... what do they want from me anyway?" he says, fluffing his favorite couch pillow. "I told them I thought it was too bad. Why make such a big deal over it and make things worse? It's not as if I can do anything about it. So let's move on, okay?" With that last statement, he puts his contented head down and is soon fast asleep. Still, the problems remain. It's too bad, but the world can sometimes be hurtful. Eventually the Philosopher will have to come to grips with his family member's strange talk about *feelings,* no matter how uncomfortable these discussions make him. Philosophers need to get used to the idea that their mates will continue to confront them about their well-developed avoidance techniques until they get some validation.

Surprisingly, the all-too-often "you don't care" comments come as a shock to him. He thinks he *does* share feelings and acts wounded when all of a sudden he becomes the object of his mate's frustration, frustration that occurs when her world is falling apart and his reaction is, "Don't you think you need to calm down?" He remains dumbfounded that she can continue to let such "insignificant" problems upset her. "Huh? ... What did I do now?" he says as he lifts his confused head up from the fluffed pillow. She stands over him in shock that he is able to rest so comfortably after she has just shared with him that her life is falling apart. "Okay," he concedes, "maybe I didn't say the right thing. But do you need to get so emotional? For the love of God, let's move on." And with that brush-off, he tunes into his quiet world again. His mate eventually gives up and calls a friend to check out why she feels like Darth Vader. "Am I expecting too much?" she asks her sympathetic

CHAPTER 7

listener. "I just need validation that I'm not crazy. Why doesn't he understand me?" she laments into the phone. The Philosopher has no idea he has this uncanny art of making everyone around him feel like they are overreacting, crazy lunatics.

But for the Philosopher, these results aren't entirely his fault. He sincerely doesn't want to hurt anyone. When it comes to empathy, the expression of a deep feeling, or offering a lot of support and understanding, he is simply inept. He remains bewildered, and more than a little confused by all the "touchy-feelie" needs of others and, if the truth be known, he thinks it's all a bit overdone. He also thinks that needing to share every intimate detail about how one feels, what one wants, and what one needs is, to say the least, B-O-R-I-N-G!

When it comes to his household role and negotiating chores, he again remains laid-back. It is here where his mate has a couple of options. She can do it herself (his favorite option), she can leave it undone (his second favorite), or she can continue to harp at him to be involved (his least favorite). Even though the Philosopher is not hung up on gender roles (he can be found in both the kitchen and the garage), he stills hold on to many traditional beliefs. One of these beliefs is that women like doing housework. And since they can do it better, he believes he should only have to *help*.

Since he feels that "helping out" is something that he gives, he prefers it to be up to him to decide when to give it. The conversation usually goes like this:

"Dear, you promised that you would clean the garage."

The Philosopher responds to his mate by saying, "Yes, honey. Don't worry, I'll get to it."

His mate, after having heard this same response many times before, says, "But *I am* worried. You have already put it off for two weeks. You keep telling me that you'll get to it. In fact, if you remember, you were going to 'get to it' last winter and now it's spring."

The Philosopher agrees. "Yes, I know. But today I'll get to it. I promise."

Of course, to him, this actual "getting to it" is quite a different matter. And the word "promise" also does not quite hold the same weight it does for others. Later he says, "Promise? Did I say promise? Well, you know what I meant. Let's not get hung up on words. I'll get to it. Don't worry. Tomorrow for sure."

The good news is that the Philosopher is drawn to rational thought like cold hands to a warm, snuggy pocket. Since his nature is compatible with concepts based on fairness and justice, adopting the ideas behind household partnerships should come easy. In fact, a household partnership could fit nicely into a life he dreams about, a life where issues can be worked out through rational negotiation and compromise compared to heavy emotions and conflict. Philosophers respond well when they know what is expected of them. They also like to work at their own pace, with no one telling them what to do or how to do it, all attributes that complement his peaceful world. Since household partnerships have a lot to do with peace, you might even find the Philosopher leading the way.

The Hunter

As is his norm, the Hunter is on red alert as he wheels his shiny clean car through the neighborhood. His eyes are meticulously surveying the lawns and homes in search of a new plant, structure, or addition that appeals to him. Suddenly he hits the brakes. The attentive Hunter has spotted something. Squealing his tires, he slams his car in reverse to back up. Rolling down the window, he calls out to his neighbor, "Hey, Rex, is that really *Agrostis nebulosa* you're growing? I've tried for years to get those ornamental grasses to sprout, but with no luck. Gosh, they're sure beautiful!" With that comment, he drives off, still scanning the vista for other ideas.

As he pulls into his driveway, his scrutiny antenna goes even higher. He smiles with satisfaction at his beautifully landscaped yard, but this smile quickly turns to a frown as he spots an eave on the corner of his house that needs some paint. He tells himself, "It must have been damaged by the broken branch that snapped during last week's windstorm." He glances at his watch. He notes he probably

CHAPTER 7

has about two hours left of daylight. He calculates that he can change his clothes, mix the paint, carry out the ladder, touch up the eave, and still have about an hour of light left to weed the vegetable garden.

For the Hunter, nothing is as important as his home. It is his hobby, his joy, and his love. There is very little in life more rewarding than having his home in perfect order. Therefore, he has an irresistible need (which his mate and children claim borders on obsessive-compulsive behavior) to make something better than it was. The adage that says, "Always leave it better than how you found it," is the battle cry of the enterprising Hunter. Although his employer relishes his ingenuity, outside employment will never take first priority over his "home on the range." Nothing "lights his fire" or sparks his passions as much as when he is working on something that belongs to him.

It is seldom that a Hunter arrives at his front door tired after a long tiring day. His energy bounces back when he steps out of his car. This vigor amazes his family, since they are no doubt normal people who like to come home, unwind, kick back, and spend the evening relaxing. They look at him pitifully because they believe he has some strange "always needs to be doing something" disease. "Poor Dad," his kids sigh, "there he goes again, off on another 'do-it-yourself' project." Because they can't relate to his inner drives, his family doesn't understand how much he loves doing what he does. They resign, accepting him as being out of control and unable to repress his urges. No doubt, this lack of understanding keeps him feeling a bit on the outside.

"Hi, everyone! I'm home," he yells, rushing through the house. No sooner does one of the Hunter's family members turn around to greet him than he disappears. Ten minutes later someone spots the top of a ladder passing by a window. A few minutes after that, the Hunter is seen in the backyard, tools strewn here and there. The screaming sounds of a power saw fills the air. As everyone watches out the window, their compassion goes out to him.

"What's he up to now, Mom?" asks one of the kids as he joins the Hunter's mate at the window.

"I have no idea," she answers. "Last night I kind of recall him muttering about some great-looking duck pond he had seen in the city park." She pauses, shakes her head and continues on, "I didn't give it much thought. I assumed he was dreaming."

Her son sympathetically puts his arm around her shoulder and gazes out the window with her. After a few moments of reverential silence he asks, "But Mom, how's he going to work it around the gazebo?"

She sighs and responds, "I don't know. I just don't know. At that time I didn't take him seriously." She returns her gaze toward the window. Again there is total silence. Suddenly, a small explosion shatters the air. It is followed by a roaring sound. The Hunter has started up the cement mixer.

There is not a task that a Hunter won't take on, even though he often gets in over his head. When, or if, this does happen, it is of little consequence. Compulsive Hunters will not be daunted by meager, incidental roadblocks (like hitting ten feet of clay while digging a moat). If there is a way, there is a Hunter leading it. However, the cost of these "do-it-yourself" home repairs depends on the skill of the Hunter. Unfortunately, some Hunters have incurred huge debt in their "home-improvement, cost-savings" projects.

Still, there's no other household personality who'll work to the death to accomplish a project as the diligent "can-do" Hunter. Family members who are not Hunters (there is only one per family; no family could survive two) do not realize the personal high, the rush of excitement, the exhilaration that the Hunter gets when a project has been completed. If they did, they would not waste their sympathy with "look at all the work he's doing." The Hunter who's creating a project is to be envied; he is one happy man.

Now even though his family appreciates his wide range of talents, they still waver between gratitude and exasperation. The gratitude is in the pride and meticulous way he keeps the home, but their frustration comes with how much time he devotes to it. When all of his free time is spent on do-it-yourself undertakings, he has little energy left over to give to the rest of the family. This

CHAPTER 7

can be a problem. His mate can easily begin to build resentment when she feels like less of a priority than one of his beloved projects.

But nothing could be further from the reality for the family-loving Hunter. He adores his family and thinks he's demonstrating his love by working hard to improve their surroundings. But since he is a "doer" more than a "talker," he generally does not share these "love thoughts" with them. This lack of intimacy is one of the issues his mate complains about most whenever she discusses her independent, strong-headed, compulsive, creative, "always on the go" Hunter with her friends. But of course, this resistance to intimacy is one of the reasons he loves his projects so much. They become his escape from the "wants and needs" of others. For even though he can build towers and cross mountains, when it comes to meeting his family's emotional needs, he has a lot in common with the Philosopher — which means he is somewhat inept.

Also, unfortunately for his mate, he ranks right up there with the Emperor in being the most gender-conscious of the household personalities. It's not that he can't ever be found in the kitchen; it's just that he believes his type of work is clearly in the realm of "helping out." And, after all, that's her job! When she brings this concern to his attention, he could not be more baffled. "My God, look how hard I work!" he exclaims. "Most wives would be thrilled to have me! I do the yard, garage, cars, barbecue, garbage, snow plowing, and everything else you hate. Come on, give me a break. I do the man's work and you do the woman's work. What could be fairer?"

His defense is certainly logical. But there is a problem. Since the bulk of his time is spent on "projects," she is left with all the parenting, banking, cleaning, entertaining, phoning, cooking, and everything else that goes into keeping the inside of the house up. He probably has never noticed (I take that back; I'm sure he has ...), but there is little creative energy needed in cleaning out the dryer's lint trap, wiping runny noses, cleaning up the dog's accidents, or changing dirty shelving paper. It simply cannot be considered in the same category as his creative projects. But since the Hunter is always playing "home improvement," these mundane, everyday, boring projects get dumped in her lap.

The Hunter's expectations involving "women's work" compound this problem. The unspoken rule governing his "home on the range" is that a reward should be waiting for him when he comes in from building the corral or whatever other project has tickled his fancy. Rewards like a spotlessly clean house, a homemade pie, a drawn bath, or a pulled-down bed are all tributes that say to him, "Thank you, darling Hunter, for busting your Hunter's butt all day, just for sweet little me." Depending on the woman's household personality, he might not receive any recognition at all. For example, if she is a Sojourner, more often than not, he'll walk in after spending twelve hours on a project and find her soaking in the tub eating bonbons. He'll then set sparks flying by brightly asking, "So what have you been doing all day?"

As a Hunter, he needs to remember that others simply don't have his energy. The rush of adrenaline that he gets from creating a project is not the same feeling his mate gets from cleaning out the kitty litter. "So ... okay," he concedes, "then why don't you find a hobby?" Once again, he has a good point. But Hunters must remember that their mate's hobby might be reading, listening to classical music, or soaking in the bathtub. Not every woman chooses to spend her free time building the Taj Mahal in her backyard. If she has free time, that is. Chances are she doesn't. For she is the one stuck with the housework while her Hunter is out doing all his outdoor projects.

As one can guess, because of his hard work and his strong division of labor, the Hunter is the hardest (except for the Emperor) to convince that a household partnership is beneficial. As far as he can see, his "home on the range" could not have a better arrangement. Remember that he truly believes he is already doing more than his fair share.

The strategy his mate needs to implement when exploring a household partnership is to distinguish outside chores from his

CHAPTER 7

hobbies. He might like this. There are some of those outdoor chores that he might be very happy to negotiate away, just as there are indoor chores that she would like to negotiate away. The other benefit of mingling the workload instead of keeping it strictly gender-related is that the two of them will have more intimacy if they work together. Besides intimacy, they also gain time. With a new arrangement, they both will end up with more time to do what they enjoy, no matter if it is building a duck pond or soaking in a tub.

The Dapper

This evening, just before leaving the office, Dapper's wife telephoned to say she would be detained at work. She was sorry to give him such late notice but he would need to be in charge of tonight's dinner and the kids. As the Dapper (who comes to this name because of his good nature and an inner desire to please his family), drives home, there is some resentment, because once again, he is to be responsible for the kids and dinner. "That's life," he concludes. His wife works and he needs to pinch-hit once in a while, but he doesn't have to like it. On his way home he stops at day care and picks up the kids. Afterwards he heads to a convenience store. His wife told him they were out of milk. By the time he drives into his driveway, he's tired.

Two hours later, as he looks out the kitchen window, a smile breaks out over his face as he watches his children playing in the backyard. He notes it is 7:30 P.M., just about time to call them in for the evening. The last of the dinner dishes are done. He's looking forward to relaxing with Monday night football. After a long day, it's now *his* time.

As he sees the remaining casserole on the counter, he wonders if his wife has eaten and whether he should keep it heated. He feels proud of his homemade chicken tetrazzini and wants her to try it. As he sets the dinner in the oven, he begins to envision his evening. "After I put the kids to bed, I'll start a fire, pop some popcorn, and turn the football game on. I certainly have earned the rest," he says to himself, "considering all I've done today." Most Dappers thinks they're special. The truth is, they are. Dappers deserves much more than an occasional evening football game for their progressive, non-macho, involved home life.

The liberated, freethinking Dapper is the least gender-conscious (except for the Partner) of the male household personalities. He has no problem doing laundry, cooking, taking care of the kids, or running household errands. He is not only involved with the buying, baking, and candlestick-making, but he's also to be found coaching his children's Little League, scheduling school conferences, and mowing the lawn. He's what's called "the modern-day man." He not only "brings home the bacon, but cooks it up in a pan."

Wait a moment. Don't confuse the Dapper with the shiny-armored knight who gallops in on the big white horse to take care of his princess. He does not enjoy playing the gallant role, and will reject most forms of chivalry. His reasons are simple. First, he doesn't want to be the only provider within the household. He enjoys his mate working and likes the concept of shared responsibility. (There is no macho ego that the Dapper needs to protect about being the breadwinner.) He learned long ago the benefits of two paychecks. Since he never wanted the full weight of the finances on his shoulder, he was always attracted to women who would share (not necessarily equally) the financial burdens of the household. Therefore he, too, willingly participates in the household duties.

The Dapper's idea of a full life is getting as much out of it as possible. This requires a balance between work, play, and home. Consequently, you won't find too many Dappers who will give up their precious free time for money or power. That doesn't mean they slouch off at work. No, they are fully aware they need a job to support their lifestyle. As committed and conscientious employees who don't make waves, they are the backbone of the work world. An employer can always expect to get the Dapper's best, but they won't get his life. Any employer who thinks they can get a Dapper to pound out sixty- or seventy-hour work weeks with a promise he will climb to the top will be disappointed. Dappers don't live to

CHAPTER 7

work. They work to live. If a Dapper's job keeps him on the road or requires long hours away from the home, he is one miserable, homesick guy who is probably looking for another job.

Because of his balanced outlook, the Dapper feels a keen responsibility to help around the house. But here again, don't expect him to be a slave to his home. They like balance. Dappers might create beautiful homes, but then resent the time it takes to keep them up. They continually struggle with balancing what they want with what it will cost to get it. "Is it worth it?" they ask. Well, if it requires more of their time—usually not.

Dappers are all different. Some love spontaneity. They want to be able to take off for a weekend to the mountains, or leave for some faraway city at a moment's notice. Others won't budge out of their homes. Their idea of fun is kicking back, relaxing, reading a book, and/or watching TV. If you hear a woman complaining she can't get her mate to ever do anything, chances are he is either the Philosopher or the Dapper.

The Dapper is the most intimate of all the male personalities (except for the Partner). Just when a woman throws up her hands and asks, "Why can't a man be more like a woman?", in walks a Dapper. And because his sensitivity gives him the ability to provide emotional support for his mate, she seldom feels lonely, even if she is stuck at home for the weekend.

Many Dappers view their mate as their best friend and confidante. Consequently, they enjoy spending time with her. Dappers normally don't stop for a drink with the guys on the way home from work. They prefer to be at home with the family. That's one of the reasons you won't find Dappers at the top of the corporate ladder. Putting a wedding anniversary first is frowned upon in board rooms.

If you ask at this point, "Okay, what's the catch? No one is that great," you are right. There are some flaws. And at the risk of hurting Dapper's sensitive feelings, there are more than one. Even though I have established that Dappers are more involved in the traditional "woman's work" than are any of their male counterparts, they still have not taken the total leap into *real* equality. They work hard to hide it, but like the rest of the male personalities, there is still this "gender thing."

Deep inside the Dapper, there's a voice that says, "You are the most generous of men for *helping* your mate out—with *her* work." In other words, Dappers still believe the home is *really* the woman's job. Therefore, he is the greatest of all human beings for doing as much as he does. Let me explain. It's true that the Dapper thinks it's within his responsibility to help out, but it's clearly defined as *help*. And he feels that this *help* needs to be appreciated.

For example, The Dapper can often be heard saying: "Honey, don't you feel lucky that I do so much? You know, I really don't know many other men who help out as much as I do. Well, I guess there's Tom. You remember him. You met him about ten years ago. He is the guy who lives in California. I think he's a housedad. Great guy and all, but he doesn't have a real job. Nope," Dapper winks at his mate, "I think I am the only great helper I know. And guess what, you lucky person, you have me all to yourself!"

The real story is that when the Dapper's mate returns home later this evening, she finds the chicken tetrazzini waiting for her. Dapper places the warm casserole on a pretty plate, pours her a glass of wine, gives her a big hug and kiss, then says, "Glad you're home, honey. I'm off to watch the game. No need to thank me for all the work I've done. You deserve it. I am glad I could help you out."

But there are other things waiting for her besides dinner, things that need her attention. The children's clothes need to be laid out for the next morning, the dog needs walking, the family room is in a shambles, one of the kid's teachers needs to be called, the kitchen stove is a mess, and the Dapper has asked her to iron him a shirt for work. The reality is that after a long, hard day she will still put in another couple of hours before she goes to bed. And during those two hours, her mate will watch football, feeling totally exonerated that he has already put in *his* time.

The problem is that she also has fallen into the belief that she needs to feel grateful to the Dapper: "What a great guy! He's done

CHAPTER 7

so much already. I couldn't even begin to ask him to *help* any more." She would feel like a total ingrate if she complained about what still needs to be done. And the sensitive Dapper would become extremely moody, irritated, or resentful if he felt criticized for what he *didn't* do.

Because this is a no-win situation, there are many more arguments in the Dapper's household than one would expect. Depending on the woman's household personality, those arguments could be a lot about who does what, when, and how much. This is a surprise twist for The Dapper, who wonders what went wrong when the chicken tetrazzini seemed so right.

What went wrong is simple. Once equality is tasted, you — the woman — want more. It's not entirely your fault. It's human nature. The good news is that the Dapper can very quickly grasp the concept that says if he is helping his mate with *her* work, it sort of makes him the employee and her the employer. Or worse yet, a mother and a child. Because Dapper often craves a storybook companion, he wants a mate as an equal — a soulmate, not a mother. Consequently, there's a natural appeal to partnership.

If a woman has a Dapper for a mate and she is thinking he can be easily swayed into a partnership, she is probably right. She just must remember to approach the subject with lots of kudos, for he will initially hear her plea as ingratitude. But eventually, since Dappers do understand fairness, they will take the leap. Lucky her. They make the best partners.

The Partner

The Partner's drive home from work is usually interrupted by at least one stop. He is either picking up the kids, the cleaning, groceries, a prescription, or doing some other needed chore. These tasks are not something he has been asked to do. He knows exactly what the kid's schedules are, since he is involved in planning them. He also knows what food is in the house, or if his shirts or his mate's suit needs to be picked up from the cleaners. He does not perceive this work as "helping out." His daily life includes sharing

ONE MAN'S "CASTLE" IS ANOTHER'S "HOME ON THE RANGE"

equally in the responsibilities of a home, raising a family, and working.

As he pulls into his driveway, he is thinking about the upcoming evening. He has no illusions that his day is over. Often it has just begun. As he contemplates dinner, he wonders if it is his turn to cook. Either way, he will be involved in the preparation, the cleanup, or doing something else. For instance, it might be his night to tutor his daughter in her math. You will not find a Partner coming home to lie on a couch while his working mate frantically runs around doing a double shift. They are partners. It's a partnership that doesn't stop at the front door. Both are involved in working to meet the family's financial responsibilities. Both are involved in taking care of the home and family. When the Partner opens the closet door to hang up his coat, he's aware there's plenty to do before he and his mate are able to spend the evening relaxing *together*. Partnership is not a natural happening. Most Partners did not just stumble into this realm of thinking. It started a long time ago in their childhoods.

He was just a young kid when Little Partner first noticed that his mom was different. She didn't look or act at all like the Beaver's mother on TV. Oh, she might have smiled a lot, but it seemed to be more about who *she* was, not who her husband was. He never had the impression that she was an extension of his father. Little Partner's mom was her own person. She was confident and did not hesitate to voice her thoughts.

Little Partner noticed something else that separated his mom from other moms. He often observed her playing. She had no problem with choosing to do something for herself, nor did she appear to feel guilty about it. Little Partner's mom thoroughly enjoyed creating a comfortable, nurturing home for her family. Even though Little Partner sensed her enjoyment, it was not hers alone. She taught him that he, too, had a responsibility in creating a comfortable home.

One of Partner's earliest memories was learning that if one gives, one gets. He also learned an important priority. Little Partner's mom taught that true enjoyment came in doing things together for

CHAPTER 7

the common good of all. Little Partners were very lucky children. They learned healthy priorities since their moms believed that people came before things.

Unlike other mothers, Little Partner's mom did not hand his sister a frying pan so she could learn to cook and him a screwdriver so he could learn to "fix things." She taught them both to do both. Little Partner needed to know how to cook as much as his sister needed to know how to fix things. It never occurred to Little Partner's mom to teach him to act and think like a "strong man," while his sister learned to act coy and dependent. Partner's sister was taught that she could depend on herself. The "weaker sex" was a myth.

"There is nothing the two of you can't do if you put your mind and soul to it. Don't ever believe anyone who tells you differently," said Little Partner's mom while walking hand-in-hand with her children through the park. "You both have been given the gift of life. With it comes your dreams. Follow them. They will guide you to the real you." These no-nonsense progressive mothers taught their Little Partner that there would be a time when *both* boys and girls needed to be strong, but there was also a time to be soft. "Both traits have merit," she would say. "The ideal is finding the balance, and to know when to be one or the other. Remember, boys need to be as soft as we are told they are strong, and girls need to be as strong as we are told they are soft."

Little Partner's mom also taught him that though boys and girls were different, they were also very much alike. For instance, they both had equal rights to talk about their sensitive feelings. They both had a right to cry. They both had rights to exercise their talents.

But life is not perfect. Little Partner also had it rough. As frustrating as it was to Little Partner, his demands were often not met. His mom refused to dote on him. She also was not always available to him. To make matters worse, she did not protect him from the big, bad world. Those were some hard times, indeed, for the Little Partner. He didn't like it at all when he learned his mom was not at his beck and call. He learned the world did not revolve around him. It was hard going for a while. Eventually he learned to make his bed, cook, clean, and do his own laundry. He also learned that his home was considered a place of pride, and there was an expectation that *all* members of the household would contribute to its well-being. Life was tough for Little Partner.

Now, Little Partner's father may or may not have been raised like Little Partner. Regardless, whether Little Partner viewed his father as supporting his mother's nontraditional views or not, his mother did not need to have support for her thinking or her actions. Her views on equal treatment and expectations for boys and girls were not up for negotiation. She did not seek consensus. She would not be compromised.

Little Partner's mom was a relentless fighter when it came to righting a wrong. She would not give in an inch if she felt something was unfair. If per chance Little Partner also had an enlightened father, all the better, but household equity genes are almost always passed down through the mothers.

So what does a Big Partner look like? The Partner is confident and assured of his identity. He believes he is equally responsible for the household. He does not have to be begged, coerced, or convinced to do his fair share. He does not see household chores through "gender eyes." Even though he doesn't enjoy cleaning (who does?), he can be found just as easily cleaning a bathroom as mowing the grass. He won't view his mate as his maid who waits on him. Nor does he see her as a secretary who does all his phone calls, his scheduling, his picking up, his putting way, or any other job he finds bothersome. He views his mate as his equal, his partner. Therefore, he equally participates in the entertaining, the shopping, and holiday preparation. He can put on a birthday party just as well as a woman and he doesn't resent it. He seldom pouts and can act all grown up when things don't go his way. He enjoys his family and his home and takes pride in maintaining it. He has a good sense of priorities and responsibilities, a positive outlook on life, and a respect for women. He desires intimacy, and enjoys working and playing together. His ego is not threatened by his mate's income and he has no problem with her equal participation in the financial support of the household. He shares equally in the management of the household income and seeks consensus before large purchases. He does not try to control or dominate others. Because of his healthy self-esteem, tolerance of others' mistakes or weaknesses comes easy. He is not critical and does not have a continual need to point out others' shortcomings.

There's more. Partners are involved fathers. They understand that their children's self-esteem is vulnerable and they are careful not to damage it. When the Partner does confront issues, he does so with sensitivity. He confidently knows his opinion carries a great deal of weight. He is aware he needs to be gentle when he comments on his children's behavior. Partners know everyone makes mistakes. He is not a perfectionist, and does not expect perfection in others. Therefore, he is more of a teacher to his children than a critic. He teaches by example. He desires to understand other people's feelings and encourages those around him to express them. He particularly wants to understand his mate's feelings and takes time to listen and respond. Simply put, a Partner enjoys pleasing you and makes efforts to do so.

A Question for the Woman: On a Scale of 1 to 10, How Does My Mate Rate As a Partner?

I'm sure by now you are saying, "Enough is enough. Come on, no one is *that* perfect!" Well, you are right. No one is always acting and feeling like a Partner. It is not a reality. We all have bad days and get in bad moods. None of us are sensitive and confident all the time. The goal is to strive toward being a Partner, but it is important to note that no one ever "arrives." No one ever does it right *all* the time.

If your mate's predominant household personality is a Partner, but you see many shortcomings while reading his profile, it is as I said: No one is perfect all the time. On a scale of 1 to 10, where does he fall? If he scored above 100, he's a 10 on a scale of 10. If he scored above 90, he is an 8 or 9 on a scale of 10. If he scored between 80 and 90, he's between a 7 or 8. If he falls below an 80 on the inventory, but considers himself a Partner anyway, he is no doubt *thinking* more about equity then practicing it.

Caution: We women have an innate desire to change our men into a 10. Even if they are an 8 or 9, we are not satisfied until they are a 10. This need to "change him" has never worked well for us. We know it, but we say we can't help it. "I just want to make him a wee bit better," we say. "He will thank me for it later." No, he won't. Change comes when he desires it himself. Men, like women, like to be the originator and the author of their own change. It's as simple as that.

If you desire your mate to change, accept him the way he is. It's a strange concept, I know. But it works.

CHAPTER 8

Two Become One—But Which One?

There are only two basic ways of structuring the relations between the female and male halves of humanity. All societies are patterned on either a dominator model—in which human hierarchies are ultimately backed up by force or the threat of force—or a partnership model, with variations in between.

— Riane Eisler, *The Chalice and the Blade* (1987)

Are You Assertive, Even-tempered, or Passive?

Now that you both know your household personalities, the fun begins. How compatible are the two of you? What are your strengths as a couple? What are your weaknesses? How adaptable are you to doing something differently?

There are three categories of household personalities: Assertive, Even-tempered, and Passive. You will find the categories of you and your mate in the box below.

Categories of Personalities

Assertive	Even-tempered	Passive
The Emperor	The Dapper	The Philosopher
The Hunter	The Sojourner	
The Rebel		The Stargazer
The Tigress		The HoneyBee

As you will note the Partner is not listed within any of the above categories. The Partner is absent from the following discussions on personality combinations simply because if a woman's mate is already a Partner there are no major issues to overcome, or behavior to change. In addition, *Dear Dinah* assumes that if a woman is lucky enough to have a Partner, she gave this book to someone else after reading the Introduction.

But to those readers who are seeking partnership this is the beginning of the "how-to" chapters. Remember to keep in mind that the following descriptions are based on predominant household personalities. Predominants are those that scored in the 80s to 90s or higher. If your household personality score did not score higher than 80, you will find some similarities in the following examples, but you probably won't have the major issues that higher-scoring couples have.

The Assertive Female with the Assertive Male

Sandy and Glen

Glen and Sandy are a working Midwest couple who struggle to balance their home and careers while raising two young boys. Sandy, a real-estate agent, identifies herself as a typical Rebel. Glen, an Emperor, is a sales manager at a wholesale auto parts store. He is known as a rising star who is very competitive, and he holds strong traditional viewpoints concerning gender. Typical of a Rebel, Sandy does not give in easily to what her Emperor calls "woman's work." Since both of their household personalities fall into the Assertive category, their home is a constant battleground over who is going to do what.

Sitting on their porch one morning, Sandy told me that ever since the day they looked deep into each other's passionate eyes and decided to become *one*, they have been struggling over *which* one. She says it is becoming increasingly upsetting to her that so many of their conversations begin and end with "you." While we both sipped our cups of tea, she shared with me the conversation they had had the previous evening.

Chapter 8

"You are unfair!" Sandy shouts at Glen. "Why am I doing all this work? I'm not your slave!"

Glen retorts, "Hey ... I work long hours at my job without complaining. Why can't you? I am sick and tired of your constant demands!"

"Demands! Is that what you call them? In case you haven't noticed, I also have a job. You are not the only one working long hours!" Sandy is clearly upset.

"You can quit that silly little job of yours any time you want. It's not as if you make that much money, anyway. Besides, your main job is the home and kids and me!" Glen defends his position.

"Over my dead body! You have spaghetti for a brain if you think I'm going to live my life around you and your needs!" Sandy attacks, trying to break through his resistance.

And so it goes, on—and on—and on. Glen and Sandy need a new idea, but what?

Ellen and Jim

Ellen, who is a Tigress, tells me that her mate Jim, a Hunter, is very much like Glen.

"He believes the house is 'woman's work,' and it's as simple as that," she moans. "Glen doesn't even try to hide the fact that his views are sexist," Ellen said, hopelessly. "He seems proud of the way he thinks. His father was the same way. I should have seen it coming. Glen firmly believes the way he was raised is exactly how it should be for us, even though his mother did not work outside the home. Oh, yes, he does the outside work, but that doesn't cut it when there is so much to do inside."

Since Ellen and Jim both have assertive personalities, their home, like Sandy and Glen's, is a constant battleground concerning who does what. Jim, a computer programmer, views Ellen's job as a nuisance. He thinks her "little" business, a gourmet coffee shop, will end when she figures out her *real* place in life (which is to make sure that he and the children are comfortable, happy, and taken care of). Ellen complains that he should *help* more, but as luck would have it, he was born a man and it's simply not his role.

"I don't ask *you* to help me outside," Jim tells his growling Tigress, "so don't ask me to help you. Everything would work out a lot better if you would just learn to cope like other women."

"In case you haven't noticed, I am working twice as much as you inside. So what, pray tell, would you ask me to help you with? When would I have time?!" Ellen snarls back at him.

These confrontations go nowhere. Like Glen and Sandy, Ellen and Jim need a new plan.

Mary and Bill

Mary, a Rebel, works as an accountant by day, and at night she is out "saving the world" with her community projects. Bill, the Hunter, is a contractor. One of his favorite things to do is retreat into his workshop every night after dinner. It comes as no surprise when Mary tells me, "We rarely see each other. The household is run by an unspoken agreement: don't ask anything from me and I won't ask anything from you."

When children came into their lives, Mary became resentful of the adjustments she had to make. While Bill's life went on relatively unaffected, Mary is now forced to limit her outside activities as she struggles to balance work and family.

Whether it's by design or not, Bill seems to have positioned himself well. He has little free time to be with the family because he is always "knocking himself out" with one of his beloved projects. Mary admittedly does not share his passion for being busy every second of the day. Consequently, she occasionally lets the house go. Bill looks at Mary and says, "I've been knocking myself out painting this house all day while you've been doing absolutely nothing, and now you want me to help with dinner? You've got to be kidding!"

And so it goes ...

The Good News and the Bad News

Is there hope for Glen and Sandy, Ellen and Jim, or Bill and Mary? Are there answers for two Assertive personalities living under the same roof? The good news is yes, there is hope for them. And yes, there are answers! Assertive couples have enormous potential.

CHAPTER 8

Assertive couples are the most adventurous and ambitious of the personality categories. If both want something to work, it damn well will. Their mutual motto is, "If it's worth doing, it's worth doing right," which fortunately includes their relationship. With that attitude, they have an excellent shot at creating a household partnership. Their "can do" spirit will help them not only climb the mountain, but also enjoy the view at the top when they get there.

The bad news is that for them to reach the summit, they must change, and that is difficult for an Assertive. It feels too much like losing.

For the Assertive female, be patient and stop doing what is not working. You are going nowhere fast with your demands and empty threats. Sandy and Mary, as Rebels, will have a harder time changing this trait than the Tigress Ellen, since their sense of injustice runs deeper.

But as a Tigress, Ellen will struggle with perfection, which becomes a stumbling block, particularly if she tries to implement the same standards at home that she does in her business. This becomes especially counterproductive if she is matched with the Emperor, who is trying to pull off the same coup. It is here that the Tigress has an edge over the Rebel. Because she is more pragmatic, she is more apt to step back from something that is not working.

What to Do Differently?

Attention to all Rebels and Tigresses! Here's a news flash! Voicing your complaints has not worked for you in the past, and it's not working for you now. It's probably a safe bet that it won't work for you in the future. Once you accept this reality, you can move on to the next logical step ... stop doing what is not working!

So what is the answer? Let's look to history and learn from what warring countries have done since the beginning of time, if they sought peace. First, they called a truce. Second, they took a break and stepped back. Each one then decided what they could live with. When they had it, they came back to the table in a spirit of negotiation and compromise. Once there, they worked out an agreement, wrote it down, and signed it into a treaty. I am suggesting that you do the same. Since you are losing the war, call a truce. As a Rebel or Tigress, you need to come to grips with what you really want, what is reasonable, and what is achievable. A later chapter provides a step-by-step process for negotiation and compromise.

Third, in a quiet moment, hand the following to your Assertive mate.

A Letter from Dinah to the Emperor or Hunter

Dear Mr. Emperor and Mr. Hunter,

As painful as this is to you, you must accept the fact that your mate is never going to break down and be the submissive subject whose only desire is to make your favorite dinner. If you are hanging around with the expectation that eventually she will come to her senses and realize you are the omnipotent and supreme head of the household, you will wait a lifetime. I know that you have noticed by now that your mate is every bit as powerful as you are. She is your equal. After all, it was this fighting spirit of hers that attracted you to her in the first place. You just want the best of both worlds, like everyone else. It doesn't make you a bad person, just one that has to change their thinking a bit to create the peace you so desire.

Later we will discuss negotiation and compromise. I encourage you to try both. These two techniques are your only hope in creating a harmonious home where partnership, not ego, is at the helm. I hope you explore this. You have nothing to lose and everything to gain.

Warmest regards,
Dinah

CHAPTER 9

It's Not Always What It Seems

Truth could never be wholly contained in words ...
at the same moment the mouth is speaking one thing,
the heart is saying another.

— Catharine Marshall

The Assertive Female with the Passive and/or the Even-tempered Male

Because opposites attract, various combinations of the Assertive female (Rebel and Tigress) and the Passive male (Philosopher) or the Even-tempered (Dapper) coexist in millions of households. These couples are easy to spot, especially when the man is the Philosopher. Their Assertive female mate is most likely labeled "the nag." When the man is the Dapper, the Assertive female is most likely labeled "impossible to please." And, I'm afraid there is a bit of truth in both perceptions. But it's not because the Rebel or Tigress isn't correct about wanting change, it's because of how she goes about trying to get it

"We sure know who wears the pants in that household, don't we? Heeheehee," giggles a group around the office water cooler. "Boy, is he ever henpecked! He probably needs to check in with her every time he walks out the door. Poor guy."

Of course, nothing could be further from the truth. The Rebel or the Tigress has tried everything except to skydive into the front yard to get their Passive mate's attention that something must change. This man's favorite reaction is to nod and mumble a couple of concessions like, "Yeah, you're right. I'll try harder next time." Then they retreat. So who's really running whom?

However, when it comes to the Dapper, have no fear, the Assertive *will* get a response. But it won't be the acknowledgment she's looking for. Dappers interpret the Assertive's frustrations as a personal slam. Therefore, these personal confrontations can get ugly and much more hurtful with a Dapper than a Philosopher. Philosophers tend to reject his Assertive female's issues as *her* problem while Dappers take them to heart. Nevertheless, the result for the Assertive female is the same. Because her communication style is combative, she will either not be heard (as in the case of the Philosopher), or she will be misunderstood (as in the case of the Dapper.) Either way, she loses.

Jane and Mike

I know Jane and Mike very well, since they live in Gary's and my neighborhood. Jane, a Tigress who is an interior designer, continually complains to me about Mike, an industrial writer who is a Philosopher. One evening she told me, "It's like he doesn't hear me. Nothing I say or do makes a dent in him." She relays a recent conversation:

"I am confused," Jane says to Mike. "I thought you said you would help Anna with her homework. I have a deadline. My sketches are needed for a meeting tomorrow. I also have to do the laundry and monthly bills. I can't do it all!"

"Oh, yes, I guess I do remember saying I would help out. Well, tonight might be a bad time. I've had a pretty rough day. Don't worry though, I'll get to it later," responds Mike.

The next night, Jane tells me she spots Mike heading for the couch. "Wait a minute!" she yells. "Don't even think about going and watching TV. We have to figure out next month's budget. You promised to help me out," she growls in frustration.

"Yeah, yeah, okay," says the Passive Mike, "but let's do it tomorrow. Tonight, I am planning on watching the game. Anyway, I really don't know anything about the finances. You're much better at it than I am. Can't you just do it? Besides, are you sure I promised? I don't remember actually promising," says the Passive Philosopher.

CHAPTER 9

Ginger and Larry

Ginger and Larry perceive themselves as the "modern-day" couple. Both have demanding jobs. Ginger, a Rebel, is an accountant executive for an advertising firm. Larry, a Dapper, is an administrator for a local medical center. They have two young children, six and eight years of age. Even though they both put in the same amount of time away from home and focused on career, Ginger tells me that she still feels ultimately responsible for making sure everything gets done in the home. She is weary from her double shift at work and in the home. Even though Larry is a good helper when it comes to the house, he looks to Ginger for his instructions.

"Larry," says Ginger, returning home late from the office, "I thought you would have cleaned up the kitchen. And why aren't the kids ready for bed? I thought you were going to shovel the snow from the porch. You know my parents are coming for the weekend. I can't do it all!"

"Would you please back off?" responds Larry, in his typical, tired Dapper manner. "It seems like I hear nothing from you but demands. Don't you appreciate any of the help that I already gave you?" says the hurt Dapper. "I made dinner, for God's sake!"

"Yes, yes ... and I am grateful," reassures Ginger, "but don't you see that your help is not enough? I am still working far more around the house than you and am tired of being the one who has to continually make the 'to-do' list. Can't you just take the initiative and do it without being asked or begged? I'm tired too! And it all falls on me."

"All right, all right!" proclaims Larry. "I didn't know we were keeping score. Just tell me what you want me to do."

The Good New and the Bad News

Is there hope for Jane and Mike and for Ginger and Larry? Are there answers for two personalities living under the same roof who are completely opposite? Yes, the good news is that the Philosopher and the Dapper are less resistant to change than their mates perceive. Rebels and Tigresses only need a new plan. Remember, if you are a

Rebel, you are the reformer. You want change, and you want it now! And as a Tigress, you can become easily irritated if you have to ask for what you need more then once. For some reason the Assertive female just expects her Passive male to know and respond immediately. "Doesn't he get it?" the Tigress growls to herself.

The bad news is that the Philosopher, who is void of any psychic connection or mind-reading, really doesn't "get it," no matter how many ways you say it. He continues to look at the Rebel as some strange being who makes mountains out of molehills, and he views the ambitious Tigress as lacking all understanding of behavior that operates differently than hers. In short, the Passive male truly does not understand why everything in his Assertive female's life has to be such a big deal.

In spite of his acute myopia, the Philosopher has a point. Both the Rebel and the Tigress could be far more effective if they understood that the Philosopher is not really stonewalling them but actually operates from a different set of beliefs and values. He simply does not think the same way his Assertive mate does and probably never will. Negotiation and compromise, as well as verbalizing with less passion, will produce better results. The Assertive female would do well to remember that the Passive male likes to talk about ideas and thoughts more than feelings. Passive males, especially Philosophers, are more impressed with *why* change should occur and what the benefits will be than they are with *how* to achieve it. And here is some more bad news. After they figure it all out, they still have a problem with doing it.

The Rebel and Tigress have a different dynamic with the Dapper. Dappers are involved with the home and actually believe they do their fair share. Therefore, they feel a lack of appreciation and respond to the Assertive's complaints with hurt and anger. The Rebel and Tigress can unknowingly sabotage the Dapper's efforts since their quest for equality comes across as always wanting more, more, and more. It seems each time a goal is met, the bar is raised to a higher notch. No doubt the Dappers view their Assertive mates as ingrates, which makes sense if the Dapper considers himself to be the great helper. The problem is that the Dapper believes he is performing a good deed when he helps out and his mate should be darn grateful, but the Rebel and Tigress believe that the Dapper's benevolence is simply not enough.

The Assertive female won't see the logic in something that applies to men but not to women. "Why is it that when I do housework, it's viewed as *my* job," asks the Rebel to the Dapper, "but when you do housework, it is considered *helping me out*? I do not understand why my work is not considered helping *you* out. Am I 'helping you out' when I go to work every day?" she asks. One has to admit that "these ingrates" do have a point.

So as you can see, even though this household at first appears less contentious than the Assertive male and female combination (since a Passive male will concede in order to avoid conflict, and an Even-tempered might just give up), they share similar problems.

What to Do Differently?

Let's start by comparing the preparation for a household partnership to the actions of a farmer who tills the soil before planting his crops. Before you move into the chapter which deals with the "how to," the ground must be cultivated. Second, the ground must be fertilized with awareness before being planted with opportunity. The successful farmer knows that all this up-front preparation increases the chances of a successful harvest. It is the same with a household partnership. The more the couple can do to prepare the ground, the greater the likelihood of a successful harvest or, in our case, a successful partnership.

It is also important for the Assertive female to know if her mate is a Philosopher or a Dapper. If the mate is a Philosopher, the key step for the Assertive woman is to take a step back. This step back provides one with a more objective viewpoint. You are now in a better position to take a closer look at your peace-loving Philosopher and learn to implement some of his gentle ways. Study how he communicates (when he does, that is) and note his nonconfrontational style. You need to approach him in the same manner, which means putting down your sledgehammer. It is only in this "safe zone" that he will begin to hear you. And remember: he is not your enemy. He does want to please you. This softer approach should not be construed as acquiescing to him, or being dishonest about your feelings. I prefer to see it as changing a behavior that's not working for you. Besides, a constantly strong, confrontational communication style is not necessarily any more honest or effective.

Third, in a quiet moment, hand the following to your Philosopher.

A Letter from Dinah to the Philosopher (the Passive)

Dear Philosopher,

Here are some hints on how you can be more effective with your Assertive female. Number one, stay with your mate. That means don't walk away every time the conversation gets a little heated. This is going to be difficult for you, since you have become comfortable with this walking-away stuff. If you truly are serious about wanting to have a happy relationship with your mate, you need to stay put, listen, and try to understand her feelings. Say things like, "Yes, I understand, that must feel frustrating, hurtful, or disappointing." No need to take on blame. Just listen and validate her feelings. If you are sincere, it will work. If you aren't, try it anyway. The sincerity will come later. Another hint: Do not try to talk her out of her feelings by saying, "Oh, it really isn't that bad." Or, "Why do you make such a huge deal over the same stuff?" Or, "Why are you getting so emotional about this?" Or, "Why are you doing this again?" If you try that "Why?" tactic (which is really asking, "Why are you such a lunatic?"), you will have two results. First, she will feel crazy. Second, she will escalate. When you ask "Why?" you are minimizing her feelings, and you have put her in the position of justifying them. By justifying them, she thinks she can prove to you and to herself that she really isn't a lunatic. This is going to take more time and can produce crazy feelings for both of you, and the issues will still go unresolved.

CHAPTER 9

> *Saying you understand someone's feeling doesn't necessarily mean you would have the same feeling in a similar situation, nor does it mean that you agree with the feelings. That is not a necessary criterion in order to validate another person's feelings. When you say "I understand," it only means you understand the feelings of your mate's frustration and yes, it is not a pleasant feeling and yes, you do understand how feeling that way could be unsettling. (You do, don't you?)*
>
> *Once you offer your mate some sincere empathy for her feelings, she will move on to the more positive subject of problem-solving. Perhaps you could even facilitate this process by saying, "I truly do understand your frustration. How about talking about how we can work together to solve the problem?" After you pick her up from the floor (since your reaction has shocked her into temporary unconsciousness), you can start discussing strategies to solve the problem.*
>
> *A warning — this understanding and empathy stuff is impossible to do while you are hanging up your coat, watching TV, reading the paper, or involved in any other behavior except looking straight into her eyes and listening. I promise you, gentle Philosopher, it will be life-changing for your relationship. If you succeed at this, you have a garden that's waiting to be planted.*
>
> Warmest regards,
Dinah

A Letter from Dinah to the Dapper (the Even-tempered)

Before I speak to the Dapper, I would like to address the Assertive woman who has a Dapper for a mate. Since the Dapper likes to participate, you must be careful not to quench his spirit. He can easily be discouraged and turn bitter if he feels his "good deeds" are not appreciated. This is a tragedy, since the Dapper is the easiest to convert to partnership. In fact, he is almost there. To cultivate the ground you should talk more about issues rather than your feelings. Since the Dapper is a post-modern-day man, at this point in the cultivation process, your feelings get in the way. I am afraid he will only hear your feelings as something that he is responsible for, or worse yet, he will interpret them as blame. Remember, he is not responsible for your feelings. A better suggestion for preparing the ground with a Dapper is to talk about fairness.

Begin by exposing the faulty belief premise your Dapper is working from. He sees himself as a helper, and a darn good one. Fertilize the new ground you have sowed with the awareness that the Dapper must come to admit that he truly does view the home as something he "helps out" with. This admission is a giant step. An upcoming chapter has a Belief and Action Inventory. Going through that exercise will help you with this process.

In a quiet moment, hand the following to your Dapper mate.

Dear Mr. Dapper,

It is critical for you to recognize that no matter how much you help out, as long as you consider it "help" you are not getting the point. You must shake the notion that being more progressive than other males places you in a seat of honor. Since most men view the home as the woman's responsibility, you cannot be given a crown because you have more awareness than most. Well, okay, maybe you should be given a medallion since you are at the top of the class, but look around at who you are comparing yourself to. The real question is, "Should the woman in your life be made to always feel grateful that she's found a man who rightfully believes he should share mutually with the household chores?" The reverse would be that you would be made to feel that you should continually be grateful that she leaves for work each morning! Now please don't misunderstand. Thankfulness is a wonderful attribute. However, in this context, "gratefulness" often denotes that we are receiving something that we don't really deserve — in this case, the "extra" help. Doesn't it seem more reasonable that, as a working couple, the mutual contribution should be expected?

Warmest regards,
Dinah

CHAPTER 10

Don't Fence Me In

Never mind.
— Gilda Radner as Emily Litella in
It's Always Something (1989)

The Even-tempered Female with the Assertive Male

This is a very unlikely pair. Most Sojourners, depending how predominant their personality is, are not attracted to the Assertive male, since they attempt to stifle their freedom. The Sojourner is usually more attracted to a Passive who is far more nonchalant about her independence. However, if she stumbles into a relationship with an Emperor or a Hunter, she doesn't stay long. Just as soon as she finds out that he has major expectations of her, she'll either set the record straight or be out the door. So if you are a Sojourner who is in a relationship with an Assertive male, I can only assume it's because he's learned that no matter how hard he tries to influence you, he can't.

Betsy and Billy

Betsy, a carefree Sojourner, is married to Billy, a competitive, gender-rigid Emperor. How it happened, I have no idea. It must have been on a lonely night long ago when the stars were out, the moon was bright, and in one of Betsy's *carpe diem* moments Billy's gallant, macho manner swept her off her feet. After they eloped, the rude awakening occurred, but by then it was too late. They had already promised "I do." And, of course, the unsuspecting Emperor had no idea that a Sojourner saying "I do" has absolutely nothing to do with "I will."

Billy (calling Betsy on the phone from his office): Hi, honey. I'm surprised I caught you in your office. I thought you were going to call in sick.

Betsy: Well, I was thinking of calling in, but after I heard the forecast predicting rain, I thought I might as well come in. So, what's up?

Billy: Something big. I have a chance to entertain some very important clients from out of town. I want to have dinner with them and ... you know ... sort of wine and dine them. It's a huge account. If I can reel them in, it means a significant bonus. So what do you think about dinner?

Betsy: I like the idea. What restaurant are you thinking of?

Billy: No, no. That won't work. The word is the guys like to be entertained in the home. It's a culture thing or something. Anyway, can you pick up some gourmet "take-out" or something that is equally impressive? By the way, what's the condition of the house?

Betsy: I don't know, haven't noticed. Why?

Billy: Well, you need to notice and you need to make sure it's in good shape and ...

Betsy (interrupting Billy): Billy, I was just thinking. Now don't go crazy on me, but I am wondering ... Do I really need to be there? You know how I hate this stuff and some of the women were talking about that new play tonight. You remember ... the one everyone is raving about? And I thought that if you really didn't need me I would ...

Billy (interrupting): Betsy! My God! What are you saying! *Of course* I need you tonight! I can't pull this off by myself! You *must* be there! You've got to get out of work early, pick up the damn dinner, go home, and get things ready. God, I hope the dishes are at least done. They are, aren't they? Can't I get you involved with my job, just once?!!!

Betsy: I don't recall you being involved with my homeless benefit.

Billy: Come on, Betsy, this is money. Let's not make this into another big deal, okay?

Betsy: Well, all right ... but this is going to cost you. (pause) Are you sure you can't do this by yourself?

Billy: Come on, Betsy, the last time I asked you for something was when I was in the hospital.

Betsy: Really? (pause) When were you in the hospital?

The Good News and the Bad News

The good news is, we don't have to fret about the Sojourner breaking the bad habit of believing she's the only one capable of putting dinner on the table. Since she doesn't view it as her job, she doesn't do it. Or she does it sparingly enough that no one in her family ever comes to expect it from her.

The bad news is that Billy and Betsy unfortunately have a conflict of needs. The Sojourner needs to fly; the Emperor needs to control her flight. Because of their conflicting needs, there is a standoff in the home. Since neither one is knocking themselves out getting everyday chores completed, there's a great deal of stress building up. They might not notice it at first because the independent Sojourner does what she wants. However, this independence comes at a price, if her Assertive mate has anything to say about it. And you can bet he does, at every opportunity. I am afraid the insouciant Sojourner's *carpe diem* is a fleeting hope when living with an Assertive man. Chances are the conflict is getting to her and she is looking for a better way.

Again, depending how high their score is, Sojourners are difficult women to get into a partnership — and the higher her score (over 100), the harder she is to convince. A partnership might mean changing something that requires more of her than she is willing to risk. The case for partnership, however, is that she hates the anxiety her procrastination produces and would welcome relief from the stress. Therefore, in order to move forward, the Sojourner has to come to admit to herself that she is in a bind, and something needs to change. Perhaps partnership is appealing, after all.

What to Do Differently?

The bottom line for the Sojourner living with the Assertive male is that one of them will need to take the lead if this change is going to happen. The Sojourner probably has a better chance of stepping forward toward creating this partnership with her strong-headed Emperor or Hunter if everything else has failed. So if a crisis is looming, she might consider taking this opportunity to implement some changes. I suspect her mate will be eager to try anything that could bring some order to his home, which means he might be ready for negotiation and compromise.

Stay tuned. An exercise in an upcoming chapter is a step-by-step approach on how to begin this process. After completing it, the Sojourner will be in a more favorable position to negotiate a fair and just household, one that I promise if you are a Sojourner can live with. Yes, you will lose some of your "whenever the mood strikes" lifestyle, but you'll gain a more manageable home, which ultimately will result in having more time to do your own thing, and reduce your stress. Wouldn't it be nice to eliminate some of those awkward and unpleasant consequences that often accompany your disorganization? You must admit that your procrastination makes your life more difficult in the long run. Of course, a household partnership won't solve all your problems with your Assertive male, but it will end the standoff.

CHAPTER 11

Why Mess Up A Good Thing? At Least For Him

Not everyone's life is what they make it. Some people's lives are what other people make them.
    – Alice Walker, *You Can't Keep a Good Woman Down* (1981)

The Passive Female with the Assertive Male

We don't have too look to far to find this couple. They probably make up the majority of our society's traditional households. The man is the leader, the decision-maker, and the head of the home. The woman sort of stands in the background perfectly contented to take the more submissive role. Most of us have grown up with this couple as our role model. During the '50s and '60s television mirrored the ideal family back to us through shows like *Ozzie and Harriet*, *Father Knows Best*, *Donna Reed*, and *Leave it to Beaver*. We were taught that the way the world works best is for the man to be "man" and the woman to be "woman."

Pat and Bob

Pat and Bob are a delightful couple who live next door to my twin sister's home in Holland, Michigan. Both Kathy's house and theirs sit high up on the sand dunes, overlooking the choppy waters of Lake Michigan. Gary and I spend many of our summer weekends nestled away in this beautiful haven.

Pat, a dual personality of Stargazer and Sojourner, works during the week at the local library. On weekends she loves to walk the beach. Bob, a typical Hunter, spends his weekdays as a business consultant. On weekends he loves to become deeply entrenched in his outdoor projects. His home is a showplace of neatly kept gardens, freshly painted eaves and decks, shiny barbecues, and squeaky-clean cars.

"Oh, no ... no indeed!" Pat answered emphatically, in response to my question as to whether Bob would ever put a load of laundry in the washing machine. As Kathy and I sat on her deck watching the sailboats below, Pat continued with her response: "Bob would jump off this balcony before he would do anything that even remotely resembles 'woman's work.' You can't imagine how frustrating that is. Ever since I went back to work, I find I need help. I am tired of doing both the housework and working an outside job," she said irritably. "I keep pleading for a housekeeper to come in a couple times a month, but Bob won't hear of it."

"Why not?" I asked. "It certainly seems reasonable." I noticed that Kathy nodded her head in agreement with me.

"Because he is compulsive with work, and thinks everyone else should be as well. He never stops. Once he can't find anything more to do with this house—I know him, he will want to sell it and start over. I guess he just assumes that I have his same passion to keep busy, so why shouldn't I be able to do all the housework, plus keep a job?"

We all became silent as we looked down from the deck and watched Bob energetically push a wheelbarrow filled with wood chips into his flower garden.

"Hey, must be nice," he yells up at us, "sitting back, enjoying the sunshine. Wish I could do that!"

"Sure he does," laughs Pat. "He'd go crazy after three minutes."

"Well ... there you have it," noted Kathy. "It seems as if he is doing what he wants. You just need to as well."

Realizing we were admiring his stamina, Bob made a special effort to dump the wheelbarrow with ease. Looking up at us, he began to pound his chest. "Still built like a man of steel!" he yelled.

Pat shook her head. "Where does he get that energy?"

"By doing something he likes doing," I answered.

CHAPTER 11

The Good News and the Bad News

The good news is that if you are a Passive female married to an Assertive male, chances are you've grown weary of the archaic role you are playing and you are ready for a drastic change. You just might be getting fed up with the expectation that it is up to you to do the daily household chores of cooking, cleaning, and laundry, and now you are willing to admit that you have created quite a mess for yourself. You have doted on your Emperor or Hunter for many years, and he has come to enjoy and expect your giving spirit. Worse yet, the children have followed the example of their father and believe you are at their beck and call. Now tired and feeling unappreciated, you agree; this is going to be a hard habit to break. But for the enterprising and "can do" HoneyBee and the creative, charming Stargazer, this will not be as hard as you anticipate.

The bad news is that many women who have Stargazer or HoneyBee personalities have adopted these roles without question. In fact, these Passives wonder why there needs to be so much commotion around equity. They like things just as they are. Their mother lived this way, their mother's mother lived this way, and so on back through the generations. Some of you Passives probably pored over every word of the book *Fascinating Womanhood* written back in the '60s as a response to the rising interest in feminism. The author, Helen B. Andelin, intrigued women everywhere with her concepts of Domestic Goddesses.

According to Andelin, Domestic Goddesses were perfect homemakers who created magic for themselves and their family simply because they learned how to make their man "feel like a man." Andelin also wrote about how important it was to greet your man at the front door so that he has someone to come home to. (Only men apparently need someone to come home to.) Andelin was convinced that a woman needed to become vulnerable, weak, and helpless so that her man could feel protective, strong, and powerful. The book was written to instruct women on how they could please their men, which is a Passive's #1 role in life.

To help you understand the impact of women's socialization,

let's take a stroll down memory lane, back to the *Ozzie and Harriet* time. The following is an actual clip from a 1950s home economics textbook found in the archives of Mary Margaret Holy Mother's High School in the midwestern town of Cresco, Iowa. The instructions were intended for high school girls, with the purpose of teaching them how to become good wives.

How to Prepare for Your Husband's Homecoming

Have dinner ready. Plan ahead, even the night before, to have a delicious meal on time. This is a way of letting him know that you have been thinking about him and are concerned about his needs. Most men are hungry when they come home and the prospect of a good meal is part of the warm welcome needed.

Prepare yourself. Take 15 minutes to rest so you will be refreshed when he arrives. Touch up your make-up, put a ribbon in your hair, and be fresh-looking. He has just been with a lot of work-weary people. Be a little gay and a little more interesting. His boring day may need a lift.

Clear away the clutter. Make one last trip through the main part of the house just before your husband arrives, gathering up school books, toys, paper, etc. Then run a dust cloth over the tables. Your husband will feel he has reached a haven of rest and order; it will give you a lift too.

Prepare the children. Take a few minutes to wash the children's hands and faces (if they are small), comb their hair, and if necessary, change their clothes. They are little treasures and he would like to see them playing the part.

Minimize all noise. At the time of his arrival, eliminate all noise of the washer, dryer, dishwasher, or vacuum. Try to encourage the children to be quiet. Be happy to see him. Greet him with a warm smile and be glad to see him.

Some don'ts. Don't greet him with problems or complaints. Don't complain if he's late for dinner. Count this as minor compared with what he might have gone through that day at work.

Make him comfortable. Have him lean back in a comfortable

chair or suggest he lie down in the bedroom. Have a cool or warm drink ready for him. Arrange his pillow and offer to take off his shoes. Speak in a low, soft, soothing and pleasant voice. Allow him to relax and unwind.

Listen to him. You may have a dozen things to tell him, but the moment of his arrival is not the time. Let him talk first.

Make the evening his. Never complain if he does not take you out to dinner or other places of entertainment. Instead, try to understand his world of strain and pressure, and his need to be home and relax.

The goal: Try to make your home a place of peace and order, where your husband can renew himself in body and spirit.

Most Passive female household personalities (Stargazers and HoneyBees) have become more enlightened and would not think of using any of the above written words for anything more than fire starter. Things have changed. You, too, have worked a full day and have no time for such nonsense. Still the Passive female is surprised when she realizes how much her lifestyle resembles that of her mother and grandmother.

What to Do Differently?

To begin with, it might be helpful to go back to the first chapter—back to Jill and Jane's letter. If you recall, they were asking if anyone had a solution short of starting World War III. Abby suggested they tell their Assertive males how they feel, or else "don't complain." Oh ... how I wish it could be that easy for you. I wish all you had to do was to tell your Emperor or Hunter how you felt about doing it all, and presto, he would see the logic of your complaint and begin to do his equal share. If it were that simple, change would have occurred centuries ago. No, it's not going to be that easy. It will take a lot more than having the Assertive man in your life whip the whipped cream or set the table to bring equity into your home. It is going to take major reform.

Begin by sitting down and pretending you are Dear Abby. What would you have told Jill and Jane? Think about it. If you had been

Abby for a day, how would you have suggested these two persons address the inequity in their household? Go back and reread the letter. What advice would you give?

It probably isn't that difficult to come up with an answer, is it? Many of us would have said, "If you don't like it, stop doing it." That's not bad advice. It's funny we can see so clearly for others, but with ourselves the solution seems much more fleeting or filled with the ever-present "buts." When someone tells you to "just stop doing it all," you say, "I would love to stop doing all the work, but how's it going to get done?" It is strange that, applied in our own situation, we view solutions as different, but that's faulty thinking. The truth is, it isn't any different. The advice you gave so confidently to Jill and Jane, who have Passive household personalities, is the same advice you should give yourself, only take out the "but."

The following is my advice to Jill and Jane. It's a tad different than Abby's.

Dinah: Jill, what do you say when your husband asks, "When will supper be ready?"

Jill: "As soon as I can make it."

Dinah: Have you always said the same thing?

Jill: Yes, almost always.

Dinah: Have you ever wondered why?

Jill: Well, I suppose it is because I believe it's my job. My husband also believes it's my job and it sort of just happens. It's been something I've done from the beginning of our relationship.

Dinah: Like a habit?

Jill (after thinking a bit): Yes, I suppose you could say that.

Dinah: Have you ever thought of saying something else to your husband when he asks you, "When is dinner going to be ready?"

Jill: Not really. Oh, I've thought a few things I could say, but no, I guess I don't know how else to respond.

CHAPTER 11

Dinah: I have a suggestion. The next time he asks, "When will supper be ready?" simply say, "I'm no longer happy with my job of always being the cook. I think we need to talk about changing some expectations, as well as sharing more of the jobs."

Jill: What good would that do? He would just get mad. He would say things like he's been working all day, so he's not going to make dinner. I don't even know how to answer when he says, "Why are you acting this way?"

Dinah: Again, you repeat, "Because I want to make some changes. I'm not happy when I feel like I'm doing it all."

Jill: Well . . . as I said before, I don't want to start World War III.

Dinah: I'm not saying it's going to be pleasant. Most change doesn't come without a revolution. But if you stay confident with your actions and don't resort to sulking, he will eventually listen to your concerns. That's how change occurs. It usually only takes one person, and then others will follow. But it is very important not to defend yourself or your actions. That's how you stay out of the war zone. Just whistle a little tune while you go about your day. Your action is important. Quit making dinner and the discussions will begin.

Jill: But what about the rest of the household work?

Dinah: Break one bad habit at a time. The rest will come.

One More Letter from Dinah to the Assertive Males

Since this is such new ground for the Passive Stargazers and HoneyBees, I am suggesting some initial habit-changing before you approach the following chapters, which address negotiating and compromise. Your partnership will have a better chance of success if you have cultivated and completed some initial groundwork. Otherwise, until you (the Stargazer or HoneyBee) take a stand for yourself, what's to negotiate? By changing a few of your bad habits up front, you are cultivating new ground in which to create your future partnership.

When you feel your Assertive male is in a receptive mood, hand him the following:

Dear Mr. Emperor and Mr. Hunter,

There is going to be a big change in your household. You are used to having little responsibility in the home and now your mate is asking for equal participation. I am sure that you can't imagine how this new "partnership" concept could possibly work to your benefit. It will take some time, but having a happy and contented partner who feels as if her needs and wants are important cannot possibly work against you. The peaceful transition to this new household is up to you. Yes, you could work to block it and expend a lot of energy to stop something that will eventually be inevitable, or else you can examine the merits, understand the fairness, and work toward creating a happier, more equitable, and enlightened household.

Warmest regards,
Dinah

CHAPTER 12

If It's Not Broken, Why Mess With It?

There is a luxury in being quiet in the heart of chaos.

– Virginia Woolf

The Even-tempered Female with the Passive Male and/or Even-tempered Male

Sue and Dick

At first glance, Sue and Dick's life is peaceful, with no noticeable stress. Their relationship is generally conflict-free and tolerant of the other's nonchalant, laid-back attitude. Maybe it's because issues don't get addressed, but that's how they like it.

Sue, a teacher and a Sojourner, is comfortable with work and home. Her husband Dick, a restaurant manager, is a typical Passive male who appears very satisfied with life. As a Passive, he does not make demands of his Sojourner and she is free to enjoy her independence. There is very little adherence within their home to societal gender roles since there are few expectations of the other. Most weekends they can be overheard having a conversation like the following:

Sue: I wonder if we should clean the house today. We've put it off the last two months and things are starting to pile up.

Dick: They are? I guess I haven't noticed. I sort of thought I would play golf today. The weather is beautiful.

Sue: Hmmm ... well ... you know that's not a bad idea.

Sure beats cleaning house. I think I'll go with you. We'll clean tomorrow.

Their philosophy is simple: They've worked all week and it's the weekend. Weekends are a time to kick back and enjoy life. As Sue, Dick, and golf clubs pull out of the garage, they notice their next-door neighbor Gus, huffing and puffing, mowing his lawn. They are immune to their own six inches of new grass, and do not even experience a tinge of guilt. However, they feel sympathetic toward Gus. It is beyond them why anyone would ruin a beautiful summer day working in the yard when the golf courses, hiking trails, waves, mountains, or beaches beckon. Their conversation continues:

Dick: Poor Gus. Someone should teach him how to have some fun.
Sue: Well ... it won't be his wife. I can't even get her to go for a walk. The other day I asked her to join me for a stroll in the park and she said the strangest thing.
Dick: What was that?
Sue: She couldn't (giggle) because she had to finish washing her windows.
Dick (now maneuvering the car around the empty garbage cans that have been lying in the driveway since the previous week): Yep, they're a strange lot all right. OOPS ... almost hit those cans again. Got to bring them in when we get back.

Off they go, to enjoy fun, laughter, and song, with not so much as a glance back at their tall grass, their peeling paint, or even the empty garbage cans now rolling into Gus's freshly mowed lawn.

Cheryl and Sam

Cheryl, a nurse, is married to Sam, a carpenter. They both work long hours and have little energy at the end of the day. Unfortunately for Cheryl, Sam has a higher need for organizing the household than she does. This creates a constant battle with Sam giving in most of

CHAPTER 12

time. The ending is simple: Sam throws in the towel, and the house becomes "just a place to kick off your shoes." Dappers don't like working alone. They eventually take the position, "If she doesn't care, neither do I." A truce is called and they live happily ever after.

Ultimately, Dappers can be great mates for Sojourners if they enjoy playing more than working around the home. They can have a great life together as long as they don't have to open their home and lifestyle with others. For instance, this is the couple that doesn't plan, inevitably is late, and being invited to their home for dinner means picking up the pizza and a six-pack. Or else, they drop off of the face of the earth for five days getting ready for Grandma's visit. So what that they carry out three months of garbage and junk? If it works for them, why invite trouble and look for change?

What to Do Differently... Or Should They?

The Even-tempered Sojourner living with her Even-tempered or Passive male might not choose to do anything differently. Again, why change something that seems to be working? But since you are reading this, you probably are seeking more organization in your life. "Just how bad is it, anyway?" asks the Sojourner and the Dapper. Let's see—do any of the following scenarios sound familiar?

- The other day you missed the beginning of a movie because you both thought the other one had brought money. Of course, neither had.

- Your washing machine is not working because no one called for repairs when you first heard a strange noise last month. Now it is completely out of commission.

- A close friend is upset with you because of your constant tardiness. You even have a few "no shows." And it seems you forget to mark her birthday on your calendar.

- You continually run out of household products at the most inconvenient time.

- You are always misplacing something important or forgetting to put something back.

- You were frustrated when your vacation was almost ruined because a credit card was "maxed out." One of you had forgotten to mail in the payment. "Didn't you mail it?" says Sojourner to her Philosopher. "No, I thought you did," he responds. "No," insists the Sojourner, "I know I laid it out for you to mail." "Oh yes, now I remember," responds the Philosopher, "but it didn't have a stamp on it."

So, if you are Sojourner living with a Philosopher or Dapper and you both want to bring some organization into your life, there is a way. As you continue to read this book, you will discover whether or not you are a true candidate for a household partnership. If you are, many of your problems could be resolved by playing the Happy Face Game with your mate. Did you notice the word "play"? I thought that would grab your attention.

I guarantee that if you follow through with negotiating your chores, you will eliminate the worry about who paid what and when. You will also enjoy your play times more by knowing that when you return you won't find your garbage cans on the roof of the house. (Gus, a Hunter, got even.)

CHAPTER 13

No Waves, No Storms

Fish are not the best authority on water.
— Jane Yolen, *Sister Light, Sister Dark* (1988)

The Passive Female with the Even-tempered and/or Passive Male

The Passive females provide a very easygoing atmosphere for their Even-tempered and/or Passive males. Therefore, these relationships can be perfect combinations. The Stargazer and HoneyBee like to be in charge of their home and will often refuse the help of their mate. Consequently, they continue to safeguard their position of caretaker. The Philosopher thrives in this environment, where there is little confrontation and almost never a demand. "Ah, life is good," says the Philosopher as he sits down to enjoy his perfectly prepared pork roast. The Dapper, however, who is more domesticated, can sometimes become irked (but probably won't always show it) when his household suggestions go on being ignored. But this Even-tempered good guy eventually adjusts; after all, his house is well cared for and he has a happy and seemingly contented mate.

Jody, a therapist and a Stargazer, usually arrives home first. She prefers this arrangement. It enables her to freshen up, begin dinner, and greet her husband Mark, the Philosopher, when he arrives home.

Typical conversations between the two Passives sound like the following:

> *Jody:* I think I am okay with it. Is it okay with you?
> *Mark:* Yes, it is fine with me—what about you?

> *Jody:* Yes. I think so ... no, I'm sure ... absolutely sure. I'm just concerned about you.
> *Mark:* Well ... I am fine with it. Whatever you want is fine with me.
> *Jody:* Are you sure you agree?
> *Mark:* Yes, yes, I'm definitely sure. Whatever you want.
> *Jody:* Okay, then that settles it. I will make the stuffed sole instead of the shrimp scampi.

What about a HoneyBee with a Dapper?

Frank, a Dapper, puts in a hectic day as an electrical engineer. He loves to come home to his wife Phyllis, a HoneyBee, who works all day as a school teacher. But who wouldn't want to come home to this HoneyBee?

Listen in to their conversation:

> *Phyllis:* I've made a beautiful beef stew, dear.
> *Frank:* Sounds wonderful. Can I help?
> *Phyllis:* No, no. It is done. Nothing left to do ... really. Just relax while I set the table.
> *Frank:* Well ... I would be glad to set the table.
> *Phyllis:* No, no. Don't bother. Please don't worry. I have it all under control.
> *Frank:* Then I'll clean up after dinner.
> *Phyllis:* No, no ... no need to. I have it all taken care of. Most of the dishes are already done. Besides, you want to watch the hockey game tonight, but thanks for offering. How nice of you, but I'll take care of it ... You do so much already.

So What's the Beef?

Once again you ask, "What's the problem here? They sound as if they are working out well together. Why mess with a happy couple?"

There is a good chance you are right. In the home of two Passives, or a Passive with an Even-tempered, there might not be that big of a problem. In fact, if all the homes were filled with Passive/Even-

CHAPTER 13

tempered male and female combinations, this book probably would never be written. Why fix what's not broken? Why create problems? Why go where uninvited? But ... at the risk of ruining a good thing, let me point out a few cracks in the foundation of these "carefree" homes.

By continuing to reinforce gender roles, Passive females unknowingly are creating a lack of intimacy within their households. A lack of intimacy leads to something very deadly in the relationship—a lack of excitement. This compliant, easygoing, always predictable (knowing how the other person is going to react) household can cause a condition that the Passives share only with their most intimate friends. They are B-O-R-E-D within the relationship. "Bored?" you cry. "But they are doing so well!" Well, yes, all these Passives and Even-tempered male relationships look happy from the outside, especially to the confrontational Assertives, but inside, these easygoing, laid-back couples are drying up from a lack of passion.

Passion in a relationship comes when deep feelings like hurts, disappointments, anger, frustration, tears, sadness, excitement, love, joy, and exhilaration are expressed. Intimacy comes when these feelings are understood and validated with each other. Unfortunately, this sort of emoting is not common among the Passives and/or Even-tempered males. It's not that the Stargazer or HoneyBee avoid these feelings; far from it. They can be as passionate as the Assertives, but because they feel more vulnerable than the Tigress or Rebel, they need to know their feelings are taken seriously before they "emote" them. Therefore, they need coaxing. They also need someone to respond. The Stargazer, specifically, will stop sharing with her Passive mate if her feelings are not validated.

The HoneyBee, the least willing of the female personalities to share her feelings, will not share them with her Philosopher more than once if he does not respond appropriately the first time. To sum it up, Passives have a lot of quiet time. Even though the Dapper is a good communicator (if he's not pouting), the level of intimacy will still improve with the conscious sharing of household duties.

What to Do Differently?

As mentioned, the Passives with a Philosopher and/or Dapper are the most unlikely couple to be reading this book or thinking about implementing a household partnership. They don't see potential benefits in changing their status quo. So if you are a Passive female contemplating a change, the one benefit you will receive immediately is an increase in your intimacy level. "How does cleaning the kitchen together increase intimacy?" the Passive asks. "Or how does changing the bed together, or playing together with our daughter Angie increase our intimacy?"

Together is the key word. Because the Passive's household has rigid gender lines, the man does his work, the woman does hers. Passives spend way too much time alone. In fact, it's not uncommon to see a Passive male sitting on the couch, drumming his fingers impatiently while waiting for his mate to finish cleaning up the kitchen, putting the kids to bed, throwing a load of laundry in the washer, and making tomorrow's lunches before they both leave for a dinner party. The thought of pitching in and sharing the work, instead of waiting impatiently, does not occur to him, nor to her. They both agreed long ago, in some cosmic cementing, that they each have their own jobs and never the two shall twine.

It does not take much imagination to visualize the difference in a relationship where both are doing last-minute chores together so they can both enjoy the evening together. Let's drop in on yet another one of the Passive's conversations to get a better look at what I mean.

This first conversation occurs between the HoneyBee and Philosopher. They are driving in their car on the way to a party. They are already behind schedule because HoneyBee had to finish all her household chores. Carefully note the intimacy level.

Conversation #1

>*HoneyBee:* I noticed when I put Michael to bed that he had a black and blue mark on his arm.
>
>*Philosopher:* Hmmm . . .

CHAPTER 13

HoneyBee: I asked him what happened and he said that Billy pushed him.

Philosopher: Oh, really? ... Who's Billy?

HoneyBee: You remember. That's the kid at school who's been picking on him for the last couple of months. Remember last week that he called him all those awful names? Don't you remember? He was so upset.

Philosopher: Yeah ... I guess ... vaguely.

HoneyBee: Well ... I'm concerned. This has happened before. I think that tomorrow I'll call his teacher. Michael says he hates school and doesn't want to go back. I'm getting worried where this is all going to end.

Philosopher: Oh, I'm sure it'll be okay.

HoneyBee: Well ... I'm not that confident. I'm also tempted to call Billy's mother. But I'm not sure if that's the right thing to do. I don't want to make it worse.

Philosopher: Well ... do what you want. I'm sure you will make the right decision. So who's going to be at the party?

Conversation #2

Compare the level of intimacy to that of conversation #1.

Stargazer: I'm happy we both were there tonight, putting Michael to bed. It sounded as if he needed talk to us.

Philosopher: Yes, so am I. I'm very bothered by his bruise, especially after learning how he got it. Did you notice how frightened he was?

Stargazer: I did. And of course, I can understand why.

Philosopher: Well ... let's call and make an appointment with his teacher. And I think we should also go and talk with Billy's parents.

Stargazer: Okay. I'll call the teacher tomorrow.

Philosopher: Great. And I'll call the parents tonight.

As One Can See ... Intimacy Involves a Lot of "We"

Conversation #1 appears a bit lonely for both Mom and Dad. No matter which one you are, you are alone with your thoughts and actions. Most decisions are usually made by yourself, even the decisions that affect your child. The HoneyBee or Stargazer just assumes she's to take charge and normally won't elicit information from the Philosopher. The Philosopher, by nature, enjoys being out of the picture. He appears uninterested and does not have a great deal to say about the situation. The truth is, his opinion really doesn't matter any longer. When you have been "away" for so long, your input is perceived more as a guest or a visitor. It might be an interesting thought, but it doesn't carry much weight. However, in conversation #2 we hear a different person. Notice how the Philosopher's *active* involvement changes the level of intimacy?

Let's drop in on another conversation. Let's hear what the Dapper has to say.

Conversation #3

Dapper: I've done my share this evening. I'm going to relax.

Stargazer: I'm confused. Share of what?

Dapper: Didn't you notice? My God ... after all I've done! I cleaned up the kitchen.

Stargazer: Yes, all the dishes are in the dishwasher, but all the pots and pans are left.

Dapper: I figured you could do that. After all, I did most of it.

Stargazer: But I did all the cooking and serving.

Dapper: Here we go again. I never feel as if I help enough for you. I don't feel appreciated.

Stargazer: I do so appreciate you! I'm always telling you how much I value your help.

Dapper: Well ... it just doesn't feel like it.

Parent/Child Versus Adult/Adult Relationship

What's happening in their conversation? A typical dynamic between the Stargazer or HoneyBee and a Dapper involves the Passive female acting as a parent to the Even-tempered male. It is most difficult to

CHAPTER 13

create adult intimacy when a parent-and-child relationship occurs every time the subject of household chores comes up.

Note the different expectations in the following conversation. Again note the intimacy level.

Conversation #4

Dapper: Boy, I'm tired. A lot of cleanup was involved in the kitchen tonight.

Stargazer: Yes. I noticed. I bet you're glad it's done.

Dapper: Is Amy in bed yet?

Stargazer: Yes, I put her to bed about fifteen minutes ago.

Dapper: I'll peek in to say goodnight.

Stargazer: My neck and back are really hurting. I think I'll lie down on the couch. Do you think you could massage them for awhile, after you see Amy?

Dapper: Yes, I'll be happy to. First, I'll need to put a load of laundry in.

Stargazer: Okay. Oh ... by the way, I have such a long day tomorrow. I don't think I can make Amy's softball game.

Dapper: Okay, I'll have to cheer louder to make up for your absence. I think we'll stop for pizza after the game.

Stargazer: Okay, then I'll just fix myself something when I get home.

Let's Both Be Grown-ups

Being connected does not just happen overnight, nor is it just about household personalities or household chores. Obviously there is much more involved, but how you view your role in the home can have a major impact on your relationship. When you expect your mate to respond to the home as an adult instead of a child, you won't always have to feel a need to reinforce the behavior as a parent would a child.

Now be honest. As you read conversation #4, did you feel a haunting sense of being uncomfortable with the traditional male and female roles reversed? Does it seem unnatural to you that Stargazer did not continually say "Thank you" for cleaning up the kitchen, "Thank you" for going in to see Amy, "Thank you" for massaging my back, "Thank you," for doing the laundry, and "Thanks" for taking care of Amy the next night? Did you also say to yourself, "Give me a break! That guy's not for real. No man I know is that accommodating!" Now go back and reread the conversation. But this time transpose the dialog. Read Dapper as Stargazer and Stargazer as Dapper, or in other words, have the woman take the traditional accommodating, nurturing role. Note your increased comfort level. If you are a Passive, it seems much more natural to you.

Regardless of the comfort level, the above conversation is what I think of when I refer to an adult-to-adult partnership. When your mate is not spoken to as a child, when they no longer feel resentful and unappreciated because you did not comment on their help, and when you mutually respect each other as an equal partner instead of someone you need to manipulate help from, barriers then dissolve and adult partnerships are free to develop.

Insanity Is Doing the Same Thing Over and Over Again but Expecting a Different Result

The above examples involved doing something differently, or changing your actions. Of course, only one person changing is not going to work forever, but it will get things started. When you begin to act differently, your mate is forced to notice.

If you want everything to stay the way it is, then do nothing differently. But if you don't think your household is working very well for you, the logical conclusion is that something more needs to change. It all sounds so simple, doesn't it? If one doesn't like something, all they have to do is change it. Yet, even though it sounds easy, the truth is, nothing is harder.

The following chapter takes a closer look at this issue of "change." Why do we resist it? What will happen if we start to change our beliefs? Or, even more dramatic, our actions? Of course, the bigger question is, "Who has to change ... him or her?" The answer is, "Both."

CHAPTER 14

Blessed Be the Beliefs That Blind Us

The tragedy of life is that people do not change.
— Agatha Christie, *There Is a Tide* (1948)

Kindred

I remember that it was a blustery Sunday morning in autumn. Almost a year had passed since I had started my quest for household equity. As powerful gusts of wind ripped dying leaves from majestic oak trees outside the church, Gary, David, Kristina, and I stood to join the congregation in singing the following hymn:

> "Blessed be the ties that bind
> our hearts in Christian love,
> the fellowship of kindred minds
> are likened to that above."

As we sat down, I thought about the words we had just sung. Looking around at the 500 parishioners, I wondered, "Just how kindred are our minds?" In fact, tilting my head and glancing over at Gary, I asked myself, "What about us? How kindred are the two of our minds?"

In the last year, many of our beliefs about the household had changed. And no matter how far apart our thinking might be in some other areas of life, our beliefs about household equity were in sync. In that area—a very critical area—I was satisfied that our beliefs had become closer, more related, and more kindred. This was the direct result, however, of our mutual desire to understand the other, and the action we took to make that happen.

I glanced outside a second time and watched the fallen leaves in their final moments, chasing each other around on the frozen ground. For a while that's how I had been feeling—swirling around with no direction, chasing some belief around about my household role that seemingly had no reality. Changing the direction and becoming a kindred spirit with Gary had been a process.

I glanced over at Gary and smiled as I thought about the last year. So much had changed. We had definitely gone from a "my job" household to an "our job" household in less then twelve months. Now that our household partnership was firmly planted, we were each reaping the harvest, but I knew that none of it would have happened if we had not been open to the process of change, especially changing our long-held beliefs about our gender.

Just this morning I had thought about how much easier it was to get to church than in previous years. Granted, David and Kristina are now young adults, but even with adults, getting up, ready, and off at a scheduled time can get hectic. But not this morning. As I say, things have changed.

At 8 A.M., I awoke first and started the coffee brewing. I then walked to the mailbox to retrieve the morning paper. Gary got up twenty minutes later and made the bed. The kids were home for the weekend and so Gary went upstairs to give them their wake-up call. During the next hour everyone got ready at their own pace, and without any help from me.

It was a far cry from when the kids were little. I remember those hated Sunday mornings when it was my job to be the recipient of panic calls and questions. "Where are my shoes?" yelled Gary, or, "I can't find my clean pants!" David cried. "I thought you were going to pick them up from the cleaners!" Kristina would call down from upstairs, "I can't go! No one woke me up on time! I can't be ready!" I would run around like some crazy woman, making beds, cooking breakfast, finding and ironing clothes. What a difference it makes when everyone is responsible for themselves!

CHAPTER 14

This morning, Gary had made breakfast. He set out cereal, fruit, bagels, jams, and juice. Everyone arrived at a different time and ate from the buffet at will. While Gary got dressed, the kids cleaned up the kitchen. In the meantime, I had put a ham in the oven for an early dinner. Since we drove my car to church, it was my job to assure we would have gas in the tank. Gary's responsibility was to bring the check for the collection. David had taken our dog Chaucer outside for a walk and Kristina had made sure Chaucer's dishes were filled with food and water. All and all, life went smoothly now that everyone was cooperating. When I thought about what the key ingredient was in instigating this drastic change, I came to the conclusion it wasn't just our beliefs becoming kindred, but also our actions.

Watch Their Feet

The recovering women who live in my agency's sober housing program love to use the phrase, "Watch their feet." It means no one gives a hoot about your words; it's your actions that count. The pastor's sermon this morning reinforced that thinking. "Faith without works is dead," he quoted from the King James Bible. Yes, it was all coming together. First, one has to be receptive to changing how one believes. Second, one has to act upon it. Otherwise, it's not worth a "diddly." It was only Gary's and the kids' actions this morning that made the difference of my feeling peaceful instead of resentful.

What's Wrong with This Picture?

As you begin to contemplate this idea of changing your beliefs, consider the following vignettes.

Vignette 1: Four businesswomen are eating in a restaurant during their lunch hour. One of them, a Stargazer, happily boasts, "My husband is my greatest helper. He takes care of our children, shops, and even makes dinner once in a while." Another responds, "Wow, aren't you lucky! What a great guy! Where did you find him?"

At the same time, four businessmen are eating in a restaurant just down the block. One of the men boasts, "My wife is my greatest helper. She takes care of our children, shops, and even makes dinner once in a while." The other men respond, "Wow, aren't you lucky! What a great gal! Where did you find her?"

Vignette 2: Jody, the HoneyBee, and Mark, the Philosopher, have busy weeks with their 40-hour jobs. This particular evening, Jody is driving home from the office reading her "to-do" list. She has to stop to pick up the cleaning and get money from the cash machine. She has to figure out what to prepare for dinner. She has to confirm plans for the Saturday night bridge game with the Nelsons. She has to help her daughter with her homework. Soon her thoughts shift to other things that did not get on the list. The laundry needs to be done and she needs to make a reassuring call to her mother-in-law to check on her dizzy spells. Jody then remembers that they're out of milk, so she'll need to stop at the supermarket around the corner from the cleaners. She might as well use the coupons she cut from the paper last weekend to shop for some additional items while she's there.

As Mark is driving home from work, he's trying to decide between the driving range and nine holes of golf, but he's vacillating. Maybe he'll just want to relax on the couch, read the paper, have a beer, and wait for dinner.

Vignette 3: For BarbAnn, a Stargazer, her work week is almost over. As she shuts off her computer, she thinks about Saturday, the day she will be hosting a slumber party to celebrate her daughter's birthday. BarbAnn already feels exhausted as she visualizes all that needs to be done: shopping, wrapping, games, cooking. "Oh, gee," she sighs, "Saturday — another one of those basic endurance contests." She sighs again, deeply feeling the weight of entertaining ten demanding eight-year-olds. She sighs a third time, thinking about Sunday: breakfast for ten, taxi service, vacuuming, dusting, scrubbing the shower, washing towels, cleaning the toilets. She feels depressed and overwhelmed. She is facing another weekend without enough hours to do all that needs to be done. Once again, there will be no time for herself.

CHAPTER 14

BarbAnn's husband, Tom, an Emperor, locks up his desk and looks up at the clock. The weekend is approaching, and he is feeling excited. On Saturday, BarbAnn will be having a good time throwing a birthday party for their daughter. He smiles, thinking about her spending the weekend doing the things she enjoys. Fortunately, he will also be doing the things he enjoys. Since he doesn't want to get in BarbAnn's way, Tom mulls over his plans. On Saturday morning he will go work out at the gym, then relax in the jacuzzi for a while. On the way home, he'll stop at the sporting goods store to pick up that new fishing reel he's been meaning to get. Sometime in the afternoon he'll arrive home, but he'll make sure he's not a nuisance. He'll be in his room napping, so he can be sharp during the poker game at Fred's that evening. Sunday is his day of rest. He can read the paper while BarbAnn and their daughter take the kids home. Perhaps later he'll finally get to read that book, or maybe he'll just putter around in the garden. If he feels ambitious, he might even put a half-hour into repairing that downspout. He'll feel good on Monday morning, knowing he spent the weekend doing the things he wanted to do.

Different Job Descriptions

After reading the above vignettes, ask your mate what, if anything, he found "wrong" with them. Ask leading questions if it helps to get things flowing. For example, in the first vignette, which conversation sounds normal and which one has never taken place in the history of the universe? Let's face it, the businessman never would have boasted about his wife doing what most people expect her to do. If he had, the other three men would have looked at him, totally befuddled, and said, "So?"

In the second vignette, Mark is going home to relax. Jody is on her way to her second shift. Discuss whether either of you see any fairness or sharing in Jody and Mark's household. Or is driving home from the office the only experience they have in common with each other?

And what do you suppose, in the third vignette, the mood of

the household will be when Tom walks in the front door and says to BarbAnn, "Boy, am I glad the weekend is here! Two whole days just to relax and do nothing!" After the blowup, Tom will think, "Boy, she sure is in a rotten mood! I'm glad I'm not going to be around her."

The Risk of Change

Change is difficult. It is defined in Webster's as "to give a different position, course, or direction, to replace with another, or to make a shift from one to another." It doesn't sound so awful, but as creatures of habit, we will go to major extremes to avoid it. No doubt, there is something about change that rocks our security. Oh, there are those rare individuals who love the excitement of the unknown and therefore revel in doing something differently. But the majority of us resist it, probably because we believe that every time we instigate a change, we somehow mess with our destiny. "What will happen if I change how I've always done this? What else will be affected?" we ask. "What if I don't like the results? Am I creating a domino effect I can't reverse? Is there any turning back? Oh my God, what if I lose control?" There is no getting around it. Change is scary.

Of course, no matter how hard we fight it, some change, like loss, comes naturally and is beyond our control. It just occurs without our consent. Jobs, homes, families, health, aging, and death are all part of living and all of those things are about change. Even though we dislike it and often fight to stop it, we cannot stop the disruption of impending change. Therefore, a primary key to individual harmony and peace of mind is how well we adapt and accept the changes—good or bad—in our lives.

But there is another side of us, one that is drawn to risk like a moth to the flame. Sometimes, for no apparent reason whatsoever, we get silly and chancy, even downright daring—daring enough to instigate change on our own. Perhaps we start off small, like painting a room a different color. If we are happy with the results, we might do something more adventurous, like adding an addition or

CHAPTER 14

putting the house up for sale and moving to the other side of town. We might even find ourselves successful with this "changing stuff" and, with increased confidence, take even greater risks, like switching careers, moving to a faraway city, or getting married. We do these things knowing full well that they could turn out disastrously. We might despise the new neighbors, the new job, or the new marriage, but on the other hand, we could just as easily find ecstasy. So we take the chance—as uncertain as it is—knowing our odds for success may be only a little better than a flip of the coin. Change and risk indeed go together. *How much* change depends on how much risk we'll take to achieve the change.

In the book *Chaos: Making a New Science*, author James Gleick writes about a process known as "the butterfly effect." According to his cause-and-effect principle, a butterfly flapping its wings in Central Park can stir up a breeze that eventually cascades into a storm over Beijing the following month. It has something to do with what's called "sensitive dependence on initial conditions." It simply means that even a minor event, such as a butterfly flapping its wings or, in our case, a woman leaving the nest for the workplace, can mushroom into major changes down the road.

This same principle underlies changing a belief that has been ingrained in our minds since birth. The beliefs we have about our gender have been with us forever, and, as we have discovered, these beliefs directly affect the roles we assume in our home. As you begin to chart a new course you will begin to stir things up, and this might well create a storm in the future.

The reality is that your household might be different a few months from now, perhaps radically different, with just a few minor changes in beliefs and actions. In fact, when these changes affect some long-held perceptions involving gender, your household will look and feel so different that you would scarcely recognize it.

I Told You So!

Remember the hysteria that happened in the '60s when all you Rebels and Tigresses first emerged from the "nest"? The result was a loud outcry from the Keepers of the Status Quo (male and female alike). "You just wait," they warned us, "once these women feel like they have the same right to work outside the home as men, we are in for it! Before you know it, they'll think they can run the country. Just watch, soon they'll pick up such foolishness as becoming doctors, or truck drivers, or even priests, for God's sake! And what happens, I ask you, if they start running for office? Can you imagine if women get into power? They have no stomach for it!" The Keepers of the Status Quo's outrage usually ends with a final profound challenge: "And who's going to be home having babies, cooking the meals, and taking care of those little darlings? The family unit will be destroyed! And you just better remember—I told you so!"

Yes, indeed. We women created quite a stir when we first started flapping our wings. But whether we felt destined to or were only doing what we had to do, we stood our ground. Our rebuttal to the Keepers of the Status Quo was, "Hey buddy, chill out! We know what's good for us. You're overreacting!" But maybe it wasn't an overreaction. I personally know Tigresses who are CEOs, physicians, attorneys, and elected officials. I know HoneyBees who are CFOs and researchers. I know Stargazers who are entrepreneurs, writers, and artists. And I know Sojourners who are professors, therapists, and pilots. The Keepers of the Status Quo were right! The world has changed. We are everywhere and into everything, including the Supreme Court. So you see, you begin to change one thing and before long a series of events occurs with major results.

But for all of the women who somehow found "the stomach for it" and who are also mothers, taking care of their "little darlings," the price has been high. Ironically, the problem here is not change, but the lack thereof. Unfortunately, even though the workplace looks entirely different, our homes still look very much the same. But beware—the butterfly effect still holds true.

Changing a Sacred Belief

We know that our belief systems are established early in life and are deeply ingrained within our subconscious. Ultimately, these beliefs

CHAPTER 14

greatly influence our behavior, whether we follow them or not. If we live by them totally, never questioning or examining them, we will soon become rigid. If we rebel and go against them without really understanding why, we will feel disappointed in ourselves, as if we have compromised some great principle.

The ideal, then, is to be willing to re-examine our beliefs and values on a continuous basis. If we are confident in ourselves, and our self-esteem is fairly well intact, we are much more receptive to challenging our existing beliefs. If, however, our self-esteem is threatened when one of our beliefs is challenged, it's usually related to our insecurities (which we all have to one degree or another). These insecurities keep us protected and defensive when we feel someone is asking us to change. But the more objective we are about our beliefs, the more receptive we can be in having them challenged—and maybe even change them.

Now, here is where risk comes in. We probably all agree that we have an overwhelming need to protect our core beliefs, the ones that truly identify us, and for some of them, we would fight to the death. Others are not so sacred, and we don't feel quite as threatened when they're challenged. But the risk comes in when we start messing around with the core of our being.

Many beliefs concerning gender roles can be considered core beliefs. They are well protected, not only by us but also by society as a whole. Questioning these gender beliefs is a risky business. We are stepping on ground held most sacred by the Keepers of the Status Quo, but examination of such beliefs is a crucial beginning to the process leading to a household partnership. That is because these core beliefs are the driving force behind our actions within the home.

In the next chapter, I'm giving you an opportunity to examine your beliefs and actions about gender roles. I warn you that this exercise is not for couples whose relationships are already on thin ice. I guarantee you that couples who participate in this exercise will end up with major disagreements regarding one another's responses.

"You must be kidding! You don't actually think that I believe that you believe that, do you?!?" or, "Come on, you don't do that!

Tell me one time that you ever did that!" are the statements that are most often spoken when couples work the Belief/Action Inventory.

So be prepared for misconceptions, disagreements, and arguments. But that's good. It is a beginning of your dialog. And don't worry, Chapter 16 will get you both on the dance floor together—learning the first steps to the dance of partnership.

CHAPTER 15

Your Beliefs and Actions Inventory

The moment we find the reason behind an emotion ... the wall we have built is breached, and the positive memories it has kept from us return, too. That's why it pays to ask those painful questions. The answers can set you free.

– Gloria Steinem

First Things First

What you believe and how you act concerning gender determines how receptive you and your mate are to change. Just what are your beliefs about gender roles? How strong are these beliefs? What about your mate's beliefs? What are they? How strong are they? Did you talk about the vignettes? Were you both surprised to find out what the other really thinks?

Before you and your mate begin to discuss the changes you are going to make, complete the following Beliefs and Actions Inventory. The first section of this exercise is designed to clarify your particular beliefs regarding gender. It is important that you answer the questions by asking yourself what you *truly believe*, not what you think you *should* believe, and what you *really do*, not what you think you *should* do. Remember that if you don't answer truthfully, you will not learn anything about yourself. This is an examination of your deepest beliefs. There are no right or wrong answers.

The second section of the exercise is designed to discover what your actions are, in spite of your beliefs. In other words, what we believe might not have anything at all to do with what we do. For example, you might believe that you shouldn't have to be responsible for doing it all, but you're still doing it all.

The third section of the exercise is designed to discover what your individual range of conflict is between your individual beliefs and actions, as well as the range of conflict between you and your mate. When you have completed this exercise, you will have a start on knowing how kindred the two of you are.

BELIEFS AND ACTIONS INVENTORY

Please answer the questions with a number from 1 to 5 on the basis of how strongly you disagree or agree.

1: strongly disagree
2: disagree
3: neither agree nor disagree
4: agree
5: strongly agree

Section I (to be answered by BOTH)
WHAT ARE MY BELIEFS?

If you do not have children, answer as if you did.

1. I believe the chores inside the house are primarily the job of the woman. _____

2. I believe a woman's innate personality makes her a better homemaker. _____

3. I believe women are more emotional than men. _____

4. I believe the mother should be more involved in parenting the children than the father since she is better at parenting. _____

5. I believe that a man who takes care of his children is "helping out" his mate since childcare is really her responsibility. _____

6. I believe a woman should do more housework if she doesn't make as much money as her mate. _____

CHAPTER 15

7. I prefer the traditional term "Mrs. John Doe" to "Ms. Jane Doe." _____

8. I believe a man has more stress than a woman. _____

9. I believe men are more cognitive and practical than women. _____

10. I believe men who are doing chores inside the home are "henpecked." _____

11. I would feel more uncomfortable seeing a boy play with a doll than I would seeing a girl play with toy trucks. _____

12. I believe a household functions more effectively if everyone knows that Dad is boss. _____

13. I believe it is more important to teach a girl how to cook than it is a boy. _____

14. When planning a social event, a holiday, or a vacation, I believe a woman knows how to make it more special than a man. _____

15. I believe most of the problems in our nation are directly related to mothers working outside the home. _____

16. I don't believe that women belong in politics; it is better left to the men. _____

17. I believe the most important job for a woman is to make sure her home is happy. _____

18. I believe it is up to the woman to delegate the household chores. _____

19. I do not consider myself a feminist. (Webster's definition is "the doctrine advocating social and political rights for women equal to those of men.") _____

YOUR BELIEFS AND ACTIONS INVENTORY

20. I believe men should do "men's work" (taking out the garbage, cleaning the garage, and mowing the lawn) and women should do "women's work" (laundry, cooking, cleaning). _____

21. I believe it is more important for a boy to be educated or trained for employment than a girl. _____

22. I believe a woman should work outside the home only if she has to. _____

23. I just don't believe men are as suited to staying home and taking care of children as women are. _____

24. I believe a man needs more free time to enjoy his leisure activities than a woman. _____

25. I believe women need to cry more than men. _____

26. I believe it's a shame that so many women have to work outside their homes. _____

27. I believe a man should expect that his wife keep his home neat and clean. _____

28. I believe there is a lot of truth to the statement, "A woman's touch is needed." _____

29. When entertaining, I think it is more appropriate for the hostess to cook and serve the dinner. _____

30. I believe men are more effective at disciplining children than women. _____

31. I have an immediate dislike for a woman who calls herself a feminist. _____

32. I believe the world would be a better place if women could stay home and take care of the children and home. _____

CHAPTER 15

33. I believe a woman has a right to feel resentful if her husband does not make enough money for her to stay home. _____

34. I believe it is more important that a man have a high-paying job than a woman. _____

35. I believe that when men show sensitivity they appear weak. _____

36. I believe that women should be more submissive to their husbands. _____

37. I believe it's awful that male breadwinners are being displaced because of women in the workforce. _____

38. I tend to tell little girls how pretty they look and little boys how smart they are. _____

39. I believe the woman should do more housework than her mate because of the simple fact that she can do it better. _____

40. It is good practice to tell a little boy that he is now the "man of the family" when his father is out of town. _____

41. I believe our nation has equal opportunity and status for women. _____

42. I don't believe there is any big deal in referring to the man as "head of the household." _____

43. The nation would be a lot better off if "men would act like men" and "women would act like women." _____

44. I believe it is primarily the man's job to support his family financially. _____

45. I believe life was a lot better before women's lib. _____

46. I would feel more comfortable about my adult sons experimenting with their sexuality than I would about my adult daughters. _____

47. I believe men are much more effective at managing the household money than women are. _____

48. If a family can only afford to send one child to college, they should choose their son over their daughter. _____

49. When I see a man working in the kitchen, I think the woman must control the home. _____

50. I feel more protective of little girls than I do of little boys. _____

Section 2 (to be answered only by WOMEN)
WHAT ARE MY ACTIONS?

Please mark only one answer.
If you do not have children, answer as if you did.
Assign the numerical values indicated by each choice.

1. My paycheck from work is mine to spend as I wish, but my mate's paycheck goes for household expenses.

    1. ____ Always true   2. ____ Mostly or somewhat true
    3. ____ Not true

2. *Answer only one of the following:*

  a. I am not teaching (or did not teach) my sons to cook, clean, do their own laundry.

    1. ____ Always true   2. ____ Mostly or somewhat true
    3. ____ Not true

  or

  b. I do not (or did not) have sons, but I notice I treat little girls more gently than little boys.

    1. ____ Always true   2. ____ Mostly or somewhat true
    3. ____ Not true

CHAPTER 15

3. I sit in the passenger seat and my mate drives the car.

   1. ____ Always true   2. ____ Mostly or somewhat true
   3. ____ Not true

4. I wait on my mate more than he waits on me.

   1. ____ Always true   2. ____ Mostly or somewhat true
   3. ____ Not true

5. I don't have my own money and/or my own checking account.

   1. ____ Always true   2. ____ Mostly or somewhat true
   3. ____ Not true

6. My mate makes major financial purchases without my knowledge or consent.

   1. ____ Always true   2. ____ Mostly or somewhat true
   3. ____ Not true

7. I do all the packing and planning for trips.

   1. ____ Always true   2. ____ Mostly or somewhat true
   3. ____ Not true

8. I do more around the house because I make less money than my mate.

   1. ____ Always true   2. ____ Mostly or somewhat true
   3. ____ Not true

9. I have very little knowledge about our family finances.

   1. ____ Always true   2. ____ Mostly or somewhat true
   3. ____ Not true

10. I do (or did) the following percentage of the parenting:

    1. ____ 75 to 100   2. ____ 60 to 75
    3. ____ around 50 or less

YOUR BELIEFS AND ACTIONS INVENTORY

11. I continually make personal sacrifices, such as not buying or doing something I want so my family or mate can spend the money to buy or do something they want.

    1. ____ Always true   2. ____ Mostly or somewhat true
    3. ____ Not true

12. My mate has more free time than I do.

    1. ____ Always true   2. ____ Mostly or somewhat true
    3. ____ Not true

13. When a sit-down meal is made in our home, I make it.

    1. ____ Always true   2. ____ Mostly or somewhat true
    3. ____ Not true

14. I am the only one who cleans the bathroom.

    1. ____ Always true   2. ____ Mostly or somewhat true
    3. ____ Not true

15. I am the only one who changes the bed linens.

    1. ____ Always true   2. ____ Mostly or somewhat true
    3. ____ Not true

16. I do all of the laundry.

    1. ____ Always true   2. ____ Mostly or somewhat true
    3. ____ Not true

17. I do all of the grocery shopping.

    1. ____ Always true   2. ____ Mostly or somewhat true
    3. ____ Not true

18. I am the only one who cleans out the refrigerator or cleans the oven.

    1. ____ Always true   2. ____ Mostly or somewhat true
    3. ____ Not true

CHAPTER 15

19. I do all of the outside errands (picking up laundry, cleaning, banking, shopping at the grocery or drug store).
    1. ____ Always true   2. ____ Mostly or somewhat true
    3. ____ Not true

20. I am the only one who washes the floors or vacuums the carpet.
    1. ____ Always true   2. ____ Mostly or somewhat true
    3. ____ Not true

21. I am the only one who folds the clothes from the dryer.
    1. ____ Always true   2. ____ Mostly or somewhat true
    3. ____ Not true

22. I am the only one who puts the groceries away.
    1. ____ Always true   2. ____ Mostly or somewhat true
    3. ____ Not true

23. I dread the holidays because all the extra work falls on me.
    1. ____ Always true   2. ____ Mostly or somewhat true
    3. ____ Not true

24. I pay all the bills; my mate has no idea what's going on.
    1. ____ Always true   2. ____ Mostly or somewhat true
    3. ____ Not true

25. *Answer only one of the following:*
    a. I am (or was) the one who stays home from work when the kids are sick.
        1. ____ Always true   2. ____ Mostly or somewhat true
        3. ____ Not true
or
    b. I pamper my mate when he is sick, but when I am sick, I am ignored.
        1. ____ Always true   2. ____ Mostly or somewhat true
        3. ____ Not true

YOUR BELIEFS AND ACTIONS INVENTORY

Section 2 (to be answered only by MEN)
WHAT ARE MY ACTIONS?

*Please mark only one answer.
If you do not have children, answer as if you did.
Assign the numerical values indicated by each choice.*

1. I never clean up after myself when I fix a snack in the kitchen.
    1. ____ Always true   2. ____ Mostly or somewhat true
    3. ____ Not true

2. I never do dishes or put them away.
    1. ____ Always true   2. ____ Mostly or somewhat true
    3. ____ Not true

3. I never consult with my mate over what money I spend.
    1. ____ Always true   2. ____ Mostly or somewhat true
    3. ____ Not true

4. I never clean out a closet, drawer, or cupboard.
    1. ____ Always true   2. ____ Mostly or somewhat true
    3. ____ Not true

5. I am NOT aware of our household's inventory (groceries, cleaning supplies, children's clothes, linens, paper products).
    1. ____ Always true   2. ____ Mostly or somewhat true
    3. ____ Not true

6. I never do the grocery shopping, other than picking up small items.
    1. ____ Always true   2. ____ Mostly or somewhat true
    3. ____ Not true

7. I usually wait to be asked to take the garbage out or to do other chores, shovel the sidewalk, or mow lawn.
    1. ____ Always true   2. ____ Mostly or somewhat true
    3. ____ Not true

CHAPTER 15

8. I tell (or told) my mate to get the kids to help.
   1. _____ Always true   2. _____ Mostly or somewhat true
   3. _____ Not true

9. I have more free time to do what I want than my mate does.
   1. _____ Always true   2. _____ Mostly or somewhat true
   3. _____ Not true

10. When I come home from or am through with my work, I relax and wait for dinner.
    1. _____ Always true   2. _____ Mostly or somewhat true
    3. _____ Not true

11. I do (or did) the following percentage of the parenting:
    1. _____ 25 or less   2. _____ 25 to 50   3. _____ 50 or more

12. I never wash or wax the floors or do vacuuming.
    1. _____ Always true   2. _____ Mostly or somewhat true
    3. _____ Not true

13. I know my mate will clean up or pick up after me.
    1. _____ Always true   2. _____ Mostly or somewhat true
    3. _____ Not true

14. There are some household chores that I simply refuse to do.
    1. _____ Always true   2. _____ Mostly or somewhat true
    3. _____ Not true

15. I never clean the bathroom.
    1. _____ Always true   2. _____ Mostly or somewhat true
    3. _____ Not true

YOUR BELIEFS AND ACTIONS INVENTORY

16. I never change our bed linens.

    1. ____ Always true   2. ____ Mostly or somewhat true
    3. ____ Not true

17. I never do the laundry.

    1. ____ Always true   2. ____ Mostly or somewhat true
    3. ____ Not true

18. I usually have to be asked, coaxed, or bribed to do housework.

    1. ____ Always true   2. ____ Mostly or somewhat true
    3. ____ Not true

19. I NEVER do little chores, such as replacing toilet paper and paper towel rolls, changing light bulbs, wiping up the kitchen counters, picking up papers, straightening cushions, putting chairs back, and straightening pictures.

    1. ____ Always true   2. ____ Mostly or somewhat true
    3. ____ Not true

20. I don't stay home from work to take care of our sick kids as much as my mate does.

    1. ____ Always true   2. ____ Mostly or somewhat true
    3. ____ Not true

21. I never cook dinner except for barbecuing.

    1. ____ Always true   2. ____ Mostly or somewhat true
    3. ____ Not true

22. I never fold clothes that I take from the dryer.

    1. ____ Always true   2. ____ Mostly or somewhat true
    3. ____ Not true

CHAPTER 15

23. I never put groceries away.

    1. ____ Always true   2. ____ Mostly or somewhat true
    3. ____ Not true

24. My mate is always complaining about picking up after me.

    1. ____ Always true   2. ____ Mostly or somewhat true
    3. ____ Not true

25. I never wait on my mate (such as bringing her coffee or something to eat).

    1. ____ Always true   2. ____ Mostly or somewhat true
    3. ____ Not true

SCORING THE BELIEF AND ACTION INVENTORY

Section I: What Are Our BELIEF TYPES?

Instructions: Add up the numbers you each gave to the questions (for example, "strongly disagree" is 1). Find your scores, and circle the corresponding belief type.

Score	Belief Type
50-85	Open-minded
86-115	Cautious
116-150	Apathetic
151-199	Resistant
200-250	Rigid

Females belief type: _____

Male belief type: _____

Section 2: What Are Our ACTION TYPES?

Instructions: Add up the numbers you each gave to the questions (for example, "always true" is 1). Find your scores, and circle the corresponding action type.

Score	Action Type
66–75	Equitable
56–65	Flexible
46–55	Traditional
36–45	Conservative
below 35	Controlled

Female's action type: _____

Male's action type: _____

Section 3: Is There a RANGE OF CONFLICT between Your Beliefs and Your Actions?

Instructions: Find your belief and action types in the chart below and assign them the corresponding number.

Belief Type	Number	Action Type	Number
Open-minded	1	Equitable	1
Cautious	2	Flexible	2
Apathetic	3	Traditional	3
Resistant	4	Conservative	4
Rigid	5	Controlled	5

Female's belief type corresponding number: _____

Female's action type corresponding number: _____

Male's belief type corresponding number: _____

Male's action type corresponding number: _____

CHAPTER 15

Now find the number that indicates the range of conflict you have within yourself (personal conflict), and the range of conflict you have as a couple (couple conflict). To do so:

1. Record both numbers (male and female) in the grid on page 173.
2. Subtract the smaller number from the larger one.
3. The range of personal conflict is determined by subtracting *horizontally*.
4. The range of couple conflict is determined by subtracting *vertically*.

Example: Your belief score is 1; your action score is 3.

1. Record these numbers in the appropriate boxes.
2. Subtract horizontally (3 – 1 = 2) to get your range of personal conflict score and record in appropriate box. Repeat for your mate's score.
3. Subtract vertically (4 – 1 = 3 and 3 – 3 = 0) to get your range of couple conflict.

Example:

	Beliefs	Actions	Range of personal conflict
Female's score	1	3	= 2
Male's score	4	3	= 1
Range of couple conflict	= 3	0	

Determine your scores:

	Beliefs	Actions	Range of personal conflict
Female's score			
Male's score			
Range of couple conflict			

The numerical value of your range of *personal conflict* between your beliefs and your actions.

Female _____ **Male** _____

The numerical value of your range of *couple conflict* between:

Beliefs _____ **Actions** _____

Section I: Your BELIEF TYPE

This first section is your individual belief type. As you read the following types, consider whether or not you are comfortable with your belief type, or do you think you might want to change a few of your tenets? Remember the butterfly, so be careful. On the other hand, remember the excitement that comes when you take a risk, so don't be *too* careful.

Open-minded

You are open-minded and have very strong beliefs about the equity between men and women. Though some view you as radical, reform has happened because of people like you. You're probably aware that your tolerance and broad-minded thinking are often threatening to others who are more frightened of change, but no matter. You will not be compromised. As a true believer regarding gender reform, you continue to look for ways to balance the scales. This makes you

CHAPTER 15

a natural in a household partnership. You view its concepts as an ideology and respond to it like a caged animal does to freedom, yet your enthusiasm can be overpowering. Remember that you need to tread softly. People who fall into this category sometimes have difficulty negotiating and/or compromising. That's because you think "fair is fair," so what's left to talk about? You will go farther and be more effective with your mate if you view the process more philosophically. The wheels of change grind slowly. A household partnership is not about winning and losing. It is about equity. Your mate will respond more positively if you remember that life cannot be fair at every second. However, with your beliefs—and a bit of patience—you will come closer to a just life than most.

Cautious

You have some strong beliefs, but you are also a cautious one who prefers to take the middle road. That's because on some issues you are confused about exactly what you do believe or should believe. Don't worry. This does not mean you are wishy-washy; it just means you were raised with one set of rules and now situations and circumstances are different. Consequently, you are still playing catch-up. One problem is that you struggle in knowing whether you think these "changes" have made life better or worse. One day you think one way, the next day another. Understanding several points of view is your strength, but it can also be your weakness. Because you can always see the other side of things, this objectivity keeps you up in the air and confused. But remember, not taking a stand is still taking a stand. How high your score is (over 151) will determine how much of your waffling is just your struggle to find the right answer or if it is actually apathy, but your strength in seeing both sides still helps you negotiate fairly and adapt to compromise quite readily. And because your basic nature desires fairness and justice, you are not uncomfortable challenging the status quo even if it adversely affects you. Because you have no problem with the basic concepts of fairness, it is within your reach. You are an ideal candidate for negotiating a household partnership.

Apathetic

Very frankly, Apathetics don't know what they believe. Since you don't hold any strong beliefs about how households should operate, you are somewhat bored with the whole idea of gender, gender roles, equity, and household partnerships. It's not by accident that you have fallen into this "yeah—maybe—well—I don't know or really care" mentality. You are a clever one. You're aware that by not taking a stand, you can avoid making a decision or being responsible for changing anything. *Au contraire, mon cher*, you cannot lie in the weeds forever. There's always somebody who will come along and chase you out. In other words, if you don't decide what you think, others will decide for you. There's one hope—if your mate is as nonchalant as you are, you're home free. Nothing will change. This has been an okay book to read, but you might as well give it to someone else. However, if your mate is getting ready to take a stand, you could be in trouble. You might have to make a choice. You're either going to have to jump in or get run over. At this point, depending on what your household personality is, you won't put up too much resistance in developing a household partnership; it's just that someone else will have to take the lead—as usual.

Resistant

Resistors have strong beliefs about men and women and the roles they should play in our society. Basically, you believe that these roles need to be the same as they were for your parents and grandparents. After all, you think what was good enough for them should be good enough for you. You resist change and have difficulty in understanding what's so wrong with the way things have always been. It is not that you don't believe in equality, but in your mind, equality has nothing to do with men and women's responsibilities in their home. You believe if men would do men's work and women would do women's work, the world would be better off. Yes, you agree, it is harder now that the woman works outside the home, but she doggoned better know that her first responsibility is in the home. Why should a man put on a sissy apron just because his mate has gone out and gotten a job? Your household personality will determine how difficult it will be for you to challenge your beliefs. If you're an Assertive, I'm afraid a household partnership is going to be awfully hard for you to swallow, but it can happen. You will just need to be spoon-fed—one compromise at a time.

Rigid

Your very strong beliefs about gender come closer to being dogma than being simply beliefs. There is just no other way to put it: you're rigid. Changing your beliefs (or dogma) will come with difficulty, if at all. It appears to you that there is something far more important at stake here than just fighting to keep the status quo. This "gender thing" has become personal for you. You fear if you give one inch, the entire foundation of your life will collapse around you. You're fighting to protect not only your lifestyle, but your whole identity. Being a man or a woman and doing what men or women do is your most important role. But knowing who you are hinges on everyone else knowing who they are, so if they change, the thought has occurred to you that you also might have to change. Yuck. Change is scary for most, but for you it is terrifying. And you'll work very hard at controlling things so that change does not occur unless you ordain it. So if the subject does come up, your pat answer is, "I like things just the way they are, thank you very much. Subject closed." A household partnership is out of the picture until you first begin to embrace some different beliefs about men and women. And, secondly, you need to realize that your fear about change has more to do with your fear of losing control than "just liking things the way they are."

Section 2: Your ACTION TYPE

This second section is about your action type. As you read the following types, again think about what you would like to change. Are your beliefs and actions in sync or do you see major discrepancies? You obviously would like to see your beliefs coincide with your actions, regardless of what they are. If they don't, you need to explore what it is that you want to change: beliefs or actions?

Equitable

Your home has few to no gender roles. When it comes to household chores, who does what is determined by factors other than who's male or who's female. Congratulations on your ability to create a household that is gender-free and built on equity. Formalizing a household partnership might help you divide the jobs by what you like compared to what needs to be done.

Flexible

The equity in your home is somewhat out of balance. One of you is doing more than his or her fair share. The problem is that there are some distinct gender lines drawn. Your actions indicate that there are efforts being made to balance the scales. You need to keep moving in that direction. Even though you've separated many of the jobs on the basis of gender, you appear flexible and have deviated considerably from traditional homes. The progress you have made should be congratulated.

Traditional

Your home looks pretty much like the home you were raised in, except that you might be sharing some parenting and finances a bit more than your parents did. Other than that, someone (no doubt the woman) is doing the traditional "woman's work"—just like Mom used to—and your home is not equitable. If your beliefs are in line with your actions, no problem, but if you are repeating your parent's roles just out of habit, you might be living contrary to your belief system. If what you do is not in alignment with what you believe, it is time to have them reconciled.

Conservative

Basically, who is female and who is male determines household chores in your home. Since the lion's share of the housework is considered "woman's work," it is probably safe to say that the woman of the household is doing the double shift. She is working a full-time job outside the home and a full-time job within the home. Unless you have a lot of paid help, she's tired. Your home is not equitable. If this is in line with your belief system, and you are the woman in this household, you might want to reexamine why you believe in martyrdom. You have fallen into the "gender trap" and have given new meaning to the term "Supermom." You have a long row to hoe if anything is going to change.

Controlled

You are not going to like this, but your household is about as far away from equity as the slave owners' were. There is no compromise, no negotiation, and no justice. If it is work and it is in the home, it's the female's job. If you both are coexisting with this archaic belief system, no problem; I'm glad you found each other. Give this book to someone you hate. You will only look at all these concepts as heresy, anyway. But, if one of you has your actions in conflict with your beliefs and you want change, it can happen. Remember the flapping butterfly wings. If one thing changes, so will something else. At this point, any change is better than what you have.

Section 3: Your RANGE OF CONFLICT (Personal and Couple's)

This third section is revealing. It's about your range of conflict between beliefs and actions. It provides you with awareness concerning your inner turmoil: how much there is and what you need to do about it, if anything. If the range is wider than you are comfortable with, you need to start thinking about how to narrow the gap. Most of us have some degree of inconsistency between what we believe and what we do; however, if you have a wide gap, you might want to begin exploring ways to change what is not working.

YOUR RANGE OF PERSONAL CONFLICT

Score = 0

If you have scored zero, you are one of the rare people whose beliefs and actions are consistent with one another. Depending on what you believe, your house might or might not be equitable. What is true, however, is that you have no conflict between what you believe and what you are doing. There is no inner turmoil.

Score = 1

A score of 1 indicates that your beliefs and actions are in minimal conflict. There is some inner turmoil and stress within your household, because you periodically find yourself compromising what you believe, but the majority of the time you are living within your home the way you believe you should be.

Score = 2

A score of 2 indicates that your beliefs and actions are in conflict and you are experiencing a good deal of inner turmoil and stress. It is also becoming more of a struggle to continue to live in such contradiction to what you believe. You need to seek a much more authentic home life, by either correcting your actions or changing your beliefs so that they can coexist more peacefully.

Score = 3

If you score a 3, no doubt you're miserable. You are living in such contradiction to your beliefs that your inner turmoil and stress could eventually affect you physically, if it hasn't already. Why continue to compromise everything you believe or do? You are not living an authentic home life and this keeps you unhappy. You need to correct this contradiction immediately. Just remember that this correction will come with a major risk to your relationship. Be prepared.

Score = 4

A score of 4 is such a serious gap between what you believe and what you do that you might want to seek professional help to get your life more in sync. No one can have this much of a gap without serious consequences to his or her emotional stability. You need to begin a journey toward understanding why you are not living a more authentic home life. You are not in a position to negotiate a household partnership until you can regain some of your damaged self-esteem. Professional help is no doubt needed to get on the path.

Score = 5

You might want to go recheck your answers and your scoring. If everything is accurate, the next step is to make an appointment with a mental health professional so you can discuss how you are coping with a life so full of contradictions, inner conflicts, and turmoil.

YOUR RANGE OF COUPLE CONFLICT

The next two parts of Section 3 explore the range of couple conflict. This is interesting! First, how different are your beliefs? Then, how differently do you act? The last section validates the couple whether they are to the far left (open-minded) or to the far right (rigid) in their beliefs. It really doesn't matter. The important issue is that you are both there together. The same is true for your actions. Whether you are to the far right (controlled) or to the far left (equitable), it won't matter as long as you fall within a comfortable range of each other. Unfortunately, problems surface when you have a range of conflict greater than 1. Exactly how wide is this range or how close are you? The following scoring will tell you how compatible your beliefs and actions are.

Range of Couple's Conflict within Your Beliefs

Score = 0

You are like two peas in a pod. You believe the same way. You are very fortunate. But your household harmony will depend on whether your actions are also congruent with your beliefs and with each other's actions.

Score = 1

This keeps life interesting. You have a healthy difference of opinion. There is no real problem here that cannot be resolved through negotiation and compromise.

Score = 2

We are definitely entering into some problem areas. This much of a difference in what the two of you believe about gender is causing some problems. To have harmony, you both need to practice the attitude that says, "I count—but you count, too." (This "how to" is found in the next chapter.) The household division of labor exercise called The Happy Face Game will also help you.

Score = 3

There is not much that the two of you agree on when it comes to gender. You are seriously apart in your thinking, and it can't help but affect your relationship whenever the subject comes up. How are you both coping with these differences? Are you just not talking about them? Is that working?

Score = 4

You both are so far apart in what you believe that one wonders how you ever came together at all. Obviously, both of you have serious differences in how you view gender and household roles. Do you talk about these differences, or have you given up on each other? This latter choice is like giving yourself a life term in prison, and it will take its toll on you.

CHAPTER 15

Score = 5

I can only say that when a couple thinks so totally differently, it is difficult to know where to start. There are so many differences in how you view men's and women's roles that you probably spend an awful lot of time apart. Or maybe one of you keeps totally quiet in order to keep the peace. Of course, this will cost that person his or her peace of mind. To avoid an all-out war, you'll need to have a third party involved if you ever plan to discuss your differences. I suggest that you seek professional help to learn other ways to live together besides not talking to each other or giving in.

Range of Couple's Conflict with Actions

Score = 0

No disagreement here; you both concur as to what is actually happening in your home. Your household harmony depends on whether you are both content about it. A household partnership will affirm that you both are satisfied with each other's household involvement.

Score = 1

You have some healthy disagreement over who is actually doing what. This inconsistency is probably due to a lack of awareness about how much, or how little, the other one is actually contributing to the household chores. A household partnership will clear up all these discrepancies.

Score = 2

You hold some major misconceptions about who is doing what. Either one of you is ignoring what the other is doing, or else you are totally unaware of what work is being done or not done. One or both of you needs a reality check. The Happy Face Game will get you back on track.

Score = 3

In the world of mental health, a couple who is this far apart is said to be living in separate realities. Maybe the reality is somewhere in the middle, but you are clearly out of touch with what each of you is doing in the house. The Happy Face Game, which addresses the division of household labor, will put an end to the charade.

Score = 4

Either one of you is blind to reality or you live in separate homes. This is more than separate realities—someone is seriously deceived. Were you joking around when you answered the questions in Section 2? Maybe you misread them. Why don't you both go back and redo the questions? No two can be this far apart from reality and still be together.

Score = 5

If you fall into this category, there is little this book can do. Seek professional help to sort out the discrepancies and falsehoods. Something is very wrong. You should redo the inventory and scoring. If, after rechecking, you still discover you fall into this category, you must be living in separate households!

Congratulations!

You have discovered important information about what you believe and what you do. If you found a range of conflict (and most do), either with yourself or as a couple, the next chapter will help you to narrow it.

CHAPTER 16

Let's Dance to the Light of the Moon

Dance is the hidden language of the soul.
– Martha Graham, in *New York Times* (1985)

The Calm after the Storm

Webster's defines "equity" as fairness and justice. It is such a simple concept; one wonders why it causes so much misunderstanding. But everyday events ranging from yelling at your teenager last Tuesday to battles raging on the Western Front were caused, without exception, by disagreements over what is fair and just. The problem is that what seems exceedingly fair to one individual is a gross miscarriage of justice to another.

While discussing the Beliefs and Action Inventory, you and your mate probably talked about what you believe to be fair and just. No doubt, you disagreed with each other and expressed it in animated fashion. But there it is. Your true thoughts and feelings are out in the open.

Immediately afterwards comes a period of "the calm after the storm." I know that feeling. Gary and I have been there—the place where sentences trail off and you find yourself with little to say. But this is a good place to be, for you have come to an end. You don't necessarily have everything worked out, but when you come together again you note that both are attempting to embrace whatever kindredness there is between you. So coming to your end can be the beginning.

Carpe Diem

It's important to seize this moment, for it is precisely here, in your dialogue, heated or not, that you begin to have your shared beliefs about fairness take root. Take more time to talk it through. You will find areas where you agree, and the areas where you don't agree might not be as important as you first thought. However, to move forward, you both must come to a place where you want to correct whatever injustice you have identified. Together you need to agree that you want a home that has an equitable partnership, without regard to gender roles. I like to think of this as learning a new dance. You might not know the steps as yet, but you like the sound of the music and you have chosen each other as your partner.

But in order for you and your mate to learn this partnership dance you must be sure you both have the same desire for a fair and just household. This is the first step to the dance — a kindred belief in equity, and a desire for a household that operates on what's fair and just.

So, let's summarize what we've covered so far. You have done the exercises and probably have a fairly good understanding of the household personalities of you and your mate. You are aware of how your personalities work together, and you know your core beliefs. You also know the range of conflict between your beliefs and actions, as well as your couple's range of conflict. So let's sit back and take stock of the current situation. Ask yourself the following questions: "Is this leading me in a direction I really want to go? If so, is my mate willing? Have we both started to feel a sense of enlightenment?" If the answer is a resounding "Yes!" you could be embarking on a whole new way of life, one that is based on the concepts of partnership. Ultimately it means an end to chores allocated by gender. In other words, you both have come to believe that you want to dance toward a household partnership filled with intimacy.

It's Time to Tango

This new joint belief can be a heady experience, but let's go for it. Picture a full moon. You and your mate are on the beach dancing

CHAPTER 16

to some faint distant music. It's a time of celebration, so slip off your shoes and dance the tango barefoot in the moonlight. As you tango away, envision a more nurturing, more intimate relationship. Envision your new partnership with added excitement and romance. Imagine a life that is void of gender roles and "woman's work." Ahhhh! ... Life is good. But wait! ... Before you get too wild and start to tango off a dock somewhere, let's take time to contemplate exactly what's happening. If you believe you are dancing in the right direction, and it appears you are, the next step you need to know is whether you and your partner are ready for action. That's when the steps get complicated.

> *Dinah's note: Before you move to step two, allow me an explanation. Soon you both will be negotiating your Household Partnership Contract. You will draw it up by playing The Happy Face Game found in Appendix B. The woman will need to prepare for this activity more carefully than the man, and though both will learn from the following sections, I have devoted the rest of this chapter and all of Chapter 17 to her preparation for playing the game.*

Step Two: A Shared Action

The second step you need to learn before negotiating your Household Partnership Contract is the action step. Our actions — our behavior — are the only criteria humans have that demonstrate what we believe. When all else is said and done, the only thing that matters is what we do. This doing is the same sort of action I referred to in the previous chapter when I wrote about "watching their feet" or the biblical concept that states, "Faith without works is dead." This action step is the key ingredient in negotiating your upcoming household contract, and for keeping it from becoming more than a piece of scrap paper with which to light a fire later on. The action step, which will prove you are doing, is the same action that supports the belief that says: "You count — but so do I."

I know how women think, and one of the most difficult tasks

for many of us is to count ourselves as much as we count others. It's one of the reasons we are so content to sit and root from the grandstands, waving our pompoms. But hopefully you are changing this thinking, and becoming convinced that your needs are every bit as important as your family's. This change in belief and its resulting action are critical. You will not be able to negotiate your household contract from an equal position of power unless you *believe* and *act like you believe* that you count as much as your mate counts.

Admittedly, this is tricky business. Embracing a new action with a mate who looks at the world a whole lot differently than you can be as difficult as a trapeze act under the big top. But don't panic. Even though you don't need to have this concept completely burned into your soul before you start negotiating, it is important that you desire to move into a deeper realm and begin to do things differently. This realm involves more than mere talking about your belief in household equity—it also involves acting as if you believe in it. The following might help.

Head to Heart

Gary is, in a word, a philosopher (not to be confused with the Philosopher household personality). We all have our mentors, people we try to emulate. Some of us follow the Beach Boys, the Grateful Dead, or Ralph Nader. But Gary sort of likens himself to a Søren Kierkegaard or a Jean-Paul Sartre. Therefore, he has trained himself to think profoundly and observe intently. As a result, he has accumulated a repertoire of sayings that he believes speak to the human condition. During the many philosophical discussions instigated by Gary, he tosses forth these "words of wisdom" like mantras. Apparently unwilling to take a chance that he is not being fully understood, he invented a series of hand motions to accompany his tenets of life.

To everyone's amazement, over the years he has perfected these movements to an art form—a stylized sign language. In fact, they are so expressive that he now often uses them in lieu of speaking. They are his trademarks. Friends and family members, seeing how

CHAPTER 16

effectively Gary can gesture home the point, have tried to imitate him, especially when the discussion gets animated. We sometimes looks like a performing group of mimes, desperately acting out our pantomimes in unison. But only Gary captures the meaning of what he is saying—or rather, not saying. Of course, I find it all endearing. Well ... most of the time.

One of Gary's favorite signs is "head to heart." This particular sign motion is not complex. With his index finger, he rapidly and repeatedly points first to his head, then to his heart. The faster his finger moves, the more he is emphasizing how difficult it is for us, as humans, to embrace within our hearts what we know to be true in our heads. With this simple motion, Gary demonstrates our continual struggle in seeking a life of authenticity—in other words, to act from our beliefs.

"You Count, But I Count, Too" Behavior

I mention this particular motion to you since you need to find methods with which to integrate the belief of "I count too" into your heart. You already know it in your head, but it's a difficult step to move a belief into one's heart, much less to act on it.

As I mentioned before, I know and work with numerous women and most feel a sense of guilt when they choose for themselves over another. If this is an area you struggle with, you must get prepared before you enter the negotiation phase, or you will get slaughtered. Since concessions are part of negotiations, unless your action matches your belief that you count as much as your mate, you will be making all of the concessions and he will make none.

This is where Gary's hand signal comes in (the one where he rapidly points from his head to his heart). He says it means, "Until your heart holds this belief, it is not yours to keep. If it's only in your head, it's merely words." Here again, Gary "the pocket philosopher" offers another observation. "If we speak only from our head and not from our heart, we are impostors." In order for you not to fall prey to this human condition, Gary contends you must view your belief as a choice. In other words, you must make an active choice to believe. But I find that the hardest part is not making the choice, but in actually changing the behavior as a result of this choice. That is where he believes the heart comes in. Once a belief is firmly planted in your heart, you can't help but act upon it.

In case you are still confused about how this actually works out, I have developed a "cheat sheet" to keep at your side while you play the Happy Face Game. You will especially need it during the negotiation process. It will act as a reminder as to what "You count, but I count too" behavior looks like.

- ✦ I will not concede to something unless I receive something of equal value.
- ✦ I will not put the needs of my mate above mine.
- ✦ I will not concede because my mate gets upset.
- ✦ I will not concede because "I have always done it" or because "I can do it better."
- ✦ I will not concede because my mate needs more free time than I do.
- ✦ I will not concede because my mate makes more money at his job than I do.
- ✦ I will not concede because I feel guilty.
- ✦ I will not concede due to thinking I can manipulate a better deal by acting like a martyr.
- ✦ I will not concede because I feel it doesn't bother me as much as it bothers him.
- ✦ *I will not concede for any other reason than it seems fair to do so.*

It's Not As Easy As It Seems

Acting as though "I count too" is brand-new behavior for many women who are not used to counting themselves as being equal to

CHAPTER 16

other family members. Self-sacrifice has been part of our heritage and change is not easy. Gary (not surprisingly) has another hand sign for this "not being easy" part (bear with me). He snaps his fingers while chanting, "change, change, change," which means, "It's not that simple, is it?" Sometimes I appreciate his insight and his expressive ways of reminding us of our humanness. Other times, I smile and think to myself, "One more snap and I punch his lights out!" But that's life with a philosopher.

Now, if this "head to heart" stuff seems like an impossible journey for you, all is not lost. Remember the saying, "Fake it till you make it," which means that if we begin to act as if it's true, after a while it will be. I don't think Gary has a hand signal for it (thank God), but I believe the saying has merit. So if you find that you can't quite muster up the belief that your needs count as much as your mate's, you are going to simply have to fake it when playing the Happy Face Game. Someday you will have no doubt that you count as much as everyone else, but until then, it'll just be our secret.

CHAPTER 17

Let's Make a Deal!

You cannot shake hands with a clenched fist.
— Indira Gandhi, press conference (1971)

The Art of Negotiation

After you have mastered the above "two-step" (step one: you believe; step two: act like you believe), you are almost ready to start dancing again. But first, there is one more step to learn. It is "how to negotiate." This is important. Within the Happy Face Game, there are matching job cards. Matching job cards go into a negotiation envelope to be negotiated after all the cards are played. Therefore, you will need to know something about negotiating styles before you start.

Negotiation is big business, and people whose business it is are paid handsomely for their skills and efforts to negotiate tough deals. Negotiating a household partnership is also a tough deal. You might not be signing an armistice (or maybe you are), but I think Henry Kissinger would be challenged. This is no small potatoes. You need to be prepared for the win-lose negotiator who could be living in your house.

Viewing the Win-Lose Style through a Matrix

The best way to understand the negotiating process is to view it in the form of a matrix. There are two individuals. They could just as easily be parent/teenager, employer/employee, lovers, or friends. For our purpose, we will make them you (the woman) and your mate (the man). Each of you wants to win. Neither wants to lose.

CHAPTER 17

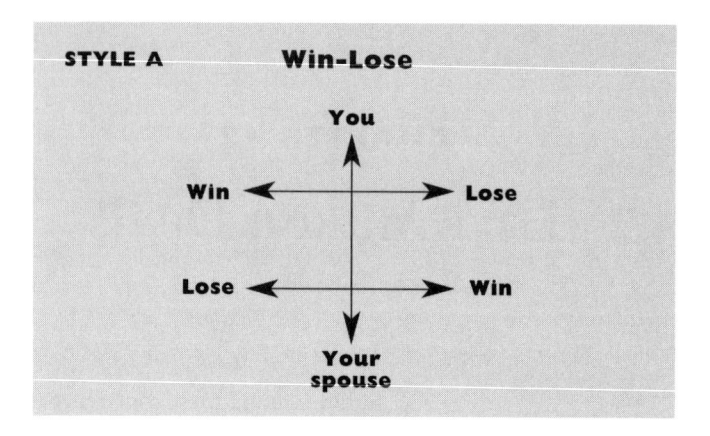

```
STYLE A            Win-Lose
                      You
                       ▲
                       |
         Win ◄─────────┼─────────► Lose
                       |
         Lose ◄────────┼─────────► Win
                       |
                       ▼
                     Your
                    spouse
```

Note how the above arrows indicate one option—"win-lose." This means that when one person wins, the other must lose. Some negotiators are "game players" who think the best possible outcome must always be at their opponent's expense. These hardball players have no mercy for the weak and only feel victory in a "win-lose" negotiation. For instance, the more venal of this group would stand off from a sinking ship and negotiate the price of life preservers while passengers thrash about in the water. It has to do with the way they view the above matrix. They see the only outcome as a vertical line. If your mate happens to be a win-lose negotiator (most Assertive household personalities are), his view may be that when drawing up the household contract, he needs to win and you need to lose. No other options come to his mind.

"But," you quickly say, "we now share the belief that there needs to be equity in the household. We came to that conclusion during the exercises, and our dance to the tango, so I am sure he won't behave in that ugly win-lose manner." Remember that we are all human, and although your mate may know it in his head, well ... as we have discussed, old ways of thinking do not suddenly extinguish themselves. Rather, they linger like a long, hard winter. So be prepared, just in case there is a bit of winter still left in him, and the seeds you are planting in your hearts may need some time to germinate and grow before they supplant the old ways you are each used to.

The Win-Lose Negotiator

For those of you facing win-lose negotiators, I have categorized them into four different types of players. I have also developed some counter-tactics for you to use while up against them. I assure you that these tactics will level the playing field.

The Boxer

One-two-three, you're out! This win-lose negotiator is a real fighter, and if this is your mate's style he will scream, swear, and attempt to shout you down. While throwing his tantrums, he looks for the right moment of weakness, then comes in with the knockout punch. His objective is to pound you into submission through intimidation. He knows all your vulnerable points and will use these weaknesses to pin you against the ropes. The boxer has a natural tendency to negotiate with aggressive body language, combative tone, and hostile demands. He doesn't want an agreement that you can live with. He wants to win. Being a "winner" strokes his ego, and he does not tolerate second place.

Countermeasures: Remember that you count, too! Refuse to give into his intimidation. Do not step down. Stay at his level. Be very conscious of your body language. Keep your back straight and lean forward in your chair. Maintain eye contact. Keep focused on the issue at hand. Try to return his emotionally charged demands with objective, nonpersonal demands of your own. Do not get into a shouting match. You will lose. Continually remind him that you will be counted. If the belligerence persists or escalates, de-escalate the situation by calling a time-out. In order to address hostile behavior, at an agreed-upon time, return to the table with some ground rules acceptable to both of you. I must advise you that if this is a continual pattern, the household partnership will have to wait; you need to attend to more immediate issues. Seek outside help.

The Chess Player

If your mate is this type of game player, his tactics are to outwit you by catching you off guard. His aim is to "get" without giving.

CHAPTER 17

His ultimate goal is to checkmate you into making all the concessions, so that you end up where you started, thanking him for being so understanding. Failing that, he will try to finesse an advantage from you without you being aware of giving it away. Suddenly the contract is signed and you find you've offered something you had no recollection of offering, like cleaning his golf clubs on a nightly basis. Your reaction will be a severe case of buyer's remorse: "How did I consent to this? Boy, am I stupid!" You then try to make the best of it, moping about with less self-esteem than when you first picked up this book. That's how the Chess Player wins.

Countermeasures: Don't play and don't concede. If you discover you're negotiating with a Chess Player, you will need to confront him right up front. Say something like, "Wait a minute, it seems like this issue is important to you. Let's put it on the table and discuss it. But just so you know, we operate on *quid pro quo* (nothing given without something returned of equal value), so what are you willing to give?" You never want to walk away from a Chess Player (or any negotiator, for that matter) unless you are confident that you have balanced the scales. Chess Players will soon give up their strategy when they know you are onto them. They know not to waste effort on a losing game.

The Poker Player

If your mate is the Poker Player, you will discover that he loves to bluff. He acts as if an issue is extremely important to him, when in fact he couldn't care less about it. By this tactic, he cons you into giving something of value for little in return. With a skillful Poker Player, the bluff can be difficult to detect. If you find yourself constantly hung up on details that appear minute to you but of great significance to him, chances are you are dealing with a Poker Player. Be aware of his objective, which is to wear you down. Eventually you will make concessions just to move on. If the Poker Player gets you to fold your hand, he wins.

Countermeasures: Calling the Poker Player's bluff may work. If not, try a bluff of your own. For instance, if the Poker Player says, "I hate mowing the grass," when you know he actually enjoys getting out and exercising behind the mower, tell him how much you hate to cook or use something else that you really like doing. This is calling his bluff. And since Poker Players hate negotiating with other Poker Players, this put-up-or-fold tactic might move the negotiations forward, so you are now able to proceed in good faith. If not, you might have to put the game on hold, and go back to re-reviewing the new belief system.

The Juggler

The Juggler's tactics are obvious. He wants to keep everything up in the air so that no decisions can be made. If this is your mate, you will hear him make comments like, "Can't we do this later? I'm just too tired tonight," or "I'm really not feeling that well," or "I had a bad day at the office," or "We aren't coming to any decisions; let's do it later." He keeps all the balls in the air, and you can never come to closure on them. Staring at all those floating balls wears you out, which is the intent. You start making concessions just to force a decision—any decision. The Juggler is driven by deeper emotions than the need to win the game. He has a deathly fear of commitment. He is almost phobic about anything that locks him into a permanent commitment. This makes negotiations with a Juggler particularly trying.

Countermeasures: During negotiations with a Juggler, maintain an open door for him. Reassure him that you are not Moses, that decisions arrived at will not be carved onto a granite tablet. Issues can be re-opened and re-negotiated on a continual basis. Insist, however, that at least one decision be made before leaving the table. Keep chipping away, one decision at a time. If the Juggler refuses to participate in a decision, make one anyway—in your favor. The Juggler, seeing he is giving away concessions by default, will become more interested in resolving issues on a mutual basis. Discontinue when negotiations become tiresome, and reschedule a later session.

The Win-Win Negotiator

If you have a competitive streak, you will not be above using some of these win-lose tactics yourself. If you continually resort to them,

CHAPTER 17

however, you'll block the development of the household contract. Besides, there is a much better tactic. To create the most effective, enduring contract, you and your mate will want to adopt the negotiating style of the Bridge Player.

The Bridge Player

Negotiating from this ideal greatly increases the chance of a successful household partnership. If both you and your mate adopt this posture, your negotiations will move along quickly, ending with a well-considered household contract. Bridge is a card game played by four players. According to the rules of the game, the cards are dealt and two of the players, who sit opposite each other, negotiate a "contract." There is an agreement on a trump suit and the number of points to be won as the hand is played out. The major difference between this style and the ones above is the relationship between the players. Bridge players negotiate, not as opponents, but as partners. In the game of bridge, two partners negotiate a contract that they both agree on and are committed to fulfilling. The partnership forms in front of the negotiations, not behind them. This is the ideal style, and is the thought process that you and your mate will want to integrate while playing The Happy Face Game.

Returning to the Matrix

Let's refer back to our negotiating matrix. The objective of the players is to draw the line diagonally, so that both negotiators win. In fact, by limiting the negotiations to diagonal lines, we can see that if one partner does not win, neither does the other. Both win or both lose. There is no other choice. In retrospect, it becomes quite obvious that a couple sharing one household cannot negotiate successfully in any other way. As far as relationships go, couples are either both winners (partners) or they are both losers.

Since you both have the same goal—to negotiate a fair and just contract—you need to acknowledge that you both are willing to make concessions. In bridge, once the contract is made, the partners

STYLE B — **Win-Win**

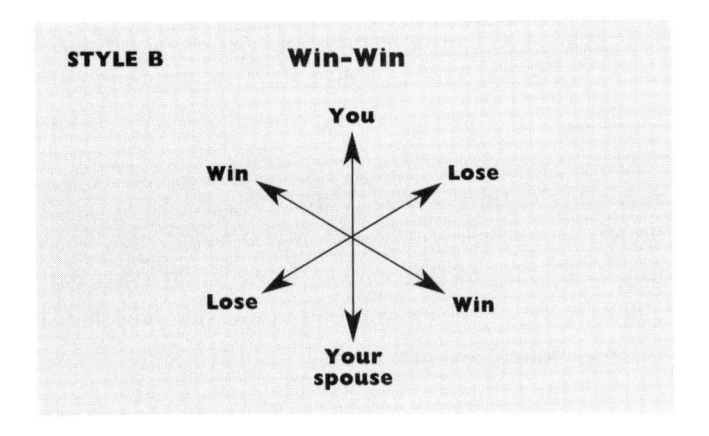

```
        You
   Win ↖ ↑ ↗ Lose
        ✕
   Lose ↙ ↓ ↘ Win
       Your
       spouse
```

share a great sense of accomplishment: slapping high five's, congratulating each other, and stroking each other's ego about how clever they both were. This same sense of accomplishment can happen between you and your mate as you sign your household contract.

Let's Meet Halfway — "The Compromise"

Webster defines *compromise* as "a settlement of differences by mutual concessions." Compromise should not be confused with *negotiation,* which Webster defines as "to deal or bargain." Compromise is the process that you and your mate will eventually use to reach an agreement. The process requires that you both are receptive to the concessions each will be asked to make. Believe it or not, Gary has another hand signal for this. It might help.

When Gary speaks of the receptivity shared by partners, he holds out both hands with palms facing each other, about a foot apart. He then tucks in all but his index finger; his thumbs are now wrapped around the three fingers with just his index fingers pointing out. He then begins to bend his index fingers alternately in and out rapidly. If you try this, you will notice how your index fingers are pointing toward each other, but never quite at the same time. Like people, they are always a little out of sync, managing to just keep missing each other, even though their desire is to connect. Gary's infamous hand signal simply means that couples need to stop for a minute, listen, and "take it in."

CHAPTER 17

"Taking it in" is Gary's terminology for being receptive to each other. Without receptivity we will be out of sync and compromise will be difficult, if not impossible, to achieve. While negotiation means taking care of yourself, compromise is a willingness to support each other to take care of themselves.

There is a big difference between you taking care of your mate and supporting him to take care of himself. That is what win-win negotiation is about: negotiating by compromising. However, beware. As mentioned, women often have a tendency to take care of others, especially if they are negotiating and compromising with an Emperor or Hunter. A good question to keep in mind is, "If you are both taking care of him, who's taking care of you?"

CHAPTER 18

The Time Has Come

Please notice what happens when I tell you ...
  We can share the power.
Please notice what happens when I tell you ...
  I won't try to control you.
Please notice what happens when I tell you ...
  I don't want you to control me.
Please notice what happens when I tell you ...
  We can be equals.
Please notice what happens when I tell you ...
  We can be partners.

– Riane Eisler and David Loye, *The Partnership Way*

It's Either Time to Dance or to Sit This One Out

The time has come. We have discovered that each household personality has its quirks, and you as a couple may have a few that are ... well, simply insurmountable. But we have come to the place where there needs to be a commitment before you move on. At the beginning of the next chapter, there is a Code of Ethics that the two of you will need to sign if you desire to move forward. In other words, this is where you dance or sit down. There might be some barriers, depending on your household personalities.

The Dapper wonders what is wrong with the present situation. "After all, I already help out so much," he complains. The Emperor laughs halfway out the door: "Surely you jest!" The Philosopher might actually commit to signing the Code of Ethics just to get his

CHAPTER 18

mate off his back, but it won't count for much. And, of course, the Hunter can't imagine that his mate is actually asking him to do more than he already is.

And the woman needs to take stock of her own personality traits, as well. Listen to those inner voices. Are you a HoneyBee? You might be thinking, "Sure, this is all well and good—for those who have the time, which I don't." Or are you a Sojourner who would gladly sign the Code of Ethics, if you could just remember where you last saw this book? Or perhaps you're a Stargazer, staring into the night and planning days of song, wine, and festivities to mark the grand signing, so caught up in the moment that you didn't notice you later conceded to doing most of the work. Maybe you're a Tigress who's somewhat irritated that this has to be done in the first place, and are we sure the spelling is correct? Or possibly you are the Rebel who has skipped the past chapters and already has her signature on the dotted line, but you neglected to educate your mate along the way.

I have never assumed that all of my readers are standing on the threshold of household partnerships, just waiting to waltz through the door. For some of you, dancing is not foremost in your mind. You have yet to learn how to walk or talk together, much less dance. This, then, is a sober moment. I may be the only author in modern times who bids her reader farewell before the end of the book. But I am afraid we have arrived on the dance floor—one of those moments in time when some of us decide we don't like the beat and want to "sit this one out," while others turn to look for a partner to boogie with.

To my readers who find themselves unable to bring their mate (and I will assume it is the male) on to the dance floor because he is saying, "It has a good beat, but it's too hard to dance to," as difficult as it is, it's time to say goodbye.

Wannabe, But Not Gonnabe

First, to my "wannabe, but not gonnabe" readers: We recognized early on that change involves risk. Although you may agree wholeheartedly with the message, you are not quite able to give up "those old, so familiar ways." Your home may not be equitable, or even content, but at least it is stable. We cannot minimize the fear of the unknown. It is real and potent. The inability to leave a zone of comfort—especially one that is socially sanctioned—has stymied many great plans of a great many people. Thank you for staying with me for this much of the journey. At this point, however, there is really no reason to continue on. Your reluctance, or your mate's, about embracing change will keep you from entering as an equal player in the forthcoming Happy Face Game. Still, change is inevitable, so I pray thee, keep this book on the shelf. You might want to return to it someday.

Gonnabe Someday, Come Hell or High Water

My other parting is to my "gonnabe someday, come hell or high water" readers. For you, my heartfelt farewell is not so much a goodbye as an "until we meet again." You are the readers who want fervently to move ahead with me, but cannot. Your mate, for whatever reason, is just not up to it. Sadly, it still takes two to tango. Even though you are convinced that this is the right path, it won't be enough. If you have come to realize that there is no way you are going to be able to bring your mate along, short of dragging him, kicking and screaming, it is time to let go. So to all of you "wannabe but can't be"s, please be patient. There will always be another dawn. Remember the insignificant little butterfly flapping its wings. Momentous changes are on the way. True, there may be a blustery storm of resistance before the dawn breaks. But then the rainbow will appear, reflecting gloriously in the sunrise, and everything will be different—how much different will depend on the severity of the storm, and how much you flap your wings. So keep the book and come back when it's time. Meanwhile, consider forming a household partnership support group. And show your children the way (remember the Partner's mom). Now I bid you goodbye and good luck. I'm confident that someday we will meet right back here. Our time will come.

CHAPTER 19

The Household Partnership

> *Just as the dominator family is the training ground for living in a warlike, male-dominant, and basically authoritarian (or dominator) society, the partnership family is where we can learn to live in a more peaceful, just, and mutually satisfying way. Here neither women nor men have to be imprisoned in the rigid straitjackets of roles that deny them part of their humanity.*
>
> – Riane Eisler and David Loye, *The Partnership Way*

Signing the Code of Ethics

Now, to my readers who are staying the course, again let me say, "Congratulations!" Much of the journey is behind you. There are only a couple of hurdles left. The first one is the signing of the Household Code of Ethics, found in Appendix A. It clarifies the mutual beliefs and actions that you as a couple will build upon in creating your Household Partnership Contract.

When you have both signed the Code of Ethics, you have made a major step in creating a fair and equitable household. Now go out to the store and buy a binder or notebook of some type. After signing, remove the Code of Ethics from the back of the book and place it in this notebook, which you have titled "Our Household Partnership." This notebook will eventually contain your individual job lists (agreed upon from the Happy Face Game) and your signed household contract.

A Time of Celebration

As the wheels of the Boeing 747 touched down at Charles de Gaulle airport, 15 miles north of Paris, Gary looked over at me, smiled, and gave the thumbs-up sign. It was quite a moment. It was our first trip to Paris and it was springtime. Gary's employer, a major North American airline, had sent him here to install a new computer system. We were six months into our partnership and, in order to make it all legal, somewhere over the Atlantic we had signed our Household Code of Ethics "into law."

There was a lot to celebrate, and we did not pass up one moment to do so. The champagne flowed right up to the last few minutes before landing. We had toasted our upcoming wedding anniversary, the completion of Gary's computer project, Paris, and—most importantly—our new household partnership. As we taxied to the gate, I looked out over the tarmac. No doubt about it, I was a new person. The quote from *The Partnership Way* that begins this chapter came back to me: I was no longer straitjacketed to a role. I felt free to be me. And what a place to begin—*vive la France!*

Negotiation of Labor

A couple of days later, at a quaint cafe along the Avenue des Champs Élysées, Gary and I developed the Happy Face Game. We tested it on the flight home to see if it covered all the bases or not—it didn't, but it certainly got us started, as it will for you. The game ends with signing of the Household Partnership Contract. We signed ours into agreement somewhere over Greenland. Numerous changes have occurred since our initial contract-signing back in May of 1991, but we have never forsaken the basic principles of negotiation, compromise, and our mutual desire for a win-win partnership.

The Happy Face Game

You are now ready to play the Happy Face Game, found in Appendix B. The Happy Face Game divides the household chores in an equitable and agreeable fashion. It does involve negotiation. Remember, negotiate in good faith, and keep in your heart the

CHAPTER 19

belief of equity in action ("You count—I count"). Good luck to both of you. You are ready to "dance by the light of the moon." You are embarking on the sea of enlightenment.

Signing the Household Partnership Contract

After you have completed the Happy Face Game and have successfully negotiated an equitable division of household chores, it is time to sign the Household Partnership Contract in Appendix C.

I suggest you set the mood before you sign. If Paris is not close by, find the most comfortable and enchanting cafe in your neighborhood. A quiet beach would also work beautifully, or perhaps a peaceful place in the park for a picnic. It would be wonderfully special if you could go off for the weekend, just the two of you, to some charming bed-and-breakfast. Forming a household partnership is a monumental occasion. Don't let this special event pass without some recognition of its importance to you and your relationship.

After the two forms are signed (the Code of Ethics and Household Partnership Contract), pat yourselves on the back. You deserve it. You did it! You are now officially partners. You are the rare ones. Share your experiences with your loved ones and friends—spread the message of equity, partnership, and enlightenment!

CHAPTER 20

The Thanksgiving Day Revelation

If you have made mistakes, even serious ones, there is always another chance for you. What we call failure, is not falling down, but the staying down.

– Mary Pickford, in *Reader's Digest* (1979)

A Year Later...

It was early morning on Thanksgiving Day, a full year after the Thanksgiving Day Caper. David and Kristina were home to celebrate the holiday. As the four of us sat in the breakfast nook, drinking coffee and nibbling on breakfast rolls, I started to explain to the kids how this Thanksgiving was going to be slightly different than past ones.

The week before, Gary and I had gone to the local delicatessen to place our order for turkey, mashed potatoes, gravy, dressing, rolls, and pumpkin pie for ten people. (Besides David and Kristina, three of their friends and a couple of ours were coming for dinner.) The evening before, Gary had picked up the entire order of food on his way home from work. It now lay neatly stacked in the refrigerator, just waiting to be heated. The pies covered with cheesecloth were sitting outside on the screened porch.

"Now we still have to prepare the salad, which you've agreed to do," I said, looking over at Gary, "and I'm responsible for the squash. However, that will be no problem because I baked it yesterday. So the only thing left to do regarding the dinner is to open a can of cranberries and uncork a bottle of wine." I got up and went over to our kitchen island to get my notebook and pen.

CHAPTER 20

"Okay, let's go over the timing, " I said as I began to pace back and forth. "An hour before dinner I will set a formal table and spruce up the flower arrangement. Twenty minutes before we sit down, Gary and I will warm everything up, and set up the buffet." I looked up from my agenda to Gary, who sat faithfully listening and nodding. "Gary," I said smiling in admiration, "immediately following placing the warm bread in the basket, you'll need to start tossing the salad." I glanced over at Kristina and David. Contrary to Gary, they weren't nodding. In fact they looked befuddled. I continued on as if I hadn't noticed, "Kristina, that will be your cue to light the candles and put the butter on the table, and David, that's your signal to open the wine and fill the water goblets. After dinner, we'll all stay in the kitchen until it's completely cleaned up. So — as you can see — there is no stone left unturned, no 'I' undotted, nor a 'T' uncrossed. This plan is so tightly woven you could bounce a nickel off of it," I said with pride. I sat back down next to Gary and paused. "Well ... what do you think?" I asked, my voice still filled with enthusiasm. "Don't you just love it when a plan comes together?"

I noticed a certain lull as David and Kristina exchanged glances. Kristina answered first. "Well ... I think I could have handled a bit more than candles and butter. Perhaps I can throw a log on the fire or dim the lights?

"That's right," said David, "it seems as if she's coasting, while I have the bulk of the work with water and wine. Doesn't seem fair to me!"

They were making fun. Gary came to my rescue.

"Now I know this is a bit different than past years, but your mother and I have planned this in a way that will remove stress and pressure from our lives. And as we all know, holidays have always been particularly overwhelming since Mom entered the work force. So personally," he said, putting his arm around me reassuringly, "I think it's great! No one has to do a lot of work, and the end product will be the same."

I could tell the kids weren't entirely sold on the idea of a "deli-bought" Thanksgiving dinner, but my attitude was, "So what?" I was intent on not allowing anything, especially senseless guilt, to interfere with my plans for a stress-free, restful day. After breakfast I was going to lie down on the couch and read the morning paper. What a difference a year had made! By purchasing "take-out," I had eliminated a whole day of cooking, as well as the last-minute three-ring circus act of getting all the food in bowls and on the table while still hot and at the same time. More importantly, it had eliminated my resentment and exhaustion that had accompanied past holiday dinners. Today would be the first Thanksgiving since I could remember that I did not feel solely responsible for creating a "moment of wonder." I was free to kick back and enjoy the holiday like the rest of the family. I loved Thanksgiving!

But surprisingly, this kicked-back, have fun, relaxed, nothing to do, eliminating stress atmosphere also eliminated some other things —some good things, things that I had forgotten about. David, a young entrepreneur of 26, is always creating ways to make it better. He mentioned a couple of times throughout the day that although he appreciated how much easier it was for me, he still missed the wonderful aromas of a cooking turkey.

"Mom, it just doesn't seem the same, you know, with the turkey-cooking smells missing and all. I am thinking that the next time we do this, we should start a crock pot of turkey stock early in the day. That way we could create an illusion that there actually is a real turkey cooking in the oven. What do you think?"

"Uh-huh," I said with a tinge of guilt (some things are impossible to change). "Well—we're just trying it out this year to see how it works. And besides, we're not eating a pretend turkey. The only difference between it and previous turkeys is someone else cooked it." I smiled, then laid my head back on the couch to finish my nap.

The Turkey Dance

Later in the day, Kristina, our traditional turkey carver, sneered at the sliced turkey warming up in the pan and said, "It looks as if the turkey is all cut up. I guess that means I won't be carving a turkey

CHAPTER 20

this year." She continued speaking in deep sighs, "Of course, this also means we won't have a wishbone ... and ... (sigh) I guess I won't be doing the turkey dance ... oh, well ... it's not important (sigh). It's good to know you don't feel stress, Mom. I think it's great that you are taking care of yourself" (sigh).

I started to feel stress. Maybe this was not such a good idea after all. I had completely forgotten about Kristina's traditional Thanksgiving Day turkey dance. It's her own improvisation, created several years ago when she was a little girl. Now at 24, and a senior dance student at the University of Minnesota, she still did the turkey dance.

Traditionally the turkey dance commenced when I announced that the little plastic thermometer had popped out of the turkey, signifying the meat was done. That was Kristina's sign to spring into the air, electric knife in hand, and begin her silly chant of, "The turkey is done. The turkey's done! The turkey's done!" All during the time she was screeching she would twirl and leap from room to room. To the laughter and enjoyment of everyone watching, she danced to what became known as the "turkey dance." Typical of Kristina, it was wonderfully creative and extraordinarily funny. David would follow behind with the video recorder, capturing her antics and our reactions. It's one of those things that you "probably have to be there for," but I was going to miss it.

There were other events I missed, like stuffing the turkey and singing that stupid, silly song, "Over the river and through the woods, to Grandmother's house we go." And I missed the rotation of turns David would set up for basting the turkey, or periodically sticking our fingers in the dressing to sample it. Also — damn it to hell! — I actually got bored with napping and reading and found I was looking forward to the time when I could warm up the dinner just so I would have something to do.

But as it turned out, what we all missed the most was the food. The warmed-up dinner did not taste nearly as good as the "homemade fixings" my Grandmother had taught me to make. And God help me, but I also missed the raving compliments about how great everything tasted. Comments like, "Once again Mom, you've truly outdone yourself," and, "Wow, Mom ... what a feast! You are great! We are so lucky to have you!" (I've always been a sucker for flattery.) No, I'm afraid the dry turkey, bland dressing, and greasy gravy didn't quite make the mark. In the final analysis, even with the company, the music, the fire, the table setting, candles, and wine, it just wasn't the same.

Sometimes We Come Full Circle

Ever since that day, I've gone back to cooking that ridiculous Thanksgiving dinner myself. Oh, yes, I get help, and I don't prepare nearly the number of dishes I use to, but as far as the holidays are concerned, not a lot has changed since the Thanksgiving Day Caper. Except I'm not nearly as resentful as I used to be, since I now feel like it's not an *expectation*, but my *choice* to keep the traditions alive—and that "except" makes a big difference.

As you seek equity, you must also seek balance. If you tip the scales too much, as I did with the carry-out Thanksgiving dinner, you may lose as much as you gain. Consequently, you gain nothing. I encourage you to keep this concept in mind as you read the following stages of household partnership.

CHAPTER 21

The Stages of the Household Partnership

It has begun to occur to me that life is a stage I'm going through.

– Ellen Goodman

Life Can Be Like a Game of Hopscotch

Everything in life is a process. Some days we jump five feet forward, only to get shoved three feet back the following day. And then again, some days we stand still and watch life go by. Perfection, or the continuous motion of moving forward, is never going to happen. Life is just too unpredictable.

I fear that if you are under the illusion that you will find "the answer" or create the perfect partnership, you will be disappointed. Since we are not perfect beings, it will be impossible to mold perfection out of imperfection. Hence, as you move through the following stages of partnership, take your time. The final stage does not come without work, arguments, and disappointments. And even then, when you feel like you have settled into it, as Gary and I mostly do, something will happen like the dreaded holiday or a sick child, and you will feel as if you are right back at the beginning. But remember, even though it feels that way, you're not. You have come quite a distance from the beginning. I encourage you to concentrate on how far you have come, instead of how far you have yet to go.

The Stages of the Household Partnership

Over the centuries numerous theories have been used to explain how the human psyche adjusts to life's changes. Many of these theories support the philosophy that life is a journey, and during our trip we all pass through similar stages. From Freud's writings to Erik Erikson's and on to Gail Sheehy's *Passages*, authors have sought to prove that in the normal course of life, people from the same cultures share an enormous amount of similarity as they pass through each life stage. But just because we share the same stages with countless other people, it doesn't make our adjustments to them any easier. Still these authors have done us a great service, for they have helped to calm our nerves. By recognizing certain benchmarks or "stages" as normal, we can relax a tad more as we pass through them. There is a certain amount of comfort in knowing that others have been where we've been, are where we are, or have gone to where we're going.

The household partnership also has its stages. There are five altogether, and each one is marked by distinct characteristics. By recognizing and understanding these unique characteristics, you (as a couple) can move through these stages as an adventure rather than an endurance test.

Patience is key. There is a greater chance of success if you do not become impatient and try to move from one stage to another too quickly. Each stage has a life and timing of its own. And, as with all of life's stages, you will pass through them in your own time and in your own way.

The ultimate goal of this chapter is to prevent a breach of your Household Partnership Contract because you or your mate lacked insight into or understanding of the process. It might help if you bear in mind that "Rome was not built in a day," and neither are partnerships.

Stage One: The New Toy

The first stage of the household partnership is easy to recognize. It's earmarked by how much fun you are having. During this stage, the partners feel energized and each of you is especially careful to fulfill your part of the contract. This is also a time when you feel sort of stuck-up and haughty. Deep inside you are congratulating yourself

CHAPTER 21

on how well you've negotiated this "new deal" of yours, and each of you is careful not to ruin a good thing. Consequently, the first stage is filled with lots of affirmations, gratitude, and superlatives. One hears things like, "Thank you, thank you. Oh, that is just wonderful," or "You are just great," or "Wow ... what a great meal you cooked," or "Gosh, the kitchen looks wonderful. You clean it better than I do," or "Gee ... what a great job mowing the lawn!"

During this first stage, no one has to be reminded about what their job is. Both of you are on your best behavior and taking care of your responsibilities. There might even be an unspoken competition going on, since no one wants to be the first to renege on the contract. The life expectancy of this first stage is about forty-eight hours.

Stage Two: Buyer's Remorse

Real life sets in, and before you know it you've moved from Nirvana into Stage Two. This second stage is more difficult. The most distinguishable characteristic is that you begin to regret you ever started the foolish game, wrote the dumb old contract, or took precious time out of your busy days to determine your personalities. "I just want to go back to the 'good ol' days,'" says the Emperor, "the way it was before all this nonsense about partnership."

This stage can just as easily be called "finding someone to blame," as the disgruntled partner asks, "Just whose idea was this, anyway?" And, since it was probably the woman's, you just might need some help to get through this time.

Pat and Dennis

Pat and Dennis both have demanding careers as tax attorneys. Pat, a Tigress, was thrilled when her husband Dennis, a Hunter, negotiated a fair and just contract. As expected, they sailed through Stage One. But now that the newness has worn off and Dennis is returning to some old habits of obsessing over his own projects, Pat is getting nervous. Just last weekend, Dennis said, "I'm sorry, but there is no time left over for me to complete my household chores. I just don't know how I agreed to do so much, considering my schedule. It seems near impossible to keep up."

Pat panicked and asked Dennis, "Have you forgotten about our commitment? I am not planning on going back to the way it was."

Couple A, B, or C?

Just how serious is this Stage Two situation? Are Pat and Dennis in danger of a total breach of contract, or can something be saved? In order to determine what corrective plan to use, they need to resolve what couple category they fall into. Are they Couple A with small problems, Couple B with medium problems, or Couple C with big papa-bear problems? Their category, as well as yours, can be determined by answering the following questions.

Questionnaire to Determine Your Category

1. At least once a week, your mate makes an excuse for why he can't fulfill his part of the partnership, such as no time, forgot, or something came up. (1 point)

2. You find yourself redoing his jobs because they're not done to your satisfaction. (3 points)

3. You find that you are both arguing about terms of the contract. Both are making statements like, "I didn't agree to that," or, "That's not what I meant." (2 points)

4. Your mate is expressing regret that he ever agreed to the Household Partnership Contract. (2 points)

5. Your mate is minimizing the validity of the household partnership contract. (4 points)

6. You are continually going back to the contract to remind him what his part is. (2 points)

7. You are feeling hopeless about how to make this work. (5 points)

8. You find yourself giving up and going back to the way it was just to get peace. (5 points)

Scoring

Couple A scores 1 to 5 points
Couple B scores 6 to 10 points
Couple C scores 11 points or more

Interpreting Your Quiz Results

Couple A

Pat and Dennis, with five points, fell into the category of Couple A. This indicates that both negotiated the contract in good faith, and though at times it doesn't feel like it, they are off to a good start. The contract, however, is being tested. It has become obvious that Dennis is not as comfortable with having everything carved in granite as Pat is. Pat must be careful not to lose everything by panicking or digging her heels in. Mutual compromise is essential in order to move into Stage Three.

Corrective Action Plan

Let's take a closer look at Pat and Dennis. It appears Dennis is not only forgetting, but is also neglecting his particular job.

This is an excellent time for Pat and Dennis to calmly schedule a partnership meeting to review and renegotiate areas of the contract that are not working. Both Pat and Dennis will need to identify the items that have become stumbling blocks. But before Pat begins the partnership meeting, she needs to ask herself the following questions:

+ How important is this issue? Is it a mountain to die on?

+ Do I need to be open for renegotiation because of some new extenuating circumstance?

+ Have we neglected to take into account a critical issue in our first negotiating round?

- What do I want changed? What do I think my partner wants to change?
- Could I renegotiate and get something back in return that would be just as satisfactory?

Hopefully Pat and Dennis can come to terms on relaxing some chores, but still staying firm on the issues that are most important. First, Dennis needs to recommit to the partnership. If he cannot leave some of his beloved projects, he will have to find extra time in his own schedule to fit them in. He must also recognize that a fair and just partnership requires sacrifice, and this change will be difficult at first. Dennis must also come to terms with the fact that he is going to have to restructure his days if he wants to keep some of his own time-consuming projects. Pat and Dennis might need to return to the negotiation table several more times before they are both satisfied. Ultimately, they are in a very good place to make the contract work.

Couple B

Couple B is the category into which most couples fall. It's here where I find that the woman is more committed to this new arrangement than the man. No doubt she has been doing the bulk of the household chores, and is very invested in the household partnership staying alive and well. She does not want to return to the "good ol' days" when her mate was only the "helper" or, even worse, not involved at all.

Wendy and Joe

Wendy, a Rebel, had high hopes when Joe, her Dapper, signed on the dotted line of their newly formed Household Partnership Contract. Even though her job as a waitress doesn't keep her out of the home as much as Joe's second shift at the plant does, she is overwhelmed with the responsibilities that her part-time outside job and full-time "inside" job of mothering three young children place upon her. Of course, she was thrilled to enter into a partnership.

CHAPTER 21

Joe has always thought of himself as a good dad—and a good helper. "I do what I can," he would say every time Wendy complained that the kids and house were becoming too much for her. The good news is Wendy saw immediate improvements after the initial signing of the contract, not only in the amount of work Joe would do, but also in his attitude. For the first couple of weeks he would come home and start his chores right away. After he finished, he still found plenty of time to do his share with the kids. His attitude appeared positive and Wendy felt confident he had grasped the concepts of partnership. He was no longer using statements about "helping out," and he did not wait to be told what to do.

But lately, Wendy notices Joe is slipping and is starting to neglect his chores, or is doing them so haphazardly that she is doing them over. When they used the above questionnaire, they scored eight points, placing them into Category B.

Corrective Action Plan

The important issue for Wendy is to remember that she is more committed to the partnership than Joe is. Therefore, she needs to be careful that it does not seem as if she is leading the way. A bossy style will cause resentment with her sensitive Dapper. Wendy needs to delicately (keep in mind that delicacy is not the easiest trait for a Rebel—this will be a challenge) implement some early intervention techniques to prevent jeopardizing what they have already created. For Wendy, and all women who find themselves in Category B, it's as important to know what not to do as it is to know what to do.

LIST OF DON'Ts

1. Don't keep track of what your partner is not doing.

2. Don't remind your partner about his agreement to do a certain chore.

3. Don't retaliate by using passive-aggressive behavior (such as not saying you're upset, but acting as if you are.)

4. Don't do your partner's job if he doesn't do it.

5. Don't entertain negative self-talk such as, "I knew he wouldn't do it," or "I knew this wouldn't work."

6. Don't sulk or pout when he doesn't do his chores.

7. Don't discuss your disappointment, anger, or frustration with the children.

8. Don't make subtle manipulating statements such as, "As soon as you get your job done, I will do mine," or "Just like I thought, you forgot."

9. Don't be obvious about following behind and redoing a job that wasn't done to your satisfaction.

10. Don't give up.

The first question you might have after reading the above don'ts is, "Why not? Why should I act all cheery and happy when he is not keeping his side of the bargain? I'm doing my share. I feel ripped off. I'm upset and I don't feel like swallowing my disappointment and anger! I'm mad!"

Of course, you will be angry when you feel your partner is backing out of the contract. In fact, major wars have been justified by the same breach. However, to achieve your objective, caution is necessary. You must remember your objective is to keep the contract as intact as possible, so concentrate on areas that you have accomplished, instead of blowing up over the areas that are weak. The weak areas that really matter should be documented for re-negotiation.

The following is a list of what to do.

LIST OF DOs

1. Maintain a daily journal about what is working, what needs improving, and what needs renegotiating.

2. Keep your part of the contract, even if your mate is neglecting his part.

CHAPTER 21

3. Keep a positive attitude concerning the areas that are working.

4. Maintain a realistic perspective about change. (Remember the butterfly.)

5. Schedule regular meetings to review and renegotiate contract issues that have been recorded in your journal.

6. Continue to reinforce how pleased you are with the partnership—if only in concept.

7. Maintain a confident attitude that you will not to return to the days of the "helper."

8. Maintain a supportive environment. If you feel like pitching in once in a while to help your mate with his chore, do it. However, be confident that the reason you are helping out is not because you "have to," or "should" do it, but because you want to. Your mate needs to help you out occasionally, as well. This creates partnership and intimacy.

9. Maintain accurate, written, and dated agreements on any renegotiation.

10. Maintain your own mental health by scheduling a time to reward yourself (e.g. when your responsibilities have been completed, use your free time for your own pleasure).

The goal of the second stage is to move to the third. By keeping scheduled partnership meetings for renegotiation, a couple shows their commitment to the contract.

For Couple B—How to Renegotiate Your Household Contract

Just as there were certain guidelines to follow when you first negotiated your household contract, there are similar guidelines, or methods, you should adhere to during renegotiation. As mentioned,

Stage Two is fragile. Disappointments have arisen, and emotions can be at an all-time high. This is a time when it is more important to talk about your actions than your feelings.

So when it is obvious that you and your partner need to return to the negotiating table, the "confrontation" needs to be non-threatening and nonjudgmental. Open the meeting by saying, "It appears that the jobs you have negotiated for are not working for you or for me. Would you like to renegotiate?" Your manner must coincide with your words. This means that, since your words sound fairly safe and non-threatening, you will want to make sure your fists are not clenched while you are talking. You will have more success convincing your mate to sit down with you if you present your position in a way that he does not feel ambushed. Claiming he is a welcher who never keeps his word is not the way to do it. Saying things like, "I am sick and tired of keeping my part of the bargain while you slough off," or, "I should have known you would find a way to keep this from working!" are fighting words that will kill any hope for renegotiation. If your mate senses hostility, he will avoid the meetings, and since these meetings are essential to keeping the partnership from defaulting, you will need to use whatever method necessary to entice your mate back to the negotiating table.

If you want success more than revenge, say something like, "I've noticed that it is difficult for you to complete your chores. Let's renegotiate and see if we can find something that works for both of us." Now that he is listening, I recommend using three key principles during your time of renegotiation.

1. Deal with the *issue*, not your feelings about the issue.
2. Be prepared to compromise. Remember that you want a win-win.
3. Don't give away the store. Never give anything away without getting something of equal value in return.

Typical of Category B couples, you will have to return to the negotiation table several times before you come to an agreement you both can live with. It will be important that, during this testing time, you continue to record your decisions. If you are dealing with the same issues over and over again, you will want to at least show some progress. Remember, developing a partnership is a process. Some processes are slower than others. Have patience.

Couple C

If you fall into the Couple C category, with eleven points or more, there is no question about what is happening. Your mate is attempting to back out of the agreement, and whenever he can find the opportunity, he is sabotaging it. Because you have been doing most of the household chores, you want change. Therefore you have been leading the charge into a partnership from the beginning. No doubt you probed and pleaded all the way through the household personality questionnaire and the inventory surveys. In his weak moment, you persuaded him to sign the Household Code of Ethics, play the Happy Face Game, and sign the contract. I don't blame you. You are no doubt desperate for change. (I have enough Rebel in me to know that I would do the same thing.)

But it has probably been obvious to you that all along the way your mate is less than enthusiastic about the idea of partnership. He has only "gone along" with your idea to keep the peace. Now you find yourself in Stage Two (you might have never even experienced Stage One) and you are angry that he is not showing any signs of commitment or change. Worse yet, he probably is not willing to renegotiate.

Corrective Action

The only corrective action plan you have at this point is to accept the fact that your mate is not interested in a household partnership. Since you are the only one committed to the contract, I am afraid it's not going to work. It now appears, if change is going to happen, it must come from you. Once you accept this, you can move on to asking yourself the question, "How do I take care of myself?" Or, "What changes can I make to increase my happiness in my home?"

Begin by making a list of the areas you have control over. As you review the list ask yourself, "What changes can I make on my own?" Are there areas of the household chores that you can forget, or do less frequently in order to give yourself more free time to do what you enjoy? Are there chores that you have consented to do for your children that they could do for themselves? Does everything always have to be done a certain way? Can you relax your standards a bit in order to have less anxiety? Are you able to hire out some of the chores?

Dominique and Tony

Right from the beginning, Dominique, a Stargazer, worried about whether Tony's heart was really in the contract. She had coaxed him into taking the personality test and the Beliefs and Actions Inventory. However, she was afraid he signed the Code of Ethics without really reading it. She then received false hopes when he seemed to enjoy playing the Happy Face Game. Nevertheless, she felt something might be wrong when she couldn't get him involved in the preparation of the notebook.

When it came to putting the partnership into action, it seemed as if Tony, the Philosopher, had forgotten everything they agreed upon. When she tried to get him back to renegotiate, he always found reasons to cancel the meetings. He was always too tired, too busy, or too involved in something (anything) else. As he walks away, he says something like: "Oh ... not right now, honey. The game is on. I promise we will do it later. Maybe tomorrow."

Dominique has just enough Rebel in her to fight back, but I'm afraid to no avail. Tony blocked every move she made. This became a classic case of the Philosopher's ability to evoke passive resistance. It worked. Dominique needs to accept reality. She cannot change someone else, especially someone who doesn't want to change.

What Are Dominique's Options?

I would not suggest to Dominique that she just cave in and throw up her hands. Nor would I suggest that she accept the fact that

CHAPTER 21

nothing is ever going to change, nor should she give up hope. She has come too far in the enlightenment process to retreat. But I am suggesting that she consider how much of a price she is willing to pay in trying to entice her passive Philosopher into a household partnership. One thing is definite: she will pay a huge price if she harbors resentment. Unresolved resentment is more difficult to live with than a non-partner.

This is probably a good time for Dominique to review her options. Basically, she has two. One option is that she can continue to do it all. The second option is she can figure out various strategies by which she can stop "doing it all" and start doing more for herself.

After she considers these two options, she might then want to ask the question, "Is my mate a partner in other areas of my life?" If her answer is "I don't know" or a definite "no," she would do well to seek outside professional help in order to gain a perspective on the relationship. But if she decides that everything else is "pretty much okay" and she can say, "Even though I don't quite have a partnership at this time, I am fairly happy," then keep the book for reference and come back to it at a later date. In the meantime, just count your blessings, and move on.

Moving into Stage Three

When you as a couple become aware that your actions are in sync with your commitment, that you both are completing most of your jobs, and that you are finding less and less need to hash over old issues, you have moved into the third stage. Make no mistake. This is still a fragile time. Your success in moving through this critical third stage and on to the fourth stage will depend on the degree you are both committed to change.

Stage Three: The Point of No Return

The third stage is most distinguished by a subtle lack of commitment. Like a couple's engagement period, partners must guard against getting too comfortable in this stage for fear they will live here forever. Some men love this stage because they feel as if they can back out of the contract at any time and for any reason. They like to think there is a disclaimer in their back pocket, which says, "If I don't like how it's going, I can return back to the way it was." Your semi-reluctant partner still enjoys this testing time and relishes the feeling that there is a back door, but this is a false perception. There is no back door. Your partner must come to grips with the fact that you have no intention of going back to the way things were. By now he is coming to realize that even if a full-fledged partnership does not develop, things will be different.

Only three things can happen in this third stage:

1. The partner will hate the added workload and bail out from the contract. This will produce a crisis.

2. The partner keeps his "I don't know if I have been sold on this yet" attitude alive, and resists the move into the fourth stage. This standoff will also produce a crisis.

3. The partner will begin to like the division of labor and soften to the idea of the contract. This couple will then move into the fourth stage.

The Chinese have given us a potentially positive perspective on crisis. The pictogram for crisis contains two characters, one for "danger" and one for "opportunity." They recognize that in every crisis, there is some sort of danger, but there is also an opportunity. I know it's difficult to see an opportunity when our world is falling apart, but if we look beyond the turmoil, there is always an opportunity for something better to take form. Crisis can be a time to regroup, rethink, and even change direction. This new direction could eventually lead to greater success. Crisis is also the time for a couple to assess whether or not they need a third person—a mediator or a professional counselor. An objective third person often can assist them in working through problem areas and moving into Stage Four.

The key ingredient during this tenuous third stage is for you

CHAPTER 21

and your mate to find support for your decision to develop a household partnership. Perhaps you can find a few other couples to form a support group. Forming household partnership support groups with other couples who are struggling for gender equity in their home can help you move through the five stages. If you can't find interested couples, form a group around your gender or household personality. Regardless of how you do it, it is important that you reach out to others and gain support in this transitional time.

You will not move into Stage Four until your beliefs and actions are in sync or kindred. When you both have accepted your partnership as a new way of life, with no turning back, you have entered Stage Four.

CHAPTER 22

The Harvest is Here

Cherish those moments when you realize that what you have planted together has bloomed.

– Dinah

Stage Four: Deeper Trust

Stage Four has some similar characteristics of the first stage. However, this stage has elements of maturity that only surface with time. Therefore, it is marked by a continued sense of commitment and trust. The contract has emerged from the danger of being breached. You are both ready to enjoy the fruits of your labor! Oh, glorious day!

Depending on which category you've emerged from (A, B, or C), you have survived a raging battle or just a few scrimmages. No doubt one or both of you have had to make more concessions than you intended, but ultimately you can rejoice in the fact that you have worked hard and have stayed with it.

As mentioned, this stage is also marked by a noticeable change in trust. You no longer feel a need to micromanage your mate. You aren't going behind his back and checking up on how well he did his job. Something else has surfaced—a new level of companionship.

You might be reminded of your first date, or your honeymoon or your first "new toy" stage. But unlike the first stage, this one feels deeper and more meaningful. Yes, something is distinctly different. It's as if you are both doing the tango but with increased confidence and in step with each other. The moon and stars mesmerize

CHAPTER 22

your minds less. There is a greater sense of clarity. A deeper awareness of the purpose of the dance has emerged. Both of you have new feelings of connectedness and intimacy which have unexpectedly accompanied the new partnership. You feel more bonded and you both are beginning to like it.

So that you do not confuse this stage with the romantic evening you had back when you were doing the tango on the dock, I have developed the following questions to help you decide if you really are in Stage Four.

STAGE FOUR
(answer true or false)

1. It is rare that my mate does not follow through on his household chores. _____

2. Arguing over household duties is rare. _____

3. We have not had to renegotiate our contract for over a month. _____

4. We both have a better feeling about our intimacy level. _____

5. Neither of us feels quite so alone with our chores. _____

6. I don't mind helping out my mate, even if it is not my job, since I trust he will do the same for me when needed. _____

7. Things are not perfect, but I feel much better about the equity in our house. _____

8. I find myself promoting the concept of household partnership with my friends. _____

9. My life feels more organized and less stressful. _____

10. I feel like my mate is becoming a real partner. _____

If you were able to answer true to six or seven of the questions, you are in Stage Four. When you can answer true to eight or more of them, you have moved into Stage Five.

Stage Five: Partnership

As a couple moves into the fifth and last stage of the household partnership, they find a new sense of independence, which strangely enough is attached to their new interdependence. The feeling is best described as being "all grown up." The woman no longer acts as a parent who is checking up on her mate—following up, monitoring, or criticizing bad behavior. Nor does she feel as if she has to continually reinforce positive behavior, as a parent does for a child. In addition, her mate no longer throws tantrums or pouts when he is asked to stick to his commitment. This "all grown up" time is the fifth or Partnership stage.

It's a time for celebration. You both deserve accolades and rewards. They are yours to relish; you've come a long way. However, a word of caution. Be cautious of thinking that says, "You have arrived," and there is nothing else to learn, or that there is never a threat of relapse. Remember that a household partnership is a process. It's always moving backward, forward, or standing still. Continued reassessment is needed to keep it moving forward.

Like a Garden, It Will Always Need Work

Today, Gary and I live in the partnership stage, but it does not mean that we are home free. No one is. I can still feel at times that old patterns surface and before I know it, I have worked a weekend away and Gary slipped by. But the same can be true for him.

I remember the first time I noticed that putting the garden to bed for winter (which is no small job in Minnesota) got lost in our negotiations and there was not a decision made as to whose job it was. In a panic, I ran for our partnership notebook to see if my worst fear was realized. If I was right and the job was overlooked, for whatever reason, I felt as if I would be stuck with it. But today I no longer panic. I know that somehow the scale will balance. Gary

CHAPTER 22

responds the same. Since he ended up with budgeting, he has most of the financial management. At the time of negotiation, we overlooked banking and tax preparation, yet he has just taken it on.

So, for us, renegotiating is mostly a thing of the past. Since we have a commitment to partnership, when we find ourselves in over our heads, the other simply helps out. Gary will come out into the garden to give me a break, or I will sit down with a calculator and let him know that I also have a handle on our finances.

Although we have our own jobs, no one is ever expected to go it alone. The longer our partnership grows, the less rigidity we feel with our "assigned" jobs. For instance, if we are in a rush to get out the door and my job is to make the bed in the morning, I do not hesitate to ask Gary for help. Nor will he hesitate to ask me to move his clothes from the washer to the dryer if he is in a rush. It now seems very much like my early relationship with my twin sister, Kathy.

From this final fifth stage, the only place to go is to continue on. On a daily basis you will perfect and integrate partnership concepts into your daily lifestyle. But, as in all the days of our life, some days will simply be better than others. And, depending on your household personalities, some of you will simply have an easier time moving through the days than others do.

Regardless of how well you have planted yourself into a household partnership, the most important issue is that neither one of you feels bound by society's rigid gender roles. As a woman, hopefully you have "come a long way" from the mindless daisy seeds that are popped into the ground to grow as expected. You are now free to grow and harvest a life that you choose. Your awakening has come and is yours forever.

Epilogue

Working in the garden ... gives me a profound feeling of inner peace. Nothing here is in a hurry. There is no rush toward accomplishment, no blowing of trumpets. Here is the great mystery of life and growth. Everything is changing, growing, aiming at something, but silently, un-boastfully, taking its time.

– Ruth Stout, *How to Have a Green Thumb Without an Aching Back* (1955)

Ten Years Later...

It has been over ten years since the Thanksgiving Day Caper. I am happy to report that our home is solidly based on the concepts of household partnership. Neither of us can remember the last time we had a negotiation meeting. We have so completely integrated a non-gender household into our lives that it's become second nature.

Kristina finished her degree in dance, and to our delight, at age thirty-four she still does the turkey dance. Today, however, it is to the delight of her own toddler. Through the utilization of new technology, David (our entrepreneur) has developed his company into a successful and thriving business. However, he still holds dear to his heart the sacred old traditions around Thanksgiving Day. For instance, last Thanksgiving he was disappointed when I finally threw away the twenty-year-old, hard-to-clean turkey roaster, and bought a bright, sparkling new, $2 aluminum, throw-away roasting pan. "It just doesn't seem the same, Mom." (I guess some things never change.)

Both "kids" are now married. Kristina married Bill five years ago, and their second child will join two-and-half-year-old Jonathan in four months! David married Molly three years ago and just had baby Barrett. Gary and I could not be more pleased with their choice of mates. Kristina's Bill is "the modern man" who rejects archaic gender roles (of course, he was raised by a "Little Partner's mother"), and David views his home and baby as his responsibility as much as Molly's. David did not look for a wife to take care of him, any more than Kristina looked for a husband to take care of her. However, they have a lot of chapters ahead of them. At their age, life usually gets more hectic. I hope they keep Dinah close by.

Gary and I are in our same country home and still have the same jobs. My twin sister Kathy left teaching, went on to graduate school, and is now working as a therapist in a county mental health clinic. She and my brother-in-law Mike still have their home on Lake Michigan where Gary and I frequently return each summer to walk, talk, and roast hot dogs on the beach.

My brother Gary left his commodities business and is now a well-known expert and author in the field of currency risk management (he has come along way from his Daniel Boone days). My brother Allen has also come quite a distance. After twenty years building a state industry, he is the retired CEO of an award-winning winery in Seattle, Washington.

All my siblings, our mates, and the grandchildren suffered the loss of my father twelve years ago when he died at eighty-one. It was November 21, five days before Thanksgiving Day. There was not an unbroken heart nor a dry eye among us as his eight beloved grandchildren (six young men and two young women) carried his casket through the snowy pines of an old cemetery to a knoll overlooking the Clinton River. He was laid to rest next to my mother.

After the funeral, we all stayed in Michigan at Kathy and Mike's house to celebrate Thanksgiving and our father's life. We resembled a scene from the movie *The Big Chill* as we all rallied and danced around, working together to prepare and put on the great meal. Still, in spite of our "avoidance humor," Dad's absence was deeply felt.

We were all exceedingly grateful that even up to the last year, Dad was still able to plant his garden. In that last summer, even though his diabetes made him so weak that he could only sit in a chair and watch us do the planting for him, he was still in the garden until the end. I remember during that last planting (and knowing it was probably the last), the nostalgia was particularly powerful. While I mounded the dirt around the tomato plant as he had taught me, and made a trench for the water as he instructed from his chair, I had flashbacks to my youth, as an eight-year-old on the Clinton River. I vividly recalled Dad hooking the pail to the hoe and dipping it down into the Clinton to gather water for the trenches. Now thirty-eight years later, the only thing he still had energy to do was to fertilize. That last summer he grew the largest and juiciest tomatoes I have ever eaten.

By the way, Dad never did find another mate after my mother died. I'm afraid some of us only get one chance at partnership. That brings me to you.

Whether you and your mate have been able to establish a partnership or not, your life together is more than, "Who is going to cook dinner tonight?" Partnership is also about having mutual dreams, aspirations, and love. It's sharing the totality of your being with another person. Partnership is, as I mentioned before, like a garden. You and your mate are the gardeners. Your garden can only flourish as much as the two of you are willing to care for, support, and nurture it. But like any abundant harvest, it's worth the effort.

Never forget that the person you've selected to plant this garden with is the same person you've chosen to bear the wind, the rain, the hurt, and the pain with. Unless you had a twin like I did, for a large part of your life you gardened alone. Then one day you found each other at the end of a row, and decided to join hands and plant a garden together. It was a big decision. But creating a garden—like a partnership—always is. My wish for you is that you make it, and that your garden be fruitful. God bless you both.

APPENDIX A

Code of Ethics

We believe our household chores should be based on what is fair and just—not on our gender. To that end, we both will strive toward creating and maintaining a home in which we are equally responsible.

We believe that each of us counts equally, and believe our actions should be based upon the axiom, "You count—and I count, too."

The needs and desires of each of us are equally important. Gender-biased cultural expectations will not outweigh the individual expectations of ourselves or our partnership.

We believe that we should be receptive to each other, supportive of each other, and respectful to each other as individuals with an equal right to opportunities to participate in the joyful gifts of life.

We believe the division of household responsibilities and duties should be based upon our individual skills, preferences, and time available, and not on our gender.

As partners, we pledge to share all housework through negotiation.

Signature _____   Signature _____
Date _____   Date _____

APPENDIX B

The Happy Face Game

I believe that the game works best if you have a third person as a moderator, but if both you and your partner have gone through the exercises, signed the Household Code of Ethics, and agree to implement a household partnership, a moderator, although helpful, will not be necessary. If you include a moderator, however, only she or he is to know the rules in advance. You and your partner will learn each rule in progression from the moderator along each step of the way. Why? Trust me. It's works better that way. And it's more fun.

If you and your partner decide to play alone, but run into difficulty, stop and wait until you can bring in a neutral moderator to help you over the stumbling blocks.

How do you find a moderator? Just give this appendix to a friend who you both trust and can confide in. Have your friend read it, then ask him or her to moderate the game for you. If your friend agrees, step back, know you're in good hands, and enjoy the game. Either way, you will end up with a Household Partnership Contract if you play fair and have fun!

Dinah

APPENDIX B

This section is to be read by the moderator:

Planting the Seed*

Back in 1774, John Chapman was born near Leominster, Massachusetts. By the time he was 25 years old, he had become a nursery man and was known for the apple trees he planted in the western portions of New York and Pennsylvania. In the early 1800s, he headed west into the Ohio River valley and Great Lakes region. There he wandered the wilderness with a bag of apple seeds on his back. Whenever he found a likely spot for planting, he would clear the land by chopping out weeds and brush by hand. Then he planted his apple seeds in neat rows and built a brush fence around the area to keep out straying animals. The trees grew, and their seeds were carried by pioneers all the way to the Pacific. Today, many apple orchards across the nation began with a single seed planted by Johnny Appleseed.

How does this possibly relate to you? Think about it. By moderating this game, you become the modern-day equivalent of Johnny or Josephine Appleseed. You will help plant the seeds of a successful household partnership. The advent of this partnership will help plow the ground for other equitable household partnerships across the land. For this, you don't need to carry a bag of seeds ... just a lot of encouragement, a presence of mind, and a belief in win-win negotiation.

Now, read the following rules and objectives. Then introduce each rule to the players as they reach that stage. Do not divulge the procedures in advance. Experience tells me that the game is more enjoyable—and often more successful—when the players are not informed of the steps until they get to them.

---

* Adapted from Johnny Appleseed Junior Ecology Club, www.appleseed.net

THE HAPPY FACE GAME

This section is to be read by the players:

Whether the game is moderated or not, remember the Code of Ethics. Remember that you both have worked through your individual household personality barriers, and you are now ready to roll up your sleeves to finalize your partnership. Yep, no doubt about it, you are both able and willing, nay, anxious! ... to share equally in the household chores. But once again, there is that nagging, worrisome question, "How?"

I assure you there is no need to worry. I have designed for you a fun way to get there. It is called the Happy Face Game. It will take you through the process of building an equitable partnership that ensures each partner has a choice in his or her selection of chores, while short-circuiting the task of "higgling and haggling" over each one.

As you play the game, I can't promise all roses and violins, but played in good faith, you will avoid most of the anguish of the hardball that surfaces with win-lose negotiators (which neither of you are, right?). You have agreed, by now, that your ultimate purpose is to create a household contract developed through win-win negotiations.

The objective of the game is to develop a division of labor in an equitable fashion that is agreeable to both household partners. This, I've been told by almost everyone I've interviewed, is impossible. But it's not impossible, as this game will prove. The Happy Face Game is played as a series of steps. These steps will avoid the pitfalls that occur when couples start discussing who is going to do what. In fact, the steps will lead you to a whole new area of sharing, which translates into greater intimacy.

So are you ready? Let's go.

APPENDIX B

Playing the Happy Face Game

The Setting

You will need at least a couple hours of uninterrupted time. Even though this is a game, it is also a serious effort that very effectively creates equanimity in the household, and therefore requires full attention with no interruptions. Create the mood. Take the phone off the hook, put the kids to bed, play some mood music, light some candles, and make a pot of tea.

Gather the Materials

Two pads of paper and two pens. Two packets of plain white 3×5" index cards, blank on one side, to be precise. Two black felt-tip markers.

Step One: Make a List of the Chores

The tough part comes first. The two players must begin by listing all the chores around the house on their pads of paper. Don't skimp; you need to write down everything from shining shoes to replacing that loose shingle that's been slapping in the wind for two-and-a-half years. Be creative, and remember to write down chores you know you only do every quarter or even once a year.

Divide by Three

Regardless of the number of chores, it *must be equally divisible by three*. If you are the moderator, instruct the players to add the one or two chores they missed, or subtract the one or two they can really forget about without devaluing the property or embarrassing the neighbors. If you don't have a moderator, then you will have to figure this out yourselves; just make sure you end up with a number of chores that can be divided by three.

Merge the List and Number the Chores

After the couple has completed their lists, the moderator (or the couple, if no moderator) combines the two lists into one on a single sheet of paper, deleting all duplicates. Then, number each chore consecutively, so it looks something like this:

1 – wash dishes
2 – wash clothes
3 – wash Tigger
4 – (etc.)

Already the preparation becomes fun, as listing chores often leads to a stimulating exchange of words and gestures between the two players. It appears that seeing certain chores down in black and white—for example, removing dead mice or darning socks—causes irritation. The prospect that that particular chore is up for negotiation will drive some over the edge. You might hear, "You've always done that! You expect me to now?" So be prepared: this interchange often ends when one of the players playfully snatches the list, crumples it into a ball, and bounces it off the other player's head. Sometimes the game is over at this point. That's when a moderator is beneficial, someone who can say, "Come on now, we've all agreed to keep playing, no matter how rough it gets. Every job is now up for negotiation?" If you don't have a moderator, your mantra is, "We've agreed to stay the course. No matter what ... we will have a contract."

Step Two: Document How Often the Chore Needs to be Done

Now the players are asked to assign a schedule to the list of chores. Often one player will want it on record that some chores (mostly housekeeping) are done on a daily or weekly basis, whereas others (mostly house maintenance–type chores) are done on a monthly or seasonal basis, or at even longer intervals. If a chore is done so irregularly or so rarely that it falls more into the category of "special project" than "repetitive chore," it probably should be deleted, and the list revised. Determining how often a chore is done, or should be done, is also fertile ground for lively conversation. (The moderator

APPENDIX B

helps the players along by assuring them that the fun part begins shortly.)

Write the schedule next to each chore. Use "D" for daily, "W" for weekly, "WW" for every other week, "M" for monthly, and "S" for seasonal (for example, stringing the outdoor Christmas tree lights). Record any other period of time in a similar fashion. The list now looks like this:

1 – wash dishes D
2 – wash clothes W
3 – wash Tigger WW
4 – (etc.)

Step Three: Record Chores, the Number, and How Often on Index Cards

Each player is instructed to number their index cards with the corresponding number of chores on the list. (For example, if there are twenty-one chores, each player receives twenty-one cards.) These cards will be their individual "decks," which they play throughout the game.

Each player must take a card and, on the blank side, write "1" at the top. Then, below the number, each player writes down the job that is at the top of the list. Next to the number, they need to write the letter(s) that designate the schedule for that job.

Here's another chance for problems. Let's say one of the players lists "changing the bed linen" with a "W" for weekly, while the other player schedules this particular chore a "M" for monthly. Even though this appears to be a huge deal initially, don't get hung up on the details. You will see that down the road, when you begin to negotiate, those issues will be resolved. So if you don't agree on the scheduling, realize that you will need to compromise. As you will note, one of you wants the lawn mowed once a week, while another wants it mowed every two weeks. One will think the checkbook should be reconciled weekly, while another believes that monthly is sufficient.

THE HAPPY FACE GAME

Continue to repeat this procedure for each of the remaining jobs on the list, until all the jobs have been identically listed, coded for scheduling, and numbered. Be sure to *make sure that the bottom half of each card remains blank*. When finished, each player should be holding an identical deck of cards that looks something like this:

| 1 D | 2 W | 3 WW |
| wash dishes | wash clothes | wash Tigger |

Step Four: Estimate the Amount of Time for Each Chore

Give each player a black felt-tip marker. Each player now retires to a separate corner of the room where he or she can work in private. They must go through each of their cards, and mark how often they estimate that the chore should take. This may be a wild guess. Nevertheless, each player should try to make a reasonable guess for each chore. Because the players are working separately, each may list a different amount of time. Be sure to leave the bottom of the cards blank. When finished, the cards should look something like this:

1 D	2 W	3 WW
wash dishes	wash clothes	wash Tigger
15 min	1 hr	½ day

APPENDIX B

Step Five: Compile in Three Different Piles According to Likes and Dislikes

The players must now carefully, thoughtfully, and agonizingly arrange the cards into three separate piles. *Each pile must contain an equal number of cards.*

The first pile will contain the cards with chores that they really, *really* don't mind doing. In fact, they may be chores that they love doing, chores that they feel they can do proudly, with a sense of contentment and accomplishment. Chores that they would do even if they had to knock on a neighbor's door and invite themselves in, just so they could do them. Well ... perhaps that's a stretch, but you get the point.

The second pile will contain the cards with chores that the player never does, hates to do, or pretends doesn't exist. These are the chores that they would pay someone else to do, if they could, that is. (This may not be an option, which explains why we're playing the game, and not, say, the monarch of Morocco and his wife.)

The third pile will contain the cards with a list of chores that fall somewhere between the first and the second piles, somewhere between love and hate. The players have listed chores that they wouldn't mind doing if it needed or had to be done and if there's no one else to do it. Not that he or she looks forward to it, mind you, but, oh-hum, no big deal either way. The attitude is, "If I have to do them, I will."

This gets tricky. The players have to decide what they like most and what they like least. At this point, the ability to agonize in silence comes in handy. They must both ask themselves, "What's more distasteful: shopping for the week's groceries, or shoveling snow? Paying bills or washing windows? Cleaning the oven or litter box? Yikes! *Every week! Every day!*" You should be listening for deep sighs over the sounds of cards shuffled back and forth. When both players call out, "Done," Step Five is complete.

Step Six: Marking the Cards

During this step, the players mark their decisions by drawing a face on every card in each pile. Pile one is the "happy face hand" and so

THE HAPPY FACE GAME

happy faces are drawn on all the cards in that pile. Pile two is the "sad face hand" and the players are instructed to draw sad faces on those cards. Pile three is the "oh, hum hand" and an oh-hum face is drawn on those cards.

After the players finish step six, the cards should look something like this:

1 D	2 W	3 WW
wash dishes	wash clothes	wash Tigger
15 min	1 hr	½ day
Happy face	**Oh, hum face**	**Sad face**

Of course, some chores might evoke some really passionate responses. A player may simply love softening his or her hands in a sink of dishwater, to the point of washing every dish by hand; or find that washing clothes is not difficult, just boring to tears; or remember that Tigger does not come gently to the bath, but spits, scratches, and draws blood every step of the way. The cards might look something like the ones below. Regardless, the other player will get the message.

1 D	2 W	3 WW
wash dishes	wash clothes	wash Tigger
15 min	1 hr	½ day

No matter how dramatic either of the players get with their drawing, the player cannot hedge his or her bet, or face. Each card must clearly designate a happy face, an oh-hum face, or a sad face.

APPENDIX B

Calling or attempting to clarify a confusing face after the play begins can lead to an unfair advantage, as will be seen. So cards that look like this:

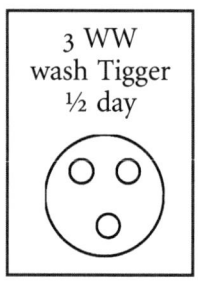

```
┌─────────────┐   ┌─────────────┐
│    1 D      │   │    2 W      │
│ wash dishes │   │ wash clothes│
│   15 min    │   │    1 hr     │
│   ╭───╮     │   │   ╭───╮     │
│   │○ ○│     │   │   │○ ⌿│─    │
│   ╰───╯     │   │   ╰─╱╱╯     │
└─────────────┘   └─────────────┘
```

or like this:
```
┌─────────────┐
│    3 WW     │
│ wash Tigger │
│   ½ day     │
│   ╭───╮     │
│   │○ ○│     │
│   │ ○ │     │
│   ╰───╯     │
└─────────────┘
```
don't count.

Step Seven Preparing the Deck in Numerical Order

After all cards are marked and restacked neatly into the three piles, face down, the players now combine their three piles back into a single deck, again, making sure to keep them in numerical order. The numbers are placed in descending order, so that when turned face down, number "1" becomes the top card.

The players are ready to return to the table. Now, sitting down and facing each other, they each place their deck, face down, in front of them. The play now is ready to commence.

Steps for Playing Out the Cards

Step One—If you have a moderator, he or she will explain how the cards are played, and will choose the player who starts first. (There's no advantage to whoever starts the play, so no big deal if

242

you aren't chosen.) If there is no moderator, the person whose birthday is closest to January 1 leads off. (A very important rule, but the reason why escapes me.)

Step Two—Cards are assigned the following face values:

| **Highest Value** | **Second Highest Value** | **Lowest Value** |
| Happy face | Oh-hum face | Sad face |

Step Three—Players alternate. Cards are played up on the table one at a time. Each play forms a two-card trick. (Just in case you are not familiar with card-playing terminology, "a trick" is another word for the cards that are being played. In this case, the two cards played in the middle of the table are called the "trick.")

Step Four—First player takes a card from top of his or her deck (card #1) and places it face up in the middle of the table. Second player does likewise. The player with the card of the highest value wins the trick, and places the cards in his or her pile of tricks won.

Step Five—Tricks with identical face values are "draw tricks" and are placed in a "draw pile" between the players. (Once again, for the benefit of non-card players, "draw" is another word for "tie.")

Step Six—Play continues until all cards are played. All the cards are now in the players' trick piles, except for those in the draw pile.

Step Seven—Now, dear players, take all your cards and list the jobs that you have "won" on a separate sheet of paper. These are your chores. This sheet listing your chores will be attached to the Household Contract when the game is over.

Step Eight—Playing the draw pile: The cards that are now left in the draw pile are chores that still need to be decided upon. How that happens is still up for grabs.

Remember Chapter 17, "Let's Make a Deal?" Well, here is where you will use those new finely tuned negotiation skills you just learned. This is the part in the game where you will truly test your desire to have an equitable household by signing a fair and just contract. So now is a time to think out of the box and to tap every creative idea you have stored away just for this moment.

APPENDIX B

It is here where you can play by your own rules. You can negotiate your cards in any manner you wish (just remember to be very conscious of *quid pro quo*). Also be aware of who, if anyone, has more job cards than the other. Also be aware of the schedule on the cards. For instance, someone might have lucked out and has several cards that list chores that only have to be done once every couple of weeks or once a month, so here is where you even the score. It is up to each of you to make the deal, but be creative.

For instance, one of you might decide to trade one sad face card for two oh-hum cards or you can decide that you will both do the job, but you will trade off and on, each month. Keep your options open. The two of you might decide to compromise by hiring someone to mow the lawn once a week (if that is one of the jobs, that is), or you might both decide that another job is not something that needs to be done—like planting the herb garden.

Then again, if they are not daily jobs, you might both decide to leave some of the job cards to be negotiated at a later date. Keep them in a basket as something to barter with as situations arise. For instance, let's say you both drew a happy face on reconciling the monthly checkbook. You really enjoy that job but so does your spouse. So you might trade that card for your choice of a movie or restaurant. You also might consider negotiation with job cards that have already been played; there is no rule that says that they can't always be thrown back on the table to renegotiate.

Once again, I remind you that this is the time that both of you need to practice your skills as "bridge players" as described in Chapter 17. Your goal is to make a contract and, even though each of you wants to end up with a good deal for yourself, you also desire a good deal for your mate. In other words, you want a win-win partnership.

Step Nine—The game is over when all the chores represented by the won tricks have been divided between the players, as well as all the chores in the draw pile. The chores of each player are now listed on a separate sheet of paper under the player's name. Attach the two lists of chores, your division of labor, to the Household Partnership Contract. See Appendix C.

Step Ten — Read your Household Partnership Contract out loud so there is no misunderstanding, then sign it, shake hands, and look in the mirror at your happy faces. You did it! You have a contract. Celebrate the new harmony that will come into your growing and vibrant relationship.

APPENDIX C

Our Household Partnership Contract

On _____ (date), we, _____ (your name) and _____ (your partner's name), have agreed to form a Household Partnership.

Whereas we are now equal partners within our home, we mutually agree to the following terms as outlined in Appendices A and B.

We also agree to amend or re-negotiate our Household Contract at the request of either partner.

This contract hereby takes effect on _____(date).

Signature _____ Signature _____

Acknowledgments

My book begins and ends with my siblings. There is no doubt that Gary, Allen, and my twin sister Kathryn were the major influences in my life. Through the worst and through the best of it, they have been there. As strange as it may seem, they quite literally raised me. Therefore, I give full credit to them for the "awakening" that I have written about in this book.

Gary, the oldest and an author, has served his role as leader well. Steadfast and loyal, no one has contributed more to this book than he did. His edits have so blended with my own voice that I no longer distinguish his words from mine. From the beginning he encouraged me to trust in myself, to believe in my work, and to recognize that I held some magic, at least *he* thought I did, which eventually helped me to believe it myself. I am deeply grateful for all his writing, editing, and support in guiding this book from conception to completion.

Allen has always been and always will be the "How can we make it better?" person. He doesn't just ask it; he also shows how to do it. His wisdom, like the fine wine he has made, continues to improve over the years. He is an example of staying on course, striving for the impossible, and never acting *too* surprised when you get it. I thank him for helping to instill the "can do" attitude in me. It carried me through all those times when all I seemed to hear was "you can't."

Kathryn, my twin, a teacher and therapist, is the best thing that has ever happened in my life. She was my first partner and the first feminist I ever knew. I think she was converted around the age of six—long before it became popular—and she remains steadfast today. I sometimes think that Kathy was Susan B. Anthony in some other life, because she lived the principles in this book long before I ever believed them or thought to write about them. She truly is my inspiration. Her words and thoughts are all through this book.

I thank my best friend Dennis, who is like a brother. He came along 25 years ago, melted in as a natural sibling, and has been a constant source of love and encouragement ever since. He read drafts of this book long before anyone else and has supported me in all my major decisions since then.

I am more grateful than I can express to:

Genie O'Malley (the most gifted woman I've ever known), the founder of Sonra Enterprises, and Authors of Unity, who with her husband Rajmar and their fabulous team of editors, designers, and copywriters brought *Dinah* to life.

David McNally, a dear and faithful friend, supporter, consultant, and best-selling author of *Even Eagles Need a Push* (a book that inspired me to write mine), and *Be Your Own Brand*. David took *Dinah* out of the ashes and put it in the hands of the "right" people. David and his dear, late wife, and a best friend to me, Jo, supported this effort from beginning to end, never doubting its value, even when I did.

Betsy Cole, a soul mate, for all her encouragement and ideas that advanced the development of this book. She never stopped believing in it or me.

Annemarie Osborn, for teaching me about manifesting one's vision.

Sara Estes, dear friend and the midwife to *Dinah*, for her countless hours of editing and advice.

I am also thankful to:

Elizabeth Lyon—a gifted writer, author, editor, and friend who gave so much of her time and expertise to this work. I will always remember that she and literary agent Natasha Kern were the first believers in *Dinah* over eight years ago.

The women at Perspectives who shaped my thinking and originally gave me the idea of this book. They include:

Jody Dunlap, a best friend and my biggest fan. She always laughed at the right places.

Shirley Shumate, dear friend, mentor, and another soul mate, who is the wisest and most compassionate woman I know.

ACKNOWLEDGMENTS

The energetic Sue Zelickson, who encouraged and supported this work from its conception.

I also thank Susan Myers and Cheryl Cochrane, both loyal friends and supporters who are wonderful role models on how to live life. I especially thank Susan for the hours she spent, way back in the beginning, editing and nurturing this work.

Jane Onan, my dear and faithful friend who believed in me before I believed in me.

I thank the spectacular "Ya-Ya"s—Dovie, Lovie, Hula Girl, and Gyspy—for all the love, support, and hours given in discussing this book. It is nice knowing that they'll be there with me, walking Stimson Beach, when the going gets rough.

I am deeply grateful for the support and love of my children. Through the years and still today, when it comes to my work and who I am, my son David and daughter Kristina are my biggest fans. (Now that they are married, they have recruited Molly and Bill to their fan club.) Their pride in my successes has made it easier for me to become someone other than *just* their mother—even though, for them, that was always enough.

I am so fortunate to have in my life two darling nephews, Tony and Joe, who have debated, challenged, *and* encouraged the development of Dinah. I thank them for all the support, love, and ideas that they have given me over the years.

There is no doubt I could not have written this book without the insight and knowledge of Gary, my husband and very best friend. I owe everything printed in this book to what we have learned *together*. I am thankful for and enormously blessed by his encouragement, wisdom, and love.

And, finally to "the group." You guys know who you are. The many years we spent together during Gary's and my early thirties was life-changing. You are still with me today, perhaps not always in view, but always in my heart. I will never forget that you taught me to grow, cry, and then to move on to a richer, fuller life. Without you, this book would never have been written.

About the Author

For the past 20 years, Jeannie Seeley-Smith has been the president of Perspectives Family Center, a human service agency in Minneapolis, Minnesota. During this time she has developed award-winning programs that help empower homeless and disadvantaged women and their children to return to the social and economic mainstream.

An advocate for a more equitable society for women, Jeannie has also become a crusader for equity within the household. She says, "Perhaps the most significant happening in our nation's last 100 years is that women have liberated themselves from society's rigid gender roles, except within the home. It is still fairly obvious that as we enter the new millennium, 'women's work' is still alive and well."

Jeannie and her husband Gary live in Chaska, Minnesota.